DEATH
by
SPELLING

Also by David Grambs

Dimboxes, Epopts, and Other Quidams:
Words to Describe Life's
Indescribable People

Words About Words

Death by Spelling

A Compendium
of Tests,
Super Tests,
and
Killer Bees

David Grambs

PERENNIAL LIBRARY

HARPER & ROW, PUBLISHERS, New York

Grand Rapids, Philadelphia, St. Louis, San Francisco
London, Singapore, Sydney, Tokyo, Toronto

Library of Congress Cataloging-in-Publication Data

Grambs, David.
  Death by spelling: a compendium of tests, super tests, and killer bees/David Grambs.—1st ed.
    p. cm.
  Summary: A quiz book of over 100 devious spelling tests along with lots of trivia and tips about words and spelling.
  ISBN 0-06-096401-4
  1. English language—Orthography and spelling—Problems, exercises, etc. [1. English language—Spelling.] I. Title.
PE1145.2.G68   1989
428.1'076—DC20   89-45136

89 90 91 92 93 DT/RRD 10 9 8 7 6 5 4 3 2 1

Grateful acknowledgment is made to *Esquire* Magazine for permission to reprint "A Spelling Test Beyond All Belief" by T.K. Brown III.

"Spelling Yiffniff" copyright © 1987 by Calvin Trillin. From *If You Can't Say Something Nice* by Calvin Trillin, published by Ticknor & Fields.

Grateful acknowledgment is made to the Scripps Howard National Spelling Bee organization for permission to reprint the "Scripps Howard National Spelling Bee Rules."

"The Spell Against Spelling" from *The Argot Merchant Disaster* by George Starbuck. Copyright © 1980 by George Starbuck. First appeared in *The Atlantic*. By permission of Little, Brown and Company.

Strictly Speaking by Edwin Newman. Reprinted by permission of Macmillan Publishing Company from *Strictly Speaking* by Edwin Newman. Copyright © 1974 by Edwin Newman.

A Civil Tongue by Edwin Newman. Reprinted by permission of Macmillan Publishing Company from *A Civil Tongue* by Edwin Newman. Copyright © 1975, 1976 by Edwin Newman.

"Our Spelling Is a Muess!" by Sandra Leman from *College Composition and Communication,* May 1975. Copyright 1975 by the National Council of Teachers of English. Reprinted with permission.

"Why Sound Must Run" from *Have a Word on Me* by Willard R. Espy. Copyright © 1981 by Willard R. Espy. Reprinted by permission of Simon & Schuster, Inc.

"Spelling Bee" by Rhoda Koenig. Copyright © 1989 News America Publishing, Inc. All rights reserved. Reprinted with the permission of *New York* Magazine.

"Poor Speller Jailed 3 Years for Bank Heist." Reprinted with permission of the *Toronto Star Syndicate*.

"Misspelled Holdup Note Leads Police to Arrest." Reprinted with permission of the *Toronto Star Syndicate*.

To Ma Brown
and Doc Henry

CONTENTS

PREFACE

Three things you can be sure of in life are death, taxes, and misspelling.

Many of us remember, not the first time we fell off a two-wheeled bicycle, but the first time we fell out of a tense little American classroom spelling bee. Or, better yet, the time we won a bee by spelling *cantaloupe* and for once felt like more than a melonhead.

Even as literate adults, we never seem quite to put behind us a tendency to misspell. We airily utter thousands of everyday and sometimes not-so-everyday words. We easily recognize and comprehend them in print. But when pen faces paper, can we, free of doubt, put them into print?

Death by Spelling is something of a competitive—or handily self-testing—odyssey through the often perilous land of English spelling. It is, to be sure, a book of spelling tests (and more), prompted by my finding that, to the best of my knowledge, no such book has been done before. This is *not* another book of basic spelling improvement tips, mnemonic devices, and rules—though you'll find plenty of so-called demon words here. For spelling enthusiasts and casualties, bookstores already offer many useful, earnest, and encouraging paperbacks on basic spelling mastery.

This book is instead a caboodle of

more than a hundred tests interspersed with various informative items, pertinent quotations, occasional drolleries, and lightly historical discourses relating to the tricky orthography of our language. But be forewarned: The tests herein are not elementary. They represent a rather extensive vocabulary, and the well-educated or well-read have a definite advantage in confronting this book. By taking all the tests in the book, you can match yourself as a speller against more than 2,500 English words.

Spelling, as you may be well aware, plays tricks with the mind. Have you never found that if you stare long enough at a familiar word, its spelling begins to appear bizarre and the word unreal? Likewise, a good speller can be perfectly sure of a word until looking at a few alternative spellings or misspellings of that word. (You may experience this once or twice in taking multiple-choice tests in this book.)

Spelling research, too, as for a book such as this one, can bring on severe orthographic discombobulation. Correct and incorrect spellings begin to play musical chairs in the mind, particularly after one has looked at, written down, and retyped countless variant and false spellings. The incorrect begins to look correct, and vice versa.

Death by Spelling is meant, above all, to be fun. Too many dull school handbooks and deadly remedial programs continue to make spelling seem as interesting as a fifth-grade tetanus, tetnus, or tetinus shot. I hope that this book will dispel, or dispell, any notion that English spelling has to be a grim business. For Ph.D.s as well as for the everyday Joe, hard-core orthography can be a realm of continual surprise, and often an occasion for outright disbelief or total confusion.

I hope the book is pleasantly edifying, too. Americans today don't need to be told that fundamental writing and reading skills in our country are not at an all-time high. Our newspapers and magazines lament this fact almost daily, and among best-selling books of late have been the jeremiads *Cultural Literacy* and *The Dictionary of Cultural Literacy*, both by E. D. Hirsch, and *The Closing of the American Mind*, by Allan Bloom.

A couple of other points here, at the price of lengthening this introduction.

Death by Spelling has a secret thesis. It is that the world is not divided into good spellers and bad spellers. Rather, it is made up of good spellers, bad spellers, and people who—often secretly or coyly—*think* they're very good spellers. Take a few of the tests here, or watch a hotshot friend or two taking them, and I think you'll see what I mean. If you give (orally) any of the book's tests to an overconfident friend, be sure to get the testee to declare, before the answers are given, the number of words he or she thinks he or she has spelled correctly. This can definitely add to the fun.

Also, the book can be used either privately or publicly, as it were. You can take any and all of these tests by yourself. If you're truly a phenomenal speller, you'll whiz through these sundry tests and exult in your triumphal score. You may even challenge friends or enemies to try the same tests and hope to do a little gloating. Then again, you just might discover here that you're not so phenomenal a speller as you thought.

You can also use *Death by Spelling* for educational or social purposes. I hope at least a few high school English teachers or freshman writing course profs will find it appealing and helpful as a classroom aid or fillip, if not as a lightweight source for a course on English and its problematical spelling.

It can also be used (preferably with a good unabridged dictionary at hand) for spelling bees, which are far from dead today. Besides school bees, various communities and corporations around the country sponsor bees for people of all ages, among these the Olsten Corporation (The Olsten Corporate Great Grown-up Spelling Bee).

But enough about educational purposes. What about purely social ones?

To your possible surprise, let me confide to you that the giving and taking of spelling tests is a marvelous participatory and spectator sport.

I discovered this little-known fact at the editorial offices of Funk & Wagnalls some fifteen years ago, when I put together a few twenty-word tests to administer to fellow editors as a dubious form of in-house, after-five recreation. These were not spelling bees, but merely a small group of people individually scribbling down the correct spellings for words called out aloud to all. And erasing lightly. And rescribbling. And erasing again, this time not so lightly.

I found that watching otherwise normal people intensely fretting, crossing out, frowning, rewriting, cursing, asking for another piece of paper, laughing, crossing out again, wagging the head, and sighing can be quite enjoyable—for the fellow spellers as well as for the test giver. This was phase one. After each test everybody was asked to predict how many words he or she "definitely" had right. The answers were then read aloud, one by one. Phase two.

Have you ever seen the look on the face of a smugly educated person who believes he or she has sixteen out of twenty definitely right when he or she learns that he or she has a total of seven words correct? Did you know that shock, bristling, protestation, smoldering, and serious ego deflation can be brought on by a mere twenty-word spelling test?

And quite a few laughs in the process, because spelling tests are utter disrespecters of race, gender, religion, class, age, and purported education. Like sidewalk banana peels, just-missed trains, and unexpected impotence, they can cause immediate and profound self-doubt, which can be fairly interesting to observe, if not to experience.

Whether you use *Death by Spelling* as an individual reader or as a party host, three important learning aids are required for each person taking one or more of the book's tests: (1) a stout pencil, (2) a stouter eraser, and (3) an extremely stout whisk broom and dustpan for the pink eraser crumbs.

If I have a motive more ulterior than the reader's enjoyment, it might be to make you just a bit more interested in our grand old English, or American, language. I shall modestly refrain from claiming any intent whatsoever to improve our national literacy.

Acknowledgments

I'd like to thank Jim Trupin for knowing whom to approach with this book idea; Rick Kot, Scott Terranella, Pamela Montgomery, Dave Cole, Terry Belanger, Terry Stoller, Irving Perkins Associates, and the copyediting department of Harper & Row for handling and helping with the sort of letter-by-letter manuscript that can be an editor's nightmare; Sondra Austin, Diane Giddis, Richard Hodges, Mary Iorns, Richard Lederer, Ellen Levine, and Rageshree Ramachandran for their specific contributions; Allen Walker Read and Edna Furness for their valuable and helpful writings; and, going back a bit, the old 42nd Street Funk & Wagnalls Gang, among them Al Bennett, Lynne Bloom, Barbara Burns, Marcus Cohen, Kathy D'Amato, Julie DeWitt, Norma Dickey, Linda Faulhaber, Norma Frankel, Herb Gilbert, Gerry Gottlieb, Frank Jay, Betty Levy, Bryna Mandel, Kathy Mark, Bill Reiss, Ellen Rosenbush, Michael Schrader, Meryl Sherman, Marilyn Silbert, Anne Skagen, John Vinton, and Linda Yosinoff.

"Do you spell it with a 'V' or a 'W'?" inquired the judge.
"That depends on the taste and fancy of the speller, my Lord," replied Sam.

Charles Dickens

Apology and Disclaimer to Mystery Novel Readers

Please be advised that *Death by Spelling* is not a juicy or devilishly clever murder mystery about the deliciously intriguing foul play and wordplay afoot in a picturesque but seething Dorset village hosting an annual convention of Oxbridge pedagogues, one of whom is a pederast, whose respective corpses are discovered in each instance next to a hefty red brick bearing a shockingly misspelled word.

Still, you shall find mysteries, verbal skulduggery, and murderous entertainment of a sort within these pages. You may even cry foul play once or twice. If so, please direct your cries at the authoritative culprit dictionaries (or at our beloved but fickle English language), not at the author, who is only an accessory/accessary to the mischief.

About the Tests

Many multiple-choice, write-in-the-word, and other tests can be found throughout the text. More tests appear, before the answer pages, as two final sections of the book: Death by Spelling College and Ultimate Death by Spelling.

The chief authorities used for spellings in *Death by Spelling* have been Webster's Third New International (Unabridged) and Webster's Ninth New Collegiate dictionaries, both published by Merriam-Webster. For words not found in these, other sources have been used, most notably the Random House Dictionary of the English Language, Second Edition Unabridged. For pronunciations (or the phonetic spellings necessary for tests not having a multiple-choice format), Random House has been my most useful guide.

The words selected for the book's tests are entirely my choices unless otherwise indicated.

People are bound to have some disagreement as to the fairness of words used on spelling tests. No group of test words will be equally familiar to all takers of a test. But I've tried to make relative general familiarity, or common usage, a guiding principle here. I've done this in part by trying to keep as much as possible to words found in the general unabridged dictionaries—or,

1

better yet, in most or all of the collegiate dictionaries (Webster's New World, American Heritage and the Random House College along with Merriam-Webster's Ninth). An obvious exception to this working rule is the group of more than fifty tests in specialized academic, professional, or hobbyist areas of expertise and so forth.

Almost all tests offer five alternative word choices. The test taker may choose to spell one or all of these in place of less familiar or more ogrelike words on the test. The alternative words, designated after the numbered words by the letters *a* through *e*, are not intended to be necessarily easier to spell; they are merely alternatives.

In the multiple-choice tests only one of the four alternatives given will be a correct spelling. (The answer pages, however, list additional acceptable spellings found in the dictionaries used as sources.)

The spellings indicated as correct answers are solely those of the dictionaries. Any agreement of the author with these spellings is purely coincidental.

> The statistics of English are astonishing. Of all the world's languages (which now number some 2,700), it is arguably the richest in vocabulary. The compendious *Oxford English Dictionary* lists about 500,000 words; and a further half million technical and scientific terms remain uncatalogued. According to traditional estimates, neighboring German has a vocabulary of about 185,000 words and French fewer than 100,000, including such Franglais as *le snacque-barre* and *le hit-parade*. About 350 million people use the English vocabulary as a mother tongue; about one-tenth of the world's population, scattered across every continent and surpassed, in numbers, though not in distribution, only by the speakers of the many varieties of Chinese.
>
> Robert McCrum, William Cran,
> and Robert MacNeil
> *The Story of English*

DSAT

DEATH BY SPELLING ADMISSIONS TEST

All right, you've duly shelled out to buy this book and are now its rightful owner. But we're sorry to tell you that actual admission to the book's tests is contingent on your passing the following test.

There are twenty words to be spelled. As is the case with most of the tests in *Death by Spelling,* five alternative words are also provided; you may choose to spell one to five of these as backups, should you find them easier than one to five of the words appearing in the main portion of the test.

Passing score: fifteen of twenty words correct.

If you get fifteen or more right, congratulations, and please proceed further into *Death by Spelling.*

If you get fewer than fifteen correct, spelling may have already placed you close to death prior to purchase of this book, and the management cannot be held responsible for being the *coup de grace.*

Death by Spelling Admissions Test

Circle the correct spelling.

1.	macaroni	maccarroni	(semolina pasta, noodles)
2.	vinigar	vinegar	(sour liquid condiment)
3.	gumption	gummtion	(shrewd initiative)
4.	gallivant	galivant	(to roam or sport about)
5.	pinapple	pineapple	(tropical fruit)
6.	mischievious	mischievous	(harmful, troublemaking, playful)
7.	introvert	intravert	(inwardly focused person)
8.	hommage	homage	(respect or tribute)
9.	aching	acheing	(hurting or throbbing)
10.	vassal	vassall	(one in feudal subservience)
11.	larangitis	laryngitis	(throat ailment)
12.	excerpt	exerpt	(selected extract)
13.	ordnance	ordinance	(military supplies or artillery)
14.	gizzard	gizzerd	(alimentary canal of bird)
15.	scintilating	scintillating	(sparkling)
16.	absorbtion	absorption	(process of being made a part of)
17.	exhileration	exhilaration	(excited cheerfulness)
18.	alumni	alumnae	(female graduates)
19.	vacuum	vaccuum	(space without matter)
20.	superintendant	superintendent	(overseer or manager)
a.	separate	seperate	(to set apart)

b.	tarrif	tariff	(import fee)
c.	priviledge	privilege	(particular benefit or favor)
d.	coroborate	corroborate	(to make certain or confirm)
e.	bachelor	batchelor	(unmarried male)

Before consulting the answers on page 284:
I think I spelled _____ words correctly on this test.
(If your estimate is correct, add one point to your score.)

ADVICE TO ORTHOGRAPHIC POCOCURANTES

Let us say right off that there is little evidence to suggest that spelling aptitude has *anything* to do with basic intelligence. Furthermore, many people are disadvantaged in having learning disabilities—often regrettably undiagnosed and unknown to themselves—that make spelling a chronically difficult problem.

Excusable or not, poor spelling is worth avoiding or overcoming. It is like being poorly dressed, poorly represented—or poorly thought of. If you tend to be an I-couldn't-care-less person, a pococurante, about correct spelling—a scribbling scofflaw—you might reconsider. Get yourself a good dictionary with hard covers, of the bigger-than-pocket-size variety, and make friends with it, surely if slowly.

For if you continue to spell negligently, putting your apathy or ignorance in ink, reasonably literate folks may draw one or all of the following unfortunate conclusions about you:

- You were educated at AK-47 High School, before dropping out, where the teachers brought in handwriting analysts to grade your spelling tests.
- You're demonstrably casual or apathetic about your mother tongue, maybe even a Young Urban Unprofessional.
- Clear thinking and attention to detail are not your strong points.
- While to others your misspellings jump out loud and clear, you're weirdly unconscious of your verbal deficiencies.

- You know your spelling is like a monkey's Scrabble game, but you evidently find reaching for a dictionary to correct things an exhausting exercise.
- You're not much of a reader, your peak literary experience having been a bowl of alphabet soup you once enjoyed as a child.
- You're a brilliant thinker or artist, even a writer, maybe even a *monstre sacré*, whose energies are too prodigious for bothering about such petty matters as spelling.

> The Roman alphabet has always been inadequate for the phonetic representation of the English language, most strikingly so for Modern English. We have, for example, only five vowel symbols, *a, e, i, o,* and *u;* that this number is wholly inadequate is indicated by the fact that the first of these alone may have as many as six different sound values, as in *cat, came, calm, any, call,* and *was* (riming with *fuzz*).
>
> Thomas Pyles and John Algeo

ABECEDARIAN

Something that pertains to the alphabet is said to be *abecedarian*. The book you're now reading, being about proper letter sequence in English words, is an abecedarian book. (If its content were composed of symbols combining letters and numbers, it would be alphanumeric or alphanumerical.)

Abecedarian also means in alphabetical order. It can mean elementary or rudimentary as well, and as a noun it means beginner or novice.

So it could paradoxically, but honestly, be said that this book's most difficult spelling tests are abecedarian (alphabet-involving) tests not for abecedarians (beginners).

> Orthography is so absolutely necessary for a man of letters, or a gentleman, that one false spelling may fix a ridicule upon him for the rest of his life; and I know a man of quality who never recovered the ridicule of having spelled *wholesome* without the *w*.
>
> Philip Dormer Stanhope, Fourth Earl of Chesterfield

COUNT THE MISSPELLINGS TEST

How good is your eye for misspellings when they appear not on a test but within a printed passage?

Read the following passage—which is no more than a kind of prose amphigory or amphigouri (nonsensical verse)—and circle all misspelled words. Then count the misspellings you've detected and write down the total number. When you have done this, turn the book upside-down for your score.

Because this passage makes as little sense as, say, the thought of an ancient Phenecian beduin, at a cotillon, using his trusty cutlas to stir a bowl of bortsch or yoghourt amidst the houp-la there, don't try to discover any edifying mcaning here as you read.

The content here is a lot of nonsensical fofarraw. One might just as capriciously conjure up the picture of an Arab shaykh, at a tolbooth, stirring a tureen of brocoli with an equally sharp cimeter or with the jungle knife called a matchet; or might imagine, for that matter, that the Phenecian or the shaykh would have on his heraldic escucheon that he was descended, not directly but paralelly (that is, alined), from an exalted calif and a chlorophyl-colored leprehaun.

Perhaps only a skalawag could be the pedler of such unreadable piffle as this passage. Or is this the fatuous verbal sculduggery of a fenagling dilletante who should have a torniquet wound tightly around his or her neck?

But the sole purpose of this passage is not to kotow to your reading interests or to win a pean of praise, much less to bring you literary ecstacy. Rather, it is to present to your eye, as a bit of an orthographic test, a whole slue or skeane of words in order to see how you react to the way they are spelled. Other than that, anything that you might find to be profitable or "minable" herein is purely accidental, or ascititious. As its reader, you are merely the unfortunate allotee, or victim, of verbal absurdity. (You would scarcely want to be even an accessary to this rambling, self-conscious writing.)

Nonetheless, please circle all misspelled words that you see here. Then count them up and write down the total number. And thank you for your patience! When you learn the correct answers on the following page, will you be appaled?

How many misspellings did you find? Twenty-five? Thirty? Thirty-five? There is not a single misspelling in the preceding passage, according to Merriam-Webster's Third New International Dictionary. All the question-able words that you noted are considered allowable, though not pref-erable, spellings. The reputable if con-troversial unabridged "Third," first published in 1961, is the long-standing final authority for all spellings in the annual National Spelling Bee.

If you're a little astonished or even "appaled" at the lexical legitimacy of such spellings, you're not alone, rest assured. Few of them would be fa-vored by current writers or editors—who, I'd say, are more prone to not catching outright misspellings than to favoring such unorthodox variants. But these spellings have been used in our language and recorded in citation files by Merriam-Webster as well as by other dictionary publishers.

You may consider this exercise a maddening prank by the author, but it's meant more as a cautionary re-minder. When it comes to English spelling, things aren't always what they seem. You never, but never, know what you'll find in your dictionary, particularly if it's a large, unabridged one.

> Another cause . . . which hath contributed not a little to the maim-ing of our Language, is a foolish Opinion, advanced of late Years, that we ought to spell exactly as we speak, which beside the obvious Inconvenience of utterly destroying our Etymology, would be a thing we should never see an End of.
>
> Jonathan Swift

Scoring Yourself on the Tests

You may score or judge yourself in any way you see fit on the tests in *Death by Spelling*, after consulting the correct answers at the back of the book. How many did you think you had right? How well do you think you should have done?

Or you may go by the Death by Spelling Scoring System shown below. This may be used for all the book's twenty-word and twenty-five-word tests. (For its two fifty-word tests, you may double the words-correct numbers below for your score.)

Please note: In all answers, not only spellings but number or form of words must be correct; if the answer is spelled as two words, a one-word answer is incorrect. Apostrophes, if there are any, must be noted. Accent marks must be indicated on words having such marks (e.g., *passé*) for the spelling to be considered correct. Capital letters need *not* be indicated in answers (they are sometimes optional in dictionaries), but remember that they are an important part of spelling and writing.

DEATH BY SPELLING SCORING SYSTEM

Number of words correct
(20- to 25-word test)

18 or more   Super Speller
                   (Go to the head of the class.)

14–17   Savvy Speller
                   (You're a wizard of literation.)

10–13   So-So Speller
                   (Your sword might be mightier than your pen.)

 6–9   Sub-Par Speller
                   (Less television might help.)

 0–5   Sarsaparilla
                   (You should be kept at a safe distance from writing implements.)

How to Add a Point to Your Score:

After taking each test and *before looking at the answers,* write down, in the box provided on the test, how many words you think you spelled correctly. Then look at the answers.

If you guessed exactly the number that the answer page shows you to have spelled right, add one point to your score.

A good sense or intuition of how well you've done on something—accurate self-evaluation—is a quality more admirable than great spelling ability. You should be rewarded for it. Besides, guessing how well you've done makes the test more fun.

> The spelling of words is subordinate. Morbidness for nice spelling and tenacity for or against some one letter or so means dandyism and impotence in literature.
>
> Walt Whitman

PRONUNCIATION KEY

This key may be referred back to in taking any of the book's tests that present the words phonetically, namely, the Words of One Syllable and Say It and Spell It tests.

In the interests of simplicity, only one pronunciation is usually given for a word; variant pronunciations are often quite acceptable.

a	mat, parry	o	opt, mom, wasp
ā	aim, ray	ō	own, growth, no
â	air, wary	ô	morbid, tall, ought
ä	ah, calm	oi	oink, soil, toy
b	bond, rabid, slab	o͝o	cook, hood
ch	chair, bachelor, cinch	o͞o	ooze, pool, boo
d	die, radon, bad	ou	ouch, clout, scow
e	end, met, delicate	p	pit, slipper, sap
ē	emit, squeal, tee, only	r	rate, barracks, cheer
f	fat, ruffle, tiff	s	sail, lasting, buss
g	gate, slogger, wig	sh	shine, ocean, push
h	hint, behest	t	toll, otter, hat
hw	which	th	thanks, ether
i	in, dig	<u>th</u>	then, other
ī	ire, fight, defy	u	uncle, mud
j	joke, major, hedge	û(r)	urn, surge, burr
k	key, liker, rack	v	vend, lover, sieve
l	lost, yellow, ill, metal	w	wilt, awake
m	my, simmer, hum	y	yell, bunion
n	new, runner, an	z	zoo, easy, these
ng	wing, sarong	zh	measure, garage
ə	vowel in unstressed syllable (weak vowel sound), as in: gallop, attend, tanager, locust, carom, debatable, poem, Connecticut, aggravate, vanilla		

A prime mark (′) follows a syllable that is stressed. Parentheses, as in n(y)o͞os (news), indicate that the sound may be pronounced or not pronounced.

> . . . the Marquess of Queensberry made his way to the Albemarle Club, where he left his card, endorsed "To Oscar Wilde posing as a somdomite"—a mis-spelling which was to become famous. The porter, with wise discretion, put the card in an envelope, and ten days later handed it to Wilde when he visited the club. As he handed it over, he calmly assured the recipient that he had not understood what it meant.
>
> Martin Fido

SCHOLASTIC APTITUDE TEST (SAT) LEVEL

Word comprehension and usage, if not spelling itself, is part of the verbal section of the Scholastic Aptitude Test, taken annually by millions of American secondary school students hopeful of college admission. The following words are among those you might find in an SAT vocabulary section, and the meanings of most of which you'd be expected to know. Can you recognize which is the properly spelled word in the three columns?

SAT Level Test

Circle the correct spelling:

1.	heterageniety	hetrogeniety	heterogeneity
2.	ansillary	ancelary	ancillary
3.	casuistry	cassuistry	cazuistry
4.	mallese	malaise	mallaise
5.	undiscried	undescried	undiscride
6.	beatific	beyatific	baetific
7.	sateyity	satteity	satiety
8.	shicanery	chicanery	chickanery
9.	frangeable	frangable	frangible
10.	disphorea	dysphoria	disforria
11.	cutanious	cutaneous	queutaneous
12.	desuetude	dessuitude	deswitude
13.	millapede	milopede	millipede

14. paucity	pauccity	pawsity
15. buccolic	bucolic	beuccolic
16. sarry	sari	sarie
17. ubiquitous	eubiquitous	ubiquetous
18. apogy	apogee	appogie
19. sizemometer	sysmometer	seismometer
20. onerous	onorous	onnorous

Before consulting the answers on page 285:
I think I spelled _____ words correctly on this test.
(If your estimate is correct, add one point to your score.)

Upon the introduction of printing, indeed, English orthography entered into that realm of Chaos and old Night in which it has ever since been floundering; it then began to put on the shape it at present bears, "if shape it may be called that shape has none."

Thomas R. Lounsbury

Why Is English Spelling So Confused?

(A Brief History)

Why, oh why, is spelling in the English language such a senseless, unpredictable muddle and, for many of us, a continual problem?

"English spelling is the world's most awesome mess," wrote linguist and author Mario Pei some years ago. "In no other language is it possible to get seven different sounds out of a combination of written letters like *ough*, *(dough, bought, bough, rough, through, thorough, hiccough)*, or conversely, spell a sound like that ordinarily represented by *sh* in fourteen different ways. . . . In no other language would it be possible to write *phtholognyrrh* for *Turner* by using the *phth* of *phthisic*, the *olo* of *colonel*, the *gn* of *gnat* and the *yrrh* of *myrrh*, or to spell, plausibly, *kaughphy* for *coffee*." English, in short, has too many sounds for its twenty-six-letter Roman alphabet.

While solutions to or simplifications of inherent spelling difficulty in English continue to be elusive, explanations as to how and why our written tongue has come to be so crabbedly irregular are not. We have only to take a brief look at the history of our language.

English, fortunately or not, did not emerge as a wondrously logical and phonetically sane creation from Jupiter's head, much less from the edict of an Oxford-Cambridge academy, a book by Noah Webster, or the mind of a strict American schoolmistress.

English vocabulary, and its modes of spelling, is so rich and varied because over the centuries it has drawn its word stock from numerous other languages. The speech we use today began evolving, some fifteen hundred years ago on the island of Britain. In that era, it was not mere word borrowing or word stealing that formed the language. It was a series of invasions.

Even before the birth of Christ, the Romans had made a foothold in the British Isles. By about 75 A.D. they had conquered the Britons (who themselves descended from two different groups of Celtic invaders that arrived centuries earlier). In the fifth century the Romans had no sooner withdrawn from Britain than the isles were invaded from the coasts of the North Sea by Teutonic (or Germanic) tribes, the Jutes and, primarily, the Saxons and the Angles. Out of this confluence came what we know as Old English.

Over the next two centuries the Anglo-Saxons had largely been converted to Christianity, and Britain became a center of learning. The Latin alphabet was introduced, replacing a runic one. Old English evolved into three dialects: Mercian (midlands), Northumbrian (north), and West Saxon and Kentish (south). But the ninth century brought fearsome invasions by Norsemen, who spoke a related language. King Alfred the Great was not able to drive the Norse invaders out, but he did halt the advance of

their "Danelaw" at a dividing line between London and Chester. (Today's maps still reflect the differences in place names and spellings on either side of this onetime boundary.)

In the ninth and tenth centuries the Danish areas of Britain were assimilated and England was unified politically. There were four dialects of Old English in use at the time, until that from Wessex gained preeminence and was adopted by church scribes. For a brief period, Anglo-Saxon spelling became homogeneous and above all phonetic, with vowels denoted in a simple way and without silent consonants.

But invasion struck again, this time in 1066, in the form of what we know as the Norman Conquest. Along with the subjugation of the Anglo-Saxons came a profound upheaval in the English language as it had been. With the occupation of the Norman rulers and clergy came the language of northern France, which the nobility established as the language of all government and of the court. The Normans did not suppress English, but now no official standard could be maintained for its spelling. Fewer books (or manuscripts) were written, and those that were, were generally in French or Latin.

But there was a positive side to these developments. Slowly but surely, the two peoples began mixing, and another "invasion" began: that of French words into English, which had remained quite alive if varied in its dialects in particular regions. Though unstandardized, English had grown less and less inflected in its word endings during those years; that is, the troublesome gender of individual words was no longer observed in practice. French, meanwhile, was never adopted by the general citizenry.

By the fourteenth century English—now Middle English—had taken its place once and for all as the language of Britain. It was now richly infused with French borrowings and possessed a vocabulary whose spellings were anything but consistent or rational; errors by Norman scribes did not help. As for French itself, by the beginning of the fifteenth century it was considered a foreign language in England.

Middle English had several dialects, but the court settled near London, and with a newly centralized government the London dialect and spellings became standard, both nationally and internationally. And now the Renaissance brought to England not only a burgeoning hunger for learning and classical culture and the spirited coining of new words but also the revolutionary discovery of the printing press.

But printing in no wise encouraged an immediate standardizing of spelling, for several reasons. Consistency of spelling was not considered all that important; the Elizabethan compositors, or typesetters, were given to altering spellings even within the same page or line for space-filling or line-balancing reasons; and many of the early printers in England were from Germany or Holland, were poorly educated, and did not know English well. Moreover, different printers favored different spellings. Shakespeare's works, with all their variant spellings, exemplify the situation at that time. There are thirteen known different spellings of Shakespeare's name recorded, and in the first printing of his sonnets (1609) the word *mistress* was spelled five different ways.

Progress in the standardization of spelling, or at least in awareness of the need for it, was made in the sixteenth and seventeenth centuries because of the publications and proposals of various scholars. But when printing houses finally began to agree on standard spellings, those spellings had often long ceased to reflect the actual pronunciation then in use.

Spelling books were printed and became popular. In the early eighteenth century consideration was given to creating an English Academy (like the French Academy, founded in 1635) to safeguard and regulate language, but most English people did not take kindly to the idea of official meddling with the language, and the idea never got very far.

By the time Samuel Johnson's milestone *A Dictionary of the English Language* was published in 1755, English spelling was fairly standardized. Although Johnson himself cannot be given credit for making spelling uniform, his dictionary was important because it gained wide acceptance and greatly helped to settle or crystallize many spellings. Yet Johnson's primary basis for spellings in his dictionary was etymology, not phonetic aptness or simplicity.

Unfortunately, English pronunciation had continued to change rapidly, especially pronunciation of its vowels. When an established spelling had finally been achieved, it was often unphonetic, not reflective of actual speech in the land. Also, many words had extraneous or silent letters inserted into them to make them more presentable etymologically—that is, to make their Latin, Greek, or French origin evident—making spelling yet more unphonetic.

Nonetheless, the dictionary thus became an institution in the eighteenth century, and henceforth the growing middle class sought "correctness" in speech and spelling. In addition, English replaced Latin as the language of scholarship, and various "authoritative" grammars were subsequently published that contributed to spelling standardization.

Meanwhile, an ocean away, America was developing its own speechways. Noah Webster's importance to uniform—and often different—spelling in the United States derives not only from his famed *American Dictionary of the English Language* (1828) but from his *American Spelling Book* (1783–85). The latter became a veritable bible to Americans, underwent several hundred revisions, and sold more than sixty million copies. At first Webster followed Johnson's (British) spellings —for example, *honour* rather than *honor*. But he included in his dictionary the variant spellings that came to be preferred by Americans, and he ultimately became an influential advocate of American independence in its language and orthography.

For a handy summary of important factors in English's complicated spelling, see "Ten Reasons Why English Spelling Is So Confused" on page 125.

> When [William] Caxton settled for the idiosyncrasies of the English he heard in the streets of London—"right" for instance reflects the fifteenth-century pronunciation "richt" (*ch* pronounced as in *loch*) —he (and printers like him) helped to fix the language on the page before its writers and teachers had reached a consensus. It is to this that English owes some of its chaotic and exasperating spelling conventions.
>
> Robert McCrum, William Cran, and Robert MacNeil
> *The Story of English*

GRADUATE RECORD EXAMINATION (GRE) LEVEL

If you're a good college speller, you're ready to move on to graduate school. A spelling test is not part of any Graduate Record Examination test. But if you're going to comprehend or use words found in a GRE aptitude test, you might as well know how to spell them.

GRE Level Test

Circle the correct spelling.

1.	acouter	accoutre	accutor
2.	beleaguer	beleagor	belieguer
3.	agglomeration	aglomoration	agglommeration
4.	paniscea	pannasea	panacea
5.	catyclism	caticlism	cataclysm
6.	tallisman	talisman	tallesman
7.	vellum	velume	vellom
8.	appothicary	apothecary	appothecary
9.	parinoiac	paranoiac	parranoiac
10.	tocsin	tocksin	toccsin
11.	codicil	codisil	codicile
12.	abberation	aberration	aberation
13.	sinosure	seinosur	cynosure
14.	dennazen	denizen	dennizen
15.	lagniappe	laniape	lanaippe
16.	appiary	apiary	appiari
17.	conivance	connivance	conivence
18.	viand	viande	vyande
19.	aquiescent	acquiescant	acquiescent
20.	mallidiction	malediction	malodiction

> *Before consulting the answers on page 285:*
> I think I spelled _____ words correctly on this test.
> (If your estimate is correct, add one point to your score.)

> Tom Sawyer stepped forward with conceited confidence and soared into the unquenchable and indestructible "Give me liberty or give me death" speech, with fine fury and frantic gesticulation, and broke down in the middle of it. . . . Tom struggled a while and then retired, utterly defeated. There was a weak attempt at applause, but it died early.
>
> "The Boy Stood on the Burning Deck" followed; also "The Assyrian Came Down," and other declamatory gems. Then there were reading exercises, and a spelling fight.
>
> Mark Twain

IDEM SONANS

Imagine an important merger being effected between two large corporations, Avocado Computer and Literal Precision Instruments, Inc. The merger is being made official and legal in a contract drawn up by corporate lawyers. Everything is detailed, printed up, and signed by all parties. Months later, when there are certain regrets by some parties regarding the union of the two companies, it is suddenly noticed that, by some fluke, Literal Precision Instruments is misspelled as "Littoral Precision Instruments" throughout the signed contract. Is the merger invalid?

Or what of the case of Cyrus T. Loot's hotly contested will? Numerous hopeful or greedy people are interested parties in who gets what as a bequest. Months after the will is finally settled, Archie Ryval, one of the bitterly disgruntled beneficiaries (who got the lamb's share), notes that the name of the hated major beneficiary,

Cupidity Sprauling, is misspelled "Humidity Sprawling" in the key introductory paragraph of the will. Can Archie call his lawyer and have the will's terms appealed?

Law is one realm in which what is writ in print is deemed to be explicitly specific, unarguable, and—well, law. Or is it? What happens when a legal instrument contains a crucial word or term that is misspelled?

The cacographic perpetrator employed by the law firm may find himself or herself looking for a new job, perhaps, but otherwise not much.

Strange but true: A misspelling of a "material" word in law, so long as the written word would have the same sound as the intended word, does not affect the legitimacy or authority of the document in civil or criminal law; or, as lawyers put it, the erroneous orthography does not "vitiate the instrument."

This principle in law is called *idem*

sonans, "having the same sound." It makes sense. Much of law derives from oral testimony. Transcription by court stenographers is often involved, as is lengthy verbiage; legalese has never been noted for economy of expression (though changes for the shorter and clearer are now being made in some chambers). Lawyers and law clerks are human, and even in the most formal prose, mistakes can be made. It seems only just and common sense that intent —obvious intent—and not error-free spelling be the binding principle in such serious matters as marital litigation, wills, and business contracts.

Still, it doesn't seem *quite* fair, does it? Lawyers—of all people—not having to be concerned about correct spelling? Should poor spellers in school, copyeditors and proofreaders, and National Spelling Bee contestants be able to plead obvious intent—*idem sonans*—when they misspell?

Further on you'll find a Law spelling test in this book. *Idem sonans* will not apply.

> Who cares about spelling? Milton spelt *dog* with two *g's.* The American Milton, when he comes, may spell it with three, while all the world wonders, if he is so minded.
>
> Augustine Birrell

WORDS OF ONE SYLLABLE TEST NO. 1

If length rather than content makes a word difficult to spell for you, you'll have nothing to fear here. This is a spelling test made up solely of one-syllable words; there will be others. Write in the correct spelling.

Words of One Syllable Test No. 1

Write in the correct spelling.

1. adz   _____ cutting tool
2. kyōō   _____ line of people
3. wēr   _____ dam in a stream
4. māz   _____ Indian corn
5. kän   _____ Asian ruler

6.	shist	_____	rock with parallel layers
7.	kwīr	_____	twenty-four or twenty-five sheets of paper
8.	krōōth	_____	ancient Celtic stringed instrument; crowd
9.	zist	_____	ancient covered portico or promenade
10.	flōō	_____	chimney channel
11.	skrip	_____	token or temporary paper currency
12.	bīt	_____	bay at a coastal bend
13.	shûr	_____	bake until set, as shelled eggs
14.	rech	_____	attempt to vomit
15.	spilth	_____	refuse or waste
16.	brôm	_____	type of carriage
17.	ängk	_____	cross whose top piece is looped; symbol of life
18.	glōz	_____	interpret or explain
19.	stûrps	_____	family branch
20.	ouf	_____	elf
a.	hwûrl	_____	circular or spiral shape
b.	brōōm	_____	mist
c.	kīn	_____	*archaic:* cows
d.	bleb	_____	blister
e.	mōōs	_____	chilled puddinglike dessert

Pronunciation key on page 10.

Before consulting the answers on page 285:
I think I spelled _____ words correctly on this test.
(If your estimate is correct, add one point to your score.)

English spelling is notoriously inconsistent and it is rather hard on those whose only wish is to be left alone that failure to master its intricacies is sometimes regarded as one of the clearest signs of an inadequate education.

G. L. Brook

SPELLING AND INTELLIGENCE

Does poor spelling have anything to do with intelligence?

This question sometimes comes up when spelling is the subject of discussion, and more than sometimes when a seemingly bright, decent, literate person has done badly on a spelling test and is nursing serious ego wounds. Is there cause to doubt his or her basic IQ?

There is good news and bad news.

The good news is that there is no evidence to prove any correlation between orthographic skills and fundamental smarts. Nor does being a good reader assure that one will be a good speller. Medical researchers have found qualitative differences in the brains of dyslexics, but they haven't in any way gotten a fix on the biology or causes of relative spelling ability. Dr. Richard E. Hodges, a dean of education at the University of Puget Sound who has studied spelling and cognition for many years, explains that no real research has been done linking spelling and intelligence, and that while it's true good spellers tend to be good readers, good readers are by no means always good spellers.

Which is not to say that people don't differ greatly in their ways, or modes, of apprehending and storing words. Some people's minds function verbally in a visual way—they "see" the word or words—while others learn words mostly by sound. Psychology tells us that learners whose mental imagery is predominantly visual are called verbiles—and that others among us are audiles, tactiles, and motiles.

Is spelling ability something innate or a skill that can be learned? Again, there is no definitive answer to this question, only continuing disagreement among experts and fevered opinions among the rest of us. One opinion is that of Kenneth G. Wilson, an English professor at the University of Connecticut who for some thirty-eight years has taught both undergraduates and Ph.D.s. "Most people," Wilson says in a *New York Times* article, "assume the ability to spell is a measure of intelligence and application, but it ain't." One of the brightest students he ever had "was a totally phonetical speller. He couldn't look words up. Someone had to transcribe [his work] before I could read [his papers]."

It has been demonstrated that having a wide vocabulary makes for a better speller; and that emotions—attitude or confidence regarding improving one's spelling—are a crucial factor, especially for young schoolchildren. What about adults? Many educated people are abysmal spellers. Not surprisingly, studies have shown that chronic spelling problems can often be traced back to a sense of spelling failure in childhood. One British educator found that childhood spelling setbacks, loss of confidence, reluctance to attend to details, apathy, and rationalization kept many educated misspellers just that, educated misspellers.

Are good writers all good spellers? Resoundingly, no. F. Scott Fitzgerald was one of America's greatest novelists and one of our notoriously bad spellers. In the first printing of *This Side of Paradise* there were about a hundred misspellings, so complained Fitzgerald himself to his editor, Maxwell Perkins, when the novel was due to be published in England.

And the bad news that goes with the good? It's simply that while poor spelling doesn't mean impaired IQ, one thing that the new science of neurolinguistics is finding is that we're all somewhat various and different in our ways, capacities, and speeds of learning. This makes it unlikely that any absolute truths or solutions will be found for making us all tip-top spellers.

> Good spelling enhances your attractiveness in social life and in your career. Good spelling facilitates studying and increases your chances of getting and holding a responsible job. And, after all, learning to spell well isn't as hard as you might think.
>
> Edna L. Furness

MULTIPLE-CHOICE TEST NO. 1

What would a book of spelling tests be without some ever-familiar multiple-choice tests? Here is the first of *Death by Spelling*'s multiple multiple-choice quizzes.

Multiple-Choice Test No. 1

Circle the correct spelling.

1. delliquess   deliquese   delliquesce   deliquesce
   (dissolve or melt)
2. hoi polloi   hoy polloi   hoy palloi   hoi palloi
   (the common crowd, the masses)
3. dipphthongal   dipfthongal   dipthongal   diphthongal
   (pert. to a gliding of vowels)
4. parasole   parosole   parasall   parasol
   (woman's light umbrella or sunshade)

5. litterateur   litterator   literateur   literatteur
   (literary person or seasoned writer)

6. lachet   latchet   latchette   lachette
   (fastening strap on a shoe)

7. hommini   hominy   homminie   homminy
   (soaked, hull-less corn kernels)

8. bombycine   bombacyne   bombacine   bombycyne
   (pert. to silkworms)

9. lainollin   lainolin   lannolin   lanolin
   (wool grease used in cosmetics)

10. reohstat   rheostat   rheostatt   reohstatt
    (electric current regulator)

11. farinah   farrinah   farrina   farina
    (meal used as breakfast cereal)

12. paparazi   papparrazi   paparazzi   papparazzi
    (celebrity-pursuing photographers)

13. otious   oshiose   ochiose   otiose
    (idle or without purpose)

14. inchoat   inchoate   incoate   incoite
    (not completely formed or manifested)

15. cunaeiform   cuneiform   cuneaform   cunnaeiform
    (using wedge-shaped characters for an alphabet)

16. murmidon   murrmidon   myrmidon   myrrmidon
    (obedient or unquestioning subordinate)

17. kaleidoscopic   kelaidoscopic   kalleidoscopic   kallaidoscopic
    (showing changing colors or patterns)

18. megilah   meggilah   megillah   megilla
    (long and involved story)

19. Mah-Jong   Majong   Ma-Jonng   Mah-Jongg
    (game of Chinese origin using 144 tiles)

20. bêttise   bêtise   baetise   bêttize
    (stupid act)

a. baccilus   bacillus   bacilus   baccillus
   (type of rod-shaped bacterium)

b. okkra   ocra   okrah   okra
   (green pods used in stews)

c. chasauble   chassible   chasible   chasuble
(priest's sleeveless vestment)

d. schmierkase   shmeerkase   schmeerkase   shmierkase
(cottage cheese)

e. keppie   keppi   kepi   kepie
(flat-topped, visored, round military cap)

Before consulting the answers on page 285:
I think I spelled ＿＿ words correctly on this test.
(If your estimate is correct, add one point to your score.)

ORTHOGRAPHY, *n.* The science of spelling by the eye instead of the ear. Advocated with more heat than light by the outmates of every asylum for the insane. They have had to concede a few things since the time of Chaucer, but are none the less hot in defence of those to be conceded hereafter.

Ambrose Bierce

Who Was Webster?

Just as we rarely think of spelling without thinking of dictionaries, we rarely think of dictionaries without conjuring up the name Webster.

The man behind the name was Noah Webster (1758–1843). The acknowledged father of American lexicography, Webster was (we are apt to forget) a contemporary of George Washington, Thomas Jefferson, Benjamin Franklin, and James Fenimore Cooper.

Webster's life was anything but dry as a reference book. Tendentious and always self-promoting, this contentious patriot was continually a focal point of controversy regarding the American language and its spelling. And his career in many ways epitomizes the many fundamental—and perennially unresolved, it seems—questions and hackles raised when men and women zealously attempt to plan, guide, or protect their national language: Should the language of the United States be thought of as different from that of England, as "the American language"? Should American pronunciation, ideally, be nationally uniform? Should dialects and the borrowing of foreign words be discouraged? Should a dictionary promulgate newly simplified spellings if readers are already accustomed to more difficult but established spellings?

Webster, a graduate of Yale, was a lawyer and a teacher and wrote not only about language (he had some familiarity with more than twenty languages) but also about economics, religion, medicine (the causes of yellow fever), and politics. His name became well known with publication in 1783 of his *The American Spelling Book,* or "blue-backed speller," which had many successive editions and became an enormously popular schoolbook in the United States, second only to the Bible in sales. (Fifty years later, when the U.S. population was less than twenty-five million, it was selling more than a million copies a year.) The book from the PBS television series "The Story of English" gives us a brief glimpse of Noah Webster at work:

> The success of the *American Speller* gave Webster, on a royalty of one cent per copy, more than enough to live on, and he now devoted the rest of his life to the zealous championing of the cause of the American language, its spelling, its grammar and its pronunciation. The story is told, by an old printer recalling his apprenticeship, of the day "a little pale-faced man came into the office and handed me a printed slip, saying, 'My lad, when you use these words, please oblige me by spelling them as here: *theater, center,* etc.'" It was Noah Webster traveling about the printing offices and persuading people to follow his "improved" conventions.

Webster published his first dictionary in 1806 and his great two-volume work, *An American Dictionary of the English Language,* in 1828, when he was seventy years old. The latter, however, containing some twelve thousand words not found in any current British dictionary, became a success only in revised editions after Webster's death.

Webster's views regarding the lexicon of our language were strong but shifting ones, and his ideas generated controversy throughout his lifetime. He at first rejected ideas of reforming, or Americanizing, English spelling, favoring such literations as *honour, metre,* and *waggon* and expressing respect for Samuel Johnson's illustrious dictionary (1755) as a spelling and pronunciation guide.

But more and more, Webster saw his mission as fostering—through Congress, education, and books—an American language that would be independent and as uniform as possible. He wanted not just to take note of dialects around the country but to discourage them. He foresaw British and American English diverging into separate languages—all well and good, he felt, as he did not want the standard for American speech to come from London. Ideally, nationally, Webster felt, spelling should not be at odds with pronunciation. It should be reformed (and now was the time to act) through the dissemination of books—his own books. He generally opposed introducing new phonetic symbols or characters into the alphabet, but at one point recommended adding "eth" *(th),* "esh" *(sh),* "eng" *(ng),* and "ezh" *(si* or *su)* and using a small mark to distinguish the voiced *th* from the unvoiced one. To simplify English spelling, he said, it was necessary to get rid of all silent letters (e.g., *ment* instead of *meant*); to supplant indefinite letters or letter combinations with definite ones (e.g., *greev* instead of *grieve*, *korus* instead of *chorus*); and to add certain marks (over or through standard letters) to distinguish between sounds when necessary, as in the case of the voiced or unvoiced *th*. Unfortunately, some of Webster's proposed new spellings were based on his inspired but erroneous etymologies.

Webster was always pragmatic enough to believe in gradual rather than sudden change in spelling. From the days when he first communicated with Benjamin Franklin, he hoped that Congress would adopt and implement his proposals. It was not to be. As George Philip Krapp notes in *The English Language in America,* the American public did not welcome such complications, and the aging Franklin did not share Webster's zeal.

Webster's ideas for a so-called Federal English never came to fruition, and in old age he found himself softening his position—not least of all, it has been pointed out, in order not to jeopardize sales of his dictionaries in England. (Among Websterian spellings that were retracted in later editions of his dictionaries were *iz, relm, mashine, yeer, bilt, tung, breth, helth, beleeve,* and *wimmen.*)

Then, as today, philologists had strong opinions pro or con such "solutions" regarding matters of language, and Webster's strong Anglophobic views gained him enemies, ridicule, and even parody from many quarters for many years. He was not only an ambitious and, to many, abrasive man but also a self-contradictory one. He repeatedly accused others of stealing his ideas or work. He often purported to have an objective, descriptivist view of American speech, yet continually insisted on perfecting the national tongue. Webster was, H. L. Mencken has noted, "not only a pedagogue but also a Calvinist, and a foe of democracy. Indeed, all his attacks on authority were arguments against the other fellow's and in favor of his own."

In many ways Webster personifies the ambivalence and insecurities many Americans felt for a half century and more after the Revolution regarding superiority or inferiority vis-à-vis England and Europe (notably France, which had a famed language academy but whose tongue Webster described as being enfeebled and not virile in sound). In 1824, while preparing his great two-volume dictionary of 1828, he visited England and made overtures to British scholars in hopes of resolving some differences between the two language camps. He now seemed to stress how similar the two species of English were; there was one English language, not two. His 1829 *Elementary Spelling Book* avowed that its pronunciations generally accorded with those of "well-bred" people in both countries.

The latter part of Webster's career was marked by a heated rivalry between him and lexicographer Joseph Worcester (1784–1865), who had worked for Webster but was a respected scholar in his own right and published his own first dictionary in 1830. Unlike Webster, Worcester was an Anglophile and had a conservative, Johnsonian, and fairly temperate and objective approach to the recording of the language; he preferred more established spellings and more refined pronunciations. (It also happened that Webster and his enterprises were identified with Yale; Worcester and his with Harvard.) Their personal differences—Webster was the aggressor, typically—grew into a celebrated "war of the dictionaries," which continued for two decades after Webster's death in 1843. The war was ultimately very much a commercial one: a no-holds-barred struggle, with unscrupulous tactics, for the American dictionary market. Worcester published his worthy *A Universal and Critical Dictionary of the English Language* in 1846, three years after Webster's death, after which the battle of the books became especially intense. In 1860 Worcester's greatest dictionary appeared, *A Dictionary of the English Language.*

Ultimately, commercial victory went to the Webster line of dictionaries, which had become Merriam-Webster by the turn of the century, but not without irony. Much of Noah Webster's own work (including many of his controversial spellings and erroneous etymologies) was done away with, and the more prudent and elegant virtues of Worcester's approach were borrowed by Webster's publishers to achieve success in the marketplace.

For all his autocratic tetchiness, we owe Webster a great deal. He had the vision to realize that American English should and would develop along its own lines. Despite his inclination to "purify" the language in sundry ways, he realized that dictionaries should be guided by actual usage, that new words —Americanisms—are not always needless or "low," and that the pronunciation of place names should be determined by local residents.

Webster also recognized that Americans, more than the British, would look to books—dictionaries—for guidance in matters of language. Many of the spelling revisions he sanctioned (*frolic, physic, center, theater, honor, favor, traveled* and *traveling, check, mask, defense*) have been adopted by Americans, as have certain American pronunciations (*schedule* and *lieutenant*).

Webster, Mencken says in *The American Language,* "was too shrewd to believe that language could really be brought under the yoke. He had observed that it was a living organism with a way of life of its own—with a process of evolution but little determined by purely rational considerations."

Even in Merriam-Webster dictionaries today, the only meaning you will find for the word *webster* is that of weaver, for which *webster* is an archaic term. But for many people the name

Webster is synonymous with lexicon— or an American one—just as Baedeker is with travel guidebook.

At the turn of the century, Merriam-Webster fought to retain exclusive right to the use of the name Webster on a dictionary cover but lost in the courts. Today, any dictionary may call itself a Webster's dictionary.

> Take care that you never spell a word wrong. Always before you write a word, consider how it is spelled, and, if you do not remember it, turn to a dictionary. It produces great praise to a lady to spell well.
>
> Thomas Jefferson

SAY IT AND SPELL IT TEST NO. 1

Here is a non–multiple-choice test that gives you each word phonetically and also provides a brief definition. If you don't do well on this one, turn a few pages and try again with another test using this format.

Say It and Spell It Test No. 1

Write in the correct spelling.

1.	mâr′dē grä	_____	pre-Lent carnival period
2.	out′lī ər	_____	person living elsewhere from where his or her business is
3.	saf′īər	_____	rich blue gem
4.	wil′fə lē	_____	perversely or obstinately
5.	wil′fo͝ol nes	_____	perverseness or obstinacy
6.	yo͝o′rə gwā	_____	South American country
7.	trans mis′ə bəl	_____	passable, as a disease
8.	zhə lā′	_____	cosmetic gel
9.	trē′klē	_____	cloyingly sweet
10.	tûrt′lit	_____	small turtle
11.	fôr′mat ər	_____	one who devises a format
12.	ə biz′məl	_____	profoundly low

13. per spik ā'shəs   _____   keenly perceptive
14. ə nēl'   _____   to strengthen through heating and
                                   cooling
15. par'əf   _____   flourish at the end of a signature
16. brāzd   _____   cooked slowly in fat in a closed pot
17. mə kad'əm   _____   type of road surface containing broken
                                     stone
18. dis kum'fit ər   _____   one who frustrates
19. kar'əl   _____   study cubicle
20. an'ə dīn   _____   relieving pain or soothing
 a. prə nouns'ə bəl   _____   capable of being pronounced
 b. fer'is hwēl   _____   amusement park vertical rotation ride
 c. ri dak'tər   _____   editor
 d. frī'ə bəl   _____   able to be crumbled
 e. jə kōōz'ē   _____   whirlpool bath or tub

Pronunciation key on page 10.

Before consulting the answers on page 285:
I think I spelled ____ words correctly on this test.
(If your estimate is correct, add one point to your score.)

AMERICA'S FIRST RUNAWAY BEST-SELLER: NOAH WEBSTER'S 'BLUE-BACKED SPELLER'

The popularity of the book was doubtless due in large measure to the fact that it presented an orderly, and as far as convention at all permitted, an economical and systematic guide to English spelling. It is historically significant therefore, not as a radical book, but because it became so widely used. In fact the *American Spelling Book* became so generally accepted as a standard that it made any thoroughgoing reform of spelling more than ever impossible. In a note to the Preface of the 1803 revision, dated March, 1818, Webster says that "the sales of the American Spelling Book, since its first publication, amount to more than five millions of copies, and they are annually increasing." A few years later, the publishers stated that one million copies were sold annually. If we remember that in 1820 the state of Illinois numbered less than 100,000 inhabitants, that the whole population of the state of New York was less than one-third of that of the present city of New York, that the whole of Massachusetts contained fewer inhabitants than Boston now does, we begin to realize the enormous consumption of these spelling books. Writing in 1837 and in answer to a letter of inquiry, Webster gave the number of copies sold to date as "at least fifteen millions." By 1865 the total circulation had been about 42,000,000 copies. From 1876 to 1890, during which time the book was under the control of D. Appleton and Company, the sales were "about eleven and one-half million copies," Ford, *Notes,* II, 448–449. "The present generation of living men and women," says a writer in the year 1865, quoted in Ford, *Notes,* II, 448, "when they go back in memory to their early school days find their thoughts resting upon this, as their only and all-important text-book." The spelling match became indeed a great social and national pastime, rivaling in interest the singing school and horse racing in pioneer and village life. It is not too much to say that for the average American citizen, especially in the North and West, throughout at least three generations, Webster's spelling book was almost the solitary means of approach to the elements of literary culture. Other spelling books appeared, some rivals, some imitations, but none ever approached the *American Spelling Book* in popularity.

George Philip Krapp

But consider also this: the Women's Campaign Fund, one of the most influential feminist organizations, has sent out a brochure soliciting contributions, and the subheading, writ large, reads: BREAK THE VISCIOUS CIRCLE. The text itself begins (in only slightly smaller print): "That viscious psychological circle has kept many women out of office." Should not these eminent postulants, some in very high office, who seek election or reelection funds, know how to spell *vicious?*

John Simon

Words of One Syllable Test No. 2

Write in the correct spelling.

1. lap   _____   inhabitant of northern Scandinavia
2. stīl   _____   step for passing over a wall or fence
3. shiv   _____   knife
4. nōos   _____   mind or reason philosophically

5.	nef	_____	table ornament or holder shaped like a ship
6.	ôk	_____	diving seabird
7.	o͝omf	_____	vitality
8.	bisk	_____	cream soup
9.	piks	_____	container for Holy Communion bread
10.	cresh	_____	Nativity scene representation
11.	bwät	_____	nightclub
12.	siv	_____	perforated straining or draining implement
13.	gôrs	_____	spiny shrub
14.	wen	_____	sebaceous skin swelling
15.	shrof	_____	coin evaluator
16.	sou	_____	make a sighing sound
17.	tōp	_____	brownish gray
18.	koin	_____	(~ of vantage) advantageous position
19.	mulkt	_____	defraud
20.	trôf	_____	animal feeding receptacle
a.	floks	_____	flowering plant
b.	fēnd	_____	demon or monster
c.	sāsh	_____	movement of the surface of water
d.	frēz	_____	sculptured entablature
e.	bo͝ors	_____	European stock exchange

Pronunciation key on page 10.

Before consulting the answers on page 286:
I think I spelled ____ words correctly on this test.
(If your estimate is correct, add one point to your score.)

The dictionary emphasizes the trivial matters of language at the expense of what is truly important. The precise spelling of a word is relatively trivial because no matter how the word is spelled, it nevertheless remains only an approximation of the spoken word. *A machine chose the chords* is a correctly spelled English sentence, but what is written as *ch* is spoken with the three different sounds heard in the words *sheen, catch,* and *kiss.*

                                                                Peter Farb

THE WEBSTERIZING OF AMERICAN SPELLING

Not until [Noah Webster's] Dictionary of 1806 was there a wholesale assault upon the authority of Johnson. [Webster] made an almost complete sweep of whole classes of silent letters: the *u* in *-our* words, the final *e* in *determine*, the silent *b* in *thumb*, the *s* in *island* and the redundant penultimate consonant in *traveler* and *wagon* (English *traveller* and *waggon*). He lopped the final *k* from *frolick* and *physick*, and transposed the *r* and *e* in many of the words ending in *-re*, such as *theatre* and *centre*. He even antedated the simplified spellers by such phonetic spellings as *tung* for *tongue* and *wimmen* for *women*. Some of these spellings simply echoed an earlier English uncertainty, others were for analogy or uniformity, or for euphony or simplicity, or because it pleased him to stir up the academic animals. Webster, in fact, delighted in controversy, and was anything but free from the national yearning to make a sensation. Many of his innovations failed to take root, and in the course of time he abandoned some himself, such as the dropping of the silent letter in such words as *head, give, built* and *realm*. Successive editions of his dictionary show further concessions, but many, like *aker* for *acre* and *cag* for *keg*, did not begin to disappear until the edition of 1847, issued by other hands after his death. Three of his favorites, *chimist* for *chemist, neger* for *Negro* and *zeber* for *zebra,* are incidentally interesting as showing changes in American pronunciation. He abandoned *zeber* in 1828, but remained faithful to *chimist* and *neger* to the last.

H. L. Mencken
The American Language

Multiple-Choice Test No. 2

Circle the correct spelling.

1. sinsimilla   sinsemilla   sensimilla   sensemilla
   (type of marijuana)

2. amersing   ammercing   amercing   ammersing
   (punishing by fining)

3. formaldahide   formaldihide   formaldehyde   formaldihyde
   (gas used in aqueous form as a preservative)

4. chrisanthemum   chrysanthemum   crysanthemum   chresanthemum
   (plant with bright flowers)

5. ukaze   ukkaize   ukase   ukaiz
   (edict)

6. farrinacious   farinaceous   farinacious   farrinaceous
   (starchy)

7. palimino   pallamino   palomino   pallomino
   (golden-colored horse)

8. cicaida   ciccaida   cicada   ciccada
   (insect that makes a shrill sound)

9. temerrarious   temorarious   temerarious   temmerarious
   (daringly bold)

10. picsecide   picescide   piscicide   piciscide
    (fish-killing agent)

11. Pocahontas   Pocohontas   Pocohontos   Poccohontas
    (Indian maiden who saved the life of Captain John Smith)

12. mellinoma   mellanoma   melinome   melanoma
    (molelike malignancy)

13. cacophany   cacaphony   caccophony   cacophony
    (harsh or unpleasant sound)

14. filiment   filliment   fillament   filament
    (electric current conductor or cathode)

15. kowtow   kowtau   kautow   kautau
    (to fawn)

16. tamboureen   tamboreen   tamborine   tambourine
    (hand-held and shaken percussion instrument)

17. prosalyte   prosilyte   proselyte   proscilite
    (one converted)

18. bourgoise   bourgoisee   bourgeoise   borgeoise
    (female middle-class person)

19. merang   maringue   merangue   meringue
    (fluffy pastry topping)

20. ptetsie fly   ptetse fly   tsetsie fly   tsetse fly
    (African fly causing sleeping sickness)

a. battik   bottik   batik   batikk
    (Indonesian fabric design)

b. wam-pam   wampam   wam-pum   wampum
    (beads once used as currency by Indians)

c. nougat   nugat   nuggate   nougate
    (nut- or fruit-studded candy)

d. tattarsall   tatersall   tattersal   tattersall
    (squared pattern used on fabrics)

e. yarmulke   yalmulke   yarlmulke   yamulke
    (Jewish skullcap)

Before consulting the answers on page 286:
I think I spelled _____ words correctly on this test.
(If your estimate is correct, add one point to your score.)

Even in so settled a matter as spelling, a dictionary cannot always be absolute. . . . The reader may want a single certainty. He may have taken an unyielding position in an argument, he may have wagered in support of his conviction and may demand that the dictionary "settle" the matter. But neither his vanity nor his purse is any concern of the dictionary's; it must record the facts. And the fact here is that there are many words in our language which may be spelled, with equal correctness, in either of two ways.

Bergen Evans and Cornelia Evans

CAUTION, DICTIONARIES AT VARIANCE

Possibly you will have a gripe or two about some of the variant spellings included as valid answers to the tests in *Death by Spelling*. I sympathize; I most assuredly outgriped you in checking dictionaries to confirm spellings for the tests and finding I had to do without many favorite word choices because variant spellings are now lexically countenanced.

Years ago, devising spelling tests was a pretty simple matter. Most words, even those tough to spell, had a single dictionary spelling. But dictionaries in recent years have been more intentful about recording alternative spellings—misspellings, to many of us—that have been appearing in print. A citation (or clipped-out example of a word's use in a book or periodical) is a citation, and dictionaries properly aim to record the language, not to prescribe it.

Still, this approach becomes a question of degree or extent—or of number of citations, and over what period of time they occur. Should a line be drawn at some point? At what point, and by whom? If there has indeed been something of a national deterioration in grammar and spelling of late, should dictionaries reflect this by including more permissive usages?

Dictionaries, however reputable, all have differences, and they can differ substantially when it comes to variant spellings. This fact was well illustrated in a comparative study by Lee C. Deighton in the early 1970s. Deighton's investigations showed that America's four major collegiate dictionaries (American Heritage, Random House, Webster's New World, and Merriam-Webster's Seventh) listed variant spellings for more than two thousand words in the common language. Complicating this—for the individual who wants, in "the dictionary," a source of firm authority—are the continuing differences among the four:

They differ as to whether some spellings occur with enough frequency to be recorded at all. They differ as to which spellings are British rather than American. They differ substantially as to whether particular compound words are to be hyphened, closed up, or written as separate words. There is disagreement on the use of hyphens in such words as *reexamine, re-examine* and *coordination, co-ordination*. There is disagreement as to whether particular spellings are current, rare, obsolete, archaic, etc.

These various differences contrast sharply with the fairly uniform spelling practice of current newspapers, magazines, books, and other publications. The question is why the dictionaries seem to be at odds with current practice. One part of the answer is that publication editors *must* make a spelling choice and stay with it consistently. The other part of the answer gets to the very nature of dictionaries. The editors of these works feel obliged to record all spellings found with reasonable frequency in their records (citations). A great many of these citations go back to the early 19th century and earlier.

All in all, Deighton found, there were some 1,770 common-usage words upon which the four dictionaries were at odds with regard to spelling.

Such differences among dictionaries still obtain today. It's enough to stop anybody from talking about "the" dictionary, or from trying to put together a book of tough spelling tests.

> Christine: Dismiss me, madam?
> Gardner: Cora, can you be so cruel?
> Mrs. Prout: Alas, yes! She has sinned the secretarial sin which is beyond forgiveness. She has misspelt!
> Gardner: Impossible!
>
> Arnold Bennet
> *The Stepmother*

TWO WORDS OR ONE

Spelling involves not only letters but also spaces, to say nothing of hyphens. Is it *such and such, such-and-such,* or *suchandsuch?* English has a way of leaving two words alone for a while, then giving them a hyphen, and then discarding the hyphen and making one solid word. New editions of dictionaries continue to show slight shifts here and there along this continuum.

Hyphens are often optional—or arguable—as when numerous modifiers are strung together. If this problem bugs you, a good style book, such as the University of Chicago Press's *A Manual of Style* ("the Chicago Manual"), can be a helpful guide. Remember that there aren't hard and fast rules here. "If you take hyphens seriously," warned John Benbow years back in *Manuscript and Proof,* the style book of the Oxford University Press, "you will surely go mad."

You'll be spared hyphens, and possible madness, in the following test, which focuses on terms that are spelled either as one word or two—at least, going by most current dictionaries. Check back again in another five years.

Two Words or One Test

Circle the correct words (or word).

1.	snow ball	snowball	13.	toll booth	tollbooth
2.	tail light	taillight	14.	step ladder	stepladder
3.	back seat	backseat	15.	night club	nightclub
4.	red brick	redbrick	16.	bow tie	bowtie
5.	waste water	wastewater	17.	bar bell	barbell
6.	sales clerk	salesclerk	18.	hammer lock	hammerlock
7.	film maker	filmmaker	19.	law suit	lawsuit
8.	pot holder	potholder	20.	window sill	windowsill
9.	bird bath	birdbath	21.	peep hole	peephole
10.	hair shirt	hairshirt	22.	art work	artwork
11.	passion flower	passionflower	23.	paper clip	paperclip
12.	locker room	lockerroom	24.	bar room	barroom

25.	lamp post	lamppost	c.	gall bladder	gallbladder
a.	land owner	landowner	d.	sea bird	seabird
b.	mouth part	mouthpart	e.	cream puff	creampuff

Before consulting the answers on page 286:
I think I spelled _____ words correctly on this test.
(If your estimate is correct, add one point to your score.)

SHH IS THE WORD

The confounding vagaries of English spelling are perhaps best summed up by the observation that the sound "sh" can be spelled at least twenty-four different ways in our language. At least, that's how many have been ferreted out by Richard Lederer, language columnist and author:

appre**ci**ate	con**sci**ous	**hs**in	By**ssh**e
o**ce**an	nau**se**ous	**ps**haw	mi**ss**ion
chaperone	**sh**oe	**s**ugar	**s**zlachta
ca**che**	man**si**on	cre**sc**endo	ini**ti**ate
fu**chs**ia	a**ss**ure	**sch**wa	na**ti**on
suspi**ci**on	A**ssh**ur		e**schsch**oltzia

If place names and more people's names were considered, possibly a longer list could be made. For the common "ay" vowel sound, Lederer discovered words representing thirty-six variant spellings.

Someone asked a Fool: "Is *kebab* with *a* or *o*?"
"With meat," he answered.

Anonymous (Sufi humor)

Say It and Spell It Test No. 2

Write in the correct spelling.

1. dis′təl _____ anatomically far from the point of attachment

2. ə man yōo en′ sēs _____ copyists or dictation takers

3. bā′ də kər _____ travel guidebook

4. glâr′ē _____ brightly reflective or dazzling

5. dī al′ə sis _____ use of membranes to separate elements of a liquid

6. tə bog′ən _____ sled curved upward at one end

7. pə trōon′ _____ old New York estate proprietor

8. kā′ tif _____ coward

9. ə ses′ə bəl _____ determinable or taxable

10. ī′ dē āt _____ to form an idea

11. pə rab′ə loid _____ type of surface in mathematics

12. im′ prest _____ loan

13. pot′ ash _____ potassium carbonate from wood ashes

14. ok sid i zā′ shən _____ dehydrogenation affected by oxygen

15. i kis′ tiks _____ science of human settlements and building

16. di mān′; di mēn′ _____ one's own land legally, estate

17. chā′ ôrl _____ Anglo-Saxon low-ranking freeman; churl

18. kib′ it sər _____ unwanted commenter or adviser

19. pros′ə li tīz _____ to convert or recruit

20. kə kōon′ _____ insect's protective envelope

a. ak′ ak′ _____ antiaircraft fire

b. bə ras′ik _____ boric

c. kath′iter _____ tube for medical insertion

d. pī ə rē′ə   _____   pus discharge

e. non ə jə när′ē ən   _____   ninety-year-old person

Pronunciation key on page 10.

Before consulting the answers on page 286:
I think I spelled ____ words correctly on this test.
(If your estimate is correct, add one point to your score.)

The late Miles Hanley, checking early New England letters and town records, noticed more than fifty spellings for forms of *receive,* including *receyve, resaived, recued, recieveing,* and *receaued.*

Charlton Laird

NOMIC SPELLING

Phonetic spelling is the writing down of a word in any way that indicates, as precisely or understandably as possible, its pronunciation.

For example, you may render the word *eraser* phonetically as i-'rā-sər *(Webster's Ninth New Collegiate Dictionary);* i rā′sər *(Webster's New World Dictionary* and the *Random House Dictionary,* Second Edition); ė·räs′ēr *(Webster's New International Dictionary,* Second Edition); ĭ-rā′sər *(American Heritage Dictionary);* and ɪ'reɪzə *(Collins English Dictionary).*

If you find dictionary or International Phonetic Alphabet (IPA) symbols too arcane to the eye, you can always respell eraser phonetically as e-RAY-ser or EE-RAY′-SER.

We don't have such options in our everyday writing, which calls for us to inscribe our thoughts in the conventional and often quite unphonetic orthography of English. Such spelling—"normal" spelling—is called nomic spelling or heteric spelling. (*Nomic* comes from the Greek word for usage, custom, law.)

Not to confuse you, but phonetically *nomic* is NAH-MIK or NO-MIK, either pronunciation being permissible.

Words of One Syllable Test No. 3

Write in the correct spelling.

1. jel   _____   gelatin
2. plad   _____   colored rectangular pattern
3. hō   _____   gardening flat-bladed tool
4. flens   _____   remove blubber from a whale
5. flem   _____   mucus
6. tēl   _____   dark greenish blue
7. hwā   _____   watery part of milk
8. kech   _____   yawllike sailing vessel
9. mou<u>th</u>   _____   speak automatically or insincerely
10. bans   _____   formal announcement of a coming marriage
11. shôm   _____   old woodwind instrument
12. krôs   _____   lacrosse stick
13. dou   _____   Arab sailing boat
14. sond   _____   atmospheric or other probe
15. dīn   _____   acceleration unit-of-force measurement
16. flesh   _____   mid-church spire
17. thrips   _____   plant-feeding insect
18. kwosh   _____   suppress
19. sto͞op   _____   tankard
20. dro͞op   _____   type of fruit, such as the cherry
a. skons   _____   candlestick bracket
b. twäl   _____   simple-weave fabric, such as linen
c. gamp   _____   blouse worn beneath a jumper
d. thyo͞o   _____   muscle
e. fôs   _____   ditch or moat

Pronunciation key on page 10.

> *Before consulting the answers on page 287:*
> I think I spelled _____ words correctly on this test.
> (If your estimate is correct, add one point to your score.)

BENJAMIN FRANKLIN'S ALPHABET

The lightning rod and Franklin stove are but two of the many creations we owe to the inventive scholar, diplomat, and patriot-of-all-trades Benjamin Franklin. In 1768, when he was sixty-two, Franklin devised a new, reformed alphabet for English. Six of its twenty-six letters were new characters. Its purpose was to make our written language more phonetic and thereby help poor spellers; each letter would represent a single sound, and there would be no more silent letters to deal with.

Like all other such spelling-reform innovations, his orthographic scheme was never adopted (Franklin never threw his full energies into promoting it, and Webster wasn't interested at the time they met). But seeing a sample of a "new" spelling can be instructive. Is it preferable to our current alphabet? Would getting used to such a new way of reading and writing just be a matter of time?

Below is a chart of Franklin's proposed new alphabet and a letter, written in that alphabet, that Franklin wrote to a friend, Mary (Polly) Stevenson. "Pali" had some reservations about the alphabet. The second letter below, in standard English letters, was Franklin's reply to her criticisms.

Franklin's Alphabet

o	old	o
a[*a*]	John, Folly	a
a	man, can	a
e	mane, lane	e
i	een, seen	i
u	tool, fool	u
ɥ[*ɥ*; Ⱶн]	um, un, in umbrage, unto, &c.	ɥ
h	hunter, happy, high	huh
g	give, gather	gi
k	keep, kick	ki
s[*s*]	sh, ship, wish	ish
ŋ[*ŋ*]	ng, ing, reaping, among	ing
n	end	en
r	art	ar
t	teeth	ti
d	deed	di
l	ell, tell	el
th[*th*]	th, think	efi

dh[*dh*; Ð]	dh, thy	edh
s	essence	es
z	ez, wages	ez
f	effect	ef
v	ever	ev
b	bees	bi
p	peep	pi
m	ember	em

Letter from Franklin to Polly Stevenson

Diir Pali,   Ritsmγnd, Dsulγi 20.–68

Yнi intended to hev sent iu ჹiz Pepers sunγr, bγt biig bizi fargat it.

Mr Kolman hez mended deeli: bγt iur gud Mγჹγr hez bin indispoz'd uith e slγit Fivγr, atended uith mγts fiibilnes and uirines. Si uiuld nat allau mi to send iu uγrd av it at ჹi tγim, and iz nau beter.

Yнi uis iu to kansider ჹis Alfabet, and giv mi Instanses af sγts Iglis Uγrds and Saunds az iu mee uink kannat perfektlγi bi eksprest bγi it. Yнi am persueeded it mee bi kamplited bγi iur help. Ði greeter difikγlti uil bi to brig it into ius. Hauevγr, if Amendments eer nevγr atemted, and thigs kantinu to gro uγrs and uγrs, ჹee mγst kγm to bi in a retsed Kandisγn at last; sγts indiid γi uink aur Alfabet and Rγitig alredi in; bγt if ui go an az ui hev dγn e fiu Senturiz langer, aur uγrds uil graduali siis to ekspres Saunds, ჹee uil onli stand far thigs, az ჹi rittin uγrds du in ჹi Tsuiniiz Languads, huits γi sγspekt mγit oridsinali hev bin e litiral Rγitig lγik ჹat af Iurop, bγt thru ჹi Tseendsez in Pronγsiesγn braat an bγi ჹi Kors af Eedses, and thru ჹi abstinet Adhirens af ჹat Pipil to old Kγstγms and amγg γჹγrs to cheer old manγr ov Rγitig, ჹi oridsinal Saunds af Leters and Uγrds eer last, and no langγr kansidered. Yнi am, mγi diir Frend, Iurz afeksγnetli.

B. FRANKLIN

Franklin Defends His Alphabet

Dear Madam,

The objection you make to rectifying our alphabet, "that it will be attended with inconveniences and difficulties," is a natural one; for it always occurs when any reformation is proposed; whether in religion, government, laws, and even down as low as roads and wheel carriages.—The true question then, is not whether there will be no difficulties or inconveniences; but whether the difficulties may not be surmounted; and whether the conveniences will not, on the whole, be greater than the inconveniences. In this case, the difficulties are only in the beginning of the practice: when they are once overcome, the advantages are lasting.—To either you or me, who spell well in the present mode, I imagine the difficulty of changing that mode for the new, is not so great, but that we might perfectly get over it in a week's writing.—As to those who do not spell well, if the two difficulties are compared, (viz.) that of teaching them true spelling in the present mode, and that of teaching the new alphabet and the new spelling according to it; I am confident that the latter would be by far the best. They naturally fall into the new method already, as much as the imperfection of their alphabet will admit of: their present bad spelling is only bad, because contrary to the present bad rules: under the new rules it would be good.—The difficulty of learning to spell well in the old way is so great, that few attain it; thousands and thousands writing on to old age, without ever being able to acquire it. 'Tis, besides, a difficulty continually increasing; as the sound gradually varies more and more from the spelling: and to foreigners it makes the learning to pronounce our language. as written in our books, almost impossible.

Now as to "the inconveniences" you mention.—The first is; that "all our etymologies would be lost, consequently we could not ascertain the meaning of many words."—Etymologies are at present very uncertain; but such as they are, the old books would still preserve them, and etymologists would there find them. Words in the course of time, change their meanings, as well as their spelling and pronunciation; and we do not look to etymology for their present meanings. If I should call a man a Knave and a Villain, he would hardly be satisfied with my telling him, that one of these words originally signified only a lad or servant; and the other, an under plowman or the inhabitant of a village. It is from present usage only, the meaning of words is to be determined.

Your second inconvenience is, that "the distinction between words of difficult meaning and similar sound would be destroyed." —That distinction is already destroyed in pronouncing them; and we rely on the sense alone of the sentence to ascertain, which of several words, similar in sound, we intend. If this is sufficient in the rapidity of discourse, it will be much more so in written sentences: which may be read leisurely; and attended to more particularly in case of difficulty, than we can attend to a past sentence, while a speaker is hurrying us along with new ones.

Your third inconvenience is, that "all the books already written would be useless."—This inconvenience would only come on gradually in a course of ages. You and I, and other living readers, would hardly forget the use of them. People would long learn to read the old writing, though they practised the new.—And the inconvenience is not greater than what has actually happened in a similar case, in Italy. Formerly its inhabitants all spoke and wrote Latin: as the language changed, the spelling followed it. It is true that at present, a mere unlearned Italian cannot read the Latin books; though they are still read and understood by many. But if the spelling had never been changed, he would now have found it much more difficult to read and write his language; for written words would have had no relation to sounds, they would only have stood for things; so that if he would express in writing the idea he has, when he sounds the word *Vescovo*, he must use the letters *Episcopus.*—In short, whatever the difficulties and inconveniences now are, they will be more easily surmounted now, than hereafter; and some time or other, it must be done; or our writing will become the same with the Chinese, as to the difficulty of learning and using it. And it would already have been such, if we had continued the Saxon spelling and writing used by our forefathers.

I am, my dear friend,
Yours affectionately,
B. Franklin

SPELLING IS NOT JUST MEMORIZING

Rageshree Ramachandran
1988 Scripps Howard National
Spelling Bee Champion

Spelling is a very serious thing. As an exercise, it is a very powerful mental discipline. One doesn't simply come across lists of words to study, but one must gradually and methodically comprise one's own lists of words. Whenever I read a book, magazine, or newspaper, or perhaps watch a movie, and come across a new or unusual word, I write it down, look it up, learn related words, and commit it to memory. But spelling is not just memorizing. It involves proper usage of words and making them part of one's vocabulary, not just some extraneous entities.

Prior to the 1988 National Spelling Bee, I spent up to three hours a day for six months studying. But I have always been learning new words and have been regularly studying for the past five years, since I was eligible to participate in spelling bees. Actually, it was a self-discovered hobby which stemmed out of my love for reading, and I was just naturally good at spelling bees. After my first two years, I started turning "competitive spelling," if you will, into a methodical process which culminated this past year. The rewards are wonderful, no matter how one fares: after spending so much time studying, one would have a clear edge over others in writing, diction, and speaking, because just participating in spelling bees enhances one's stage presence as well.

And I don't intend to stop studying now that I have won the National Spelling Bee. Learning new vocabulary terms is a useful and healthy practice at any time of life. It certainly aids me in, for example, writing and taking English tests, where so many words either have foreign roots that I have studied or are related to words that I know.

It is necessary to know what it is like up on stage. For me, when I get my word, it's not a do-or-die sort of thing. By careful thinking and finding related words or identifying the root word, I can confidently spell a word I have never heard of before.

Multiple-Choice Test No. 3

Circle the correct spelling.

1. flytyer   flytier   fly tier   fly tyer
   (maker of fishing flies)
2. ensorcellment   insorsellment   ensorclement   insorclement
   (bewitchment)
3. carrefour   cariforre   carrifore   carefour
   (crossroads or square)

4. jalapeño   jaliapeño   jalliapeno   jalapenno
   (Mexican pepper)

5. Roorshach   Roorschach   Rorschach   Rorshach
   (psychological inkblot test)

6. strycknine   strichnine   strychnine   strichnyne
   (type of poison)

7. bimilinnary   bimillinary   bimilinary   bimillenary
   (2000th anniversary)

8. aquarelist   acquarellist   aquarellist   aquerelist
   (watercolorist)

9. fiefee   fieffee   feoffee   feofee
   (recipient of a fee)

10. cocotte   coccotte   cocqotte   cocquot
    (prostitute)

11. schedaddle   skiddadle   skidaddle   skedaddle
    (to run away)

12. bizarrerie   bazaarery   bazaarerie   bizarrery
    (peculiar happenings, appearance, etc.; strangeness)

13. nayade   niade   naiad   nayad
    (water sprite)

14. tai quon do   tae quon do   tae kwon do   tai kwon do
    (Korean martial art)

15. aolian   aolean   aeolian   aolaean
    (musically making a sighing, windlike sound)

16. pailiasse   palliasse   paliasse   pailliasse
    (straw mattress)

17. banquette   bankette   bancquette   banc-ette
    (upholstered seat built in to a wall)

18. koine   quoine   coine   coinee
    (dialect that has spread)

19. anopheles   anofeles   annopheles   anophelies
    (malaria-causing mosquito)

20. *kapishe*   *capisce*   *cappisce*   *kappische*
    (Italian: Understand?)

a. lachrymose   lachrimose   lacrymose   lacrimose
   (tearful)

b. beddizzen   beddizen   bedizzen   bedizen
(to dress gaudily)

c. Kwonset   Kwonsit   Quonset   Quonsette
(semicircular prefabricated building of corrugated metal)

d. croupiée   croupier   croupie   croopier
(casino gaming tables employee)

e. obloquie   obloquey   obloqoy   obloquy
(bad reputation)

Before consulting the answers on page 287:
I think I spelled ___ words correctly on this test.
(If your estimate is correct, add one point to your score.)

EYE DIALECT

When is it that you see misspellings in a book, and not merely one or two of them, but whole paragraphs or even pages of them, and scarcely take notice? And when the misspellings are meant to be there?

"Wen yer reedin' dyilog lines spoke in dylekt," says the person giving you the answer.

Eye dialect is the term for misspelled, or phonetically respelled, words used in literature (and journalism and comic strips, for that matter) to indicate a provincial or less than educated speaker, or just to have a humorous effect. Such creative spelling is used especially by writers of a folk or ethnic stamp, such as Mark Twain, Artemus Ward, and Joel Chandler Harris, but eye dialect has been used by thousands of other novelists and poets, from Shakespeare to Langston Hughes and countless modern writers of fiction. Try to find a historical romance or hard-boiled American detective novel that doesn't have some colorful-character spelling.

Note that eye dialect need not always be a rendering of anomalous pronunciation. Is *wuz* said any differently from *was*? Or *wimmin* from *women*? The intent in such usages is mostly to draw attention to the speaker's class, local origins, or poor education.

An interesting thing about eye dialect is that such phonetic misspellings are very much like the simplified spellings advocated by English spelling reformers. It is partly because so many people associate such reformist spellings with comic strip characters and fictional yokels that the spelling reform movement has never succeeded.

> Correct spelling is aided by a photographic memory and some familiarity with etymology, especially Latin and Greek. Misspelling is a not innocuous disease against which writers should inoculate themselves with a potion of Latin and Greek roots and regular checkups at Dr. Webster's, the best resort for a spell.
>
> John B. Bremner

MINUTE MINUTE WALTZ

As in minute (small and requiring attention to detail) and minute (sixty seconds). No more luxurious mulling over and erasing. It's time to learn at first hand if you can beat the second hand. Besides a pencil here, you need a wristwatch, stopwatch, or visible clock. You've got exactly one minute to circle the correct spellings. Can you handle deadline stress as well as a confident proofreader?

Minute Minute Waltz Test

Circle the correct spelling.

1. bonhomie   bonhommie   bonnehommie   bonhommey
   (geniality)
2. segway   segue   seggway   seggue
   (to proceed or continue without pause)
3. shelfull   shelffull   shelf-full   shelfful
   (quantity filling a shelf)
4. éppéist   épéeiste   épéeist   épéist
   (fencer using a dueling-type sword)
5. comeuppence   comupence   comeuppance   come-up-ence
   (deserved punishment, rejection, etc.)
6. mopyness   mopeyness   mopiness   mopieness
   (sluggishness)
7. abutall   abuttal   abbutal   abuttle
   (land boundary legally)
8. transferance   transferrence   transference   transferrance
   (turning over or conveying)

9. villify   vilify   vilefy   villefy
   (to defame)
10. consumé   consomé   consummé   consommé
    (a clear soup)

Before consulting the answers on page 287:
I think I spelled _____ words correctly on this test.
(If your estimate is correct, add one point to your score.)

Say It and Spell It Test No. 3

Write in the correct spelling.

1. də vwaurs′   _____ respects or formal farewell
2. kon fer ē′   _____ conference participant
3. myōō′sə lij   _____ adhesive substance
4. ser′ēd   _____ dense or crowded
5. sham′ē   _____ goatlike antelope
6. tōōt′lij   _____ guardianship, protection, or
                                    instruction
7. kōō tor ē âr′   _____ female high-fashion dress designer
8. swan yā′   _____ elegantly groomed
9. shif′ə rōb   _____ wardrobe-chest of drawers
10. pret′səl   _____ salted, doughy cracker in twisted
                                    shape
11. di sēd′ənt   _____ dead person
12. luv′ē duv′ē   _____ very affectionate or suspiciously so
13. per i pə tet′ik   _____ moving around
14. jōō′dē iz əm   _____ Jewish religion or culture
15. flō til′ə   _____ military fleet
16. shal′ət   _____ green onion
17. eks kûr′sis   _____ digression
18. tə ra′zo; tə rä′tso _____ mosaic flooring
19. gal ə mō′frē   _____ hodgepodge
20. sē fol′ə jē   _____ study of elections

a. brag ə dō′shē ō   _____   cocky boasting
b. vī res′əns; vir res′əns   _____   greenishness
c. fi′jit ē nes   _____   restlessness
d. mar ē ä′chē   _____   Mexican folk musical group
e. tas′əl   _____   ornamental bunched-cords pendant

Pronunciation key on page 10.

Before consulting the answers on page 287:
I think I spelled _____ words correctly on this test.
(If your estimate is correct, add one point to your score.)

SPELLING REFORM: QUOTEWORTHY DIFFERING OPINIONS

The English spelling-system is best left alone, except in minor particulars. Attempts to simplify or respell the language are likely to be unavailing for a long time to come.

> Robert Burchfield

. . . the English race will not be content to sit down forever with a system of spelling which has nothing to recommend it but custom and prejudice, nothing to defend it but ignorance, nothing but superstition to make it an object of veneration.

> Thomas R. Lounsbury

[Spelling reform] is as hypothetical and deceptive as [the name] "The Conifers" for a house with a dwarf larch in the garden. Briefly, the spelling of English cannot be reformed, and should not be even if it could; a phonetic alphabet is out of the question for English. There is a two-fold objection, of time and place, even without our calling on the centuried traditions that have composed our spelling.

> Basil Cottle

In this country [the spelling reform movement] has been handicapped by the fact that, to Americans, phonetic spelling suggests the grotesqueries of the comic writers, stretching from Seba Smith to Milt Gross, and by the further fact that popular interest in and respect for spelling prowess, fostered by the institution of the spelling bee, still survive more or less.

H. L. Mencken

We instinktively shrink from eny chaenj in whot iz familyar; and whot kan be more familyar dhan dhe form of wurdz dhat we hav sen and riten more tiemz dhan we kan posibly estimat?

Sir Isaac Pitman

It is apparent that any attempt to influence spelling appreciably in the direction of simplicity is doomed. Periodicals that attempt this are likely to acccomplish nothing more than to inconvenience their staffs and make their readers smile. The fact that not one of the *Chicago Tribune's* millions of readers commented on its virtual abandonment of fonetic (oops) phonetic spelling in 1955, after years of persistence in such oddities as *frate* for *freight* and *sofomore* for *sophomore,* seems to indicate the subscribers thought they were seeing typographical errors all that time.

Roy H. Copperud

To spell words as they used to be pronounced is not etymological, but antiquarian.

W. W. Skeat

The tinkers with spelling agree on one point; they all say: "make it phonetic—let us spell as we pronounce." Very nice, but *whose* pronunciation? I listen daily to the local weather bureau, where I have singled out by ear six announcers, of whom one is a woman and one almost certainly a black—a man with a splendid deep voice. The six pronounce the same words differently: the black drops the g in -*ing* like a British aristocrat; the young woman says *an'*, not *and.* Some of the others say *humi-ity,* also without a *d.* There is *tempracher* and *temperchoor; Tyusday* and *Toosday;* the word *center* occurs as *cent'er* and as *cent-ter* (a New Yorkism); the number 20 is spoken as *twanny, twenny,* and *twennt-ty.* This is but a sampling of the wide diversity of sounds actually uttered to signify common words.

Jacques Barzun

Misspellers Unite—If You Can

(Spelling Reform)

If you continually struggle with spelling, you may now and then have gritted your teeth, bitten the eraser off your pencil, and had a brilliant idea. Instead of your having to improve your spelling, why doesn't somebody improve—simplify—the exasperating language?

Neither Noah Webster nor Benjamin Franklin, as we've already noted, succeeded in overhauling our alphabet. But that was more than 150 years ago. Why hasn't there been a *law* passed to rid English of all useless silent letters, unnecessary double *l*'s and double *t*'s, and that *-able* or *ible* mess?

Why not indeed?

Reforming our way of spelling would, it has been argued, save time and expense in elementary education and in all writing and printing. It would allow people to spell as they pronounce, and possibly focus more attention on good pronunciation and make it more standardized everywhere. It would make it easier for foreigners to become Americanized (or Anglicized) and make English a more accessible international language. Words now spelled the same but having different meanings, such as *bow, tear, lead, read,* and *sow,* would be differentiated (although there would be a vice versa, blurring distinctions between, say, *to, two,* and *too*).

A simple and sanely phonetic English spelling system would save both pupils and teachers a lot of grief. It might even, one proponent has vowed, spare children the "atrophy of logical faculties"—so illogical is our present spelling.

The history of our language shows that not only born misspellers but exasperated teachers and professors, copyeditors, and foreign students of English have had the same original thought. Spelling reform has been passionately espoused, opposed, and debated over the past two hundred years, involving not only Franklin and Webster but Sir Isaac Pitman; Mark Twain; George Bernard Shaw; Alfred, Lord Tennyson; and Teddy Roosevelt. But it has remained an ignis fatuus, a perennially lost cause.

Proposals to homogenize our orthography go back to the beginning of the thirteenth century (before printing was introduced into England, in 1476, by William Caxton). A monk named Ormin, or Orm, ventured some simplified spellings in his *Ormulum*, a work in Middle English paraphrasing the scriptures. Orm's intent was to make the written word reflect pronunciation more accurately. He doubled consonants after short vowels, retaining single consonants after long vowels. Thus he spelled *fire fir* and *fir firr;* the Middle English word for "went," pronounced with a long *o,* Orm spelled *for,* whereas the preposition we know as *for* he spelled *forr*. But—possibly a harbinger of reactions to later high-minded reform efforts—Orm's ideas did not catch on.

In the sixteenth century Sir John Cheke, a professor of Greek at Cambridge University, urged ridding the language of silent final *e*'s and all silent consonants (e.g., *dout* instead of *doubt*). But despite his having influential support, English, as H. L. Mencken later put it in *The American Language,* "went on its wild way." In the following century, John Wilkins's "Essay Towards a Real Character and a Philosophical Language" (1668) proposed a new, international phonetic alphabet without success. (Wilkins was a Cambridge master and later a bishop.) And exactly a hundred years later, encouraged by Webster, Franklin devised his alphabet but never published the document, confessing that he felt too old for such a crusade. As for Webster, his views changed over the years. Initially opposing any spelling changes, he favored considerable change by 1790, then came to advocate only moderate (and inconsistent) changes.

Since then, in both England and the United States, many others have put forth spelling reform schemes. They have ranged from systems of radically new phonetic symbols (some like those of shorthand) to less ambitious modifications of the alphabet or of particular common words.

Post-Revolution and Victorian American individuals hopeful of re-spelling our language included (to name a few of them) Jonathan Fisher, a clergyman and artist (1793); William Thornton, a

Scottish physician in the United States (1793); James Ewing, a businessman (1798); Abner Kneeland, a Baptist Minister and later a free-thinker (1813); Michael H. Barton, a Quaker educator (1803–1833); Ezekiel Rich, a minister (1844), and Amasa D. Sproat, a druggist (1857).

In the past century, reform has been promoted by various organizations on both sides of the Atlantic, most notably by the Simplified Spelling Board in the United States and the Simplified Spelling Society in England—all to no end. A brief chronology gives some idea how much time and effort have gone into the cause, if only intermittently:

- **1876.** The American Philological Association (APA) appoints a committee to explore the subject and recommends eleven revised spellings: *ar, catalog, definit, gard, giv, hav, infinit, liv, tho, thru,* and *wisht.*
- **1876.** The Spelling Reform Association is established at a convention in Philadelphia and endorses the eleven spellings just listed. For a more thorough overhauling of the language's orthography, a complete phonetic alphabet is devised.
- **1879.** England forms a similar body, the British Spelling Reform Association. Members include Charles Darwin and Alfred, Lord Tennyson.
- **1886.** The APA makes recommendations pertaining to thirty-five hundred words, including *cach, truble, tung,* and *ruf.* These proposals have little success.
- **1898.** The National Education Association revives the 1886 APA scheme, shortening the list and nominating twelve changes: *tho, altho, thru, thruout, thoro, thoroly, thorofare, program, prolog, catalog, pedagog,* and *decalog.*
- **1906.** The Simplified Spelling Board is organized with a supportive subsidy from Andrew Carnegie and issues a list of three hundred proposed simplified spellings. President Theodore Roosevelt orders their adoption by the Government Printing Office (GPO), causing great official and public outcry. Ultimately, and briefly, only the White House uses the new spellings—twelve of them. When Taft becomes President, the New York *Sun* refers to the defeated candidate Roosevelt with a one-word headline: "THRU."
- **1908.** In England the Simplified Spelling Society is founded and begins issuing a long series of pamphlets and books. Its aim is to reform spelling without new characters, new phonetic values, or

new accents; for example, *onor, laebor, kulor*. The society accepts the goals of the Simplified Spelling Board with regard to the general populace but urges special spelling innovations in elementary schools.

- **1921.** The National Education Association, which has urged reform since 1898, withdraws its endorsement of the Simplified Spelling Board's handbook (published in 1919).
- **1931.** The Chicago *Tribune*—which will champion the cause of simplified spelling—adopts more than eighty such spellings, including *iland, rime, fantom, crum, jaz,* and *lether*. Over the next fifty years the *Tribune* modifies this list, in some cases because of public pressure.

With these highlights we may also mention Anglic, a Swedish project to adapt, or "generalize," English for worldwide use. Though the project was endorsed in London in 1930 by the International Phonetic Association and other groups, it was not a phonetic system, and the rival Simplified Spelling Board was not so enthusiastic about it. With the death of its deviser, R. E. Zachrisson, and World War II, its promotion came to a halt.

But spelling reform, however well-intentioned or ingenious the plan, has found support neither with the British nor with the American citizenry. More often than not, its advocates have quarreled over methods or specifics, and more often than not the great misspelling populace has remained mightily indifferent, resistant, or bemused regarding such meddling with our time-honored language. Another curious fact is that most reformist ideologues have not practiced—or spelled—what they preached in their own writings and correspondence.

Why, finally, do most people oppose or even ridicule the idea of changing our approved spellings? It seems to come down to the truth, sad or not, that such an undertaking, here and now in the twentieth century, is too quixotic—either too little too late or too much too late; and that to many people, the most idealistic and educated spelling reformer is some sort of crank.

Speaking more historically, two events in particular dealt serious blows to the movement. One was the abortive zeal of Teddy Roosevelt in trying to coerce adoption in Washington of simplified spellings; in doing so, he underrated the natural resistance of the American public, and by politicizing the issue he caused his measures to backfire. The other setback to the cause was Andrew Carnegie's failure to provide for further financial support to the movement after his death.

Opponents of spelling reform point to specific, inherent disadvantages or problems stemming from such orthographic utopianism. Simplified phonetic spellings, besides appearing (for quite a while, at least) illiterate or cartoon-dialoguelike, would obscure the etymologies of words. This argument has been called fallacious, since even now our traditional spellings are often unreliable indices of derivation, and because only people knowing some Latin and Greek (if not Old English and Old French) can profit from etymological spelling. But the fact remains that one of the things people cherish about English is that its spellings very much reflect its rich and various history.

Besides the etymological argument, antireformists point out that with simplified spellings, words now pronounced the same but spelled differently (*night* and *knight, son* and *sun, bare* and *bear*) would no longer be differentiated, and that there are many more of these words (homophones) than there are words spelled the same but pronounced differently (homographs). Would the newly spelled word's context always make the meaning clear? Phonetic spellings, opponents say, will obscure the connections between related words— between, for example, sage (*saj?*) and sagacity (*sugasitee?*). What's more, many words in our language (so-called eye words) are mostly encountered in print and rarely need to be pronounced. What about the spelling of new loan words? Should they be immediately converted, respelled?

And who likes the look of simplified spellings? This "aesthetic" argument has been rejected by reformers, but clearly many people would not look kindly on any change in the look of English. What about people's surnames and geographical names, which couldn't very well be changed? (Even fanatics for spelling reform tend to agree about this.) Also, opponents say, would-be reformers exaggerate the difficulties of English spelling. (Poor spellers may disagree.) Above all, isn't English just too rich and mixed a language to be simplified—or infantilized —forcibly through spelling? It's logical to want to reform a difficult spelling system. But is it the nature of English or any other tongue to be comfortably logical?

There are all these criticisms, to say nothing of the unimaginable problems that would ensue in dispensing with hundreds of years of printed material and literature as we know it today. Too many people, from language scholars to the common reader, find the idea of spelling reform not only impracticable but downright foolish or even comical. "When the Simplified Spelling Board began making its list longer and longer and wilder and wilder," H. L. Mencken comments in *The American Language,* "the national midriff began to tickle and tremble, and soon the whole movement was reduced to comedy."

Jacques Barzun, in *A Word or Two Before You Go,* points out that a spell-as-you-speak method of teaching would never work because "a *nearly* adequate phonetic system—one matching the sounds we speak—would require not twenty-six letters but forty-three. This addition means added difficulty for the child starting school. And as to phonetic detail, it is a question how far a child—indeed, any person—is aware of how he does pronounce." We should also remember, Barzun says, that English belongs not only to the United States but to the British Isles, Australia and New Zealand, the Indian subcontinent, many islands, large areas of Africa, and thousands of Europeans, Asians, and Latin Americans, who "have learned English and modified its utterance in countless ways. Some cannot say *th*, others invert *v* and *w*, while the sounds of *r, l, b,* and *d,* and the vowels vary indefinitely. What makes them all 'speak English' is the central, conventional spelling of the words that they voice as they please or as they can."

Rest assured, nonetheless, that the spelling reform movement will never be stone dead. (Among American groups currently espousing the cause are Better Education thru Simplified Spelling, Inc., in Detroit, and the Typographic Council for Spelling Reform, which advocates a so-called Soundspel alphabetic system.) If it has made no other lasting dent in our language, it has probably in some way encouraged the endemic whimsical, quasi-phonetic spellings, such as "lite," that we see everywhere in business and advertising today.

PAIRS OR PEARS (HOMOPHONES)

You thought you could escape these classic sound-alike word dilemmas in a book of spelling tests? These little pairings illustrate once again what a difference a single letter can make in the meaning of a word.

Pairs or Pears (Homophones) Test

Check True or False.

1. ( ) True   carat: unit of weight   karat: unit of fineness for gold
   ( ) False
2. ( ) True   rillets: streamlets   rillettes: seasoned ground-meat
   ( ) False   appetizer
3. ( ) True   principle: main or chief   principal: fundamental
   ( ) False   assumption or tenet
4. ( ) True   forward: ahead   foreword: prefatory part of a book
   ( ) False

5. ( ) True   miner: nonadult   minor: coal worker
   ( ) False

6. ( ) True   stationary: writing paper   stationery: not moving
   ( ) False

7. ( ) True   flair: illuminating blaze   flare: style
   ( ) False

8. ( ) True   valance: edging drapery   valence: chemical number
   ( ) False

9. ( ) True   pallet: crude bed   palette: artist's paint-daub holder
   ( ) False

10. ( ) True   censor: incense container   censer: moral arbiter
    ( ) False

11. ( ) True   discrete: separate or individual   discreet: quietly
    ( ) False   considerate

12. ( ) True   leach: bloodsucking worm   leech: dissolve through
    ( ) False   percolation

13. ( ) True   breach: rear of a gun's barrel   breech: break or
    ( ) False   rupture

14. ( ) True   immanent: impending   imminent: dwelling within
    ( ) False

15. ( ) True   millenary: women's hats   millinery: group of a
    ( ) False   thousand

16. ( ) True   council: lawyer   counsel: advisory group
    ( ) False

17. ( ) True   gluttonous: eating voraciously   glutinous: sticky
    ( ) False

18. ( ) True   capital: top of an architectural column
    ( ) False   capitol: state legislative building

19. ( ) True   shear: cut   sheer: transparent
    ( ) False

20. ( ) True   affect: bring about   effect: make a pretence of
    ( ) False

21. ( ) True   calender: time chart   calendar: cloth- or paper-
    ( ) False   smoothing machine

22. ( ) True   pedal: power using the feet   peddle: sell
    ( ) False

23. ( ) True   hangar: airplane shelter   hanger: closet wire
    ( ) False   implement

24. ( ) True   trooper: theatrical performer   trouper: mounted
    ( ) False   policeman

25. ( ) True   complement: flattering remark
   ( ) False   compliment: something that completes
a. ( ) True   apothem: pointed saying
   ( ) False   apothegm: perpendicular from the center of a polygon
b. ( ) True   auger: tool for boring   augur: foretell
   ( ) False
c. ( ) True   indite: write down or compose   indict: accuse
   ( ) False
d. ( ) True   grandam: grandmother   grande dame: imposing lady
   ( ) False
e. ( ) True   spoor: small reproductive plant body
   ( ) False   spore: animal trace or droppings

> *Before consulting the answers on page 287:*
> I think I spelled ____ words correctly on this test.
> (If your estimate is correct, add one point to your score.)

GEORGE BERNARD SHAW VS. ENGLISH SPELLING

The English language cannot be spelt, because there is no English alphabet. We make shift with a Latin alphabet which has only five vowels. The vowels we use, mostly diphthongs, are innumerable: no two inhabitants of these isles use the same set; but the sounds they utter are so far recognizably alike as to be intelligibly represented by 18 letters. The consonants, as to which there is much less difference of utterance, require 24 letters.

Our attempts to make a foreign alphabet of 26 letters do the work of 42 are pitiable. We write the same vowel twice to give it a different sound, and thus get five additional vowels. We couple two different vowels, or even triple them, in various permutations, which give us much more than 18 vowel spellings. We also double the following consonant (compare "table" and "dabble," for instance) or make two consonants represent simple sounds like the consonants in "thee" and "she," for which the Latin alphabet does not provide.

These devices would make our alphabet phonetic enough for

practical purposes if we used them consistently; but as our use of them is not consistent no one can pronounce a line of English from English writing or print.

And yet our phoneticians . . . have wasted a century raising an empty laugh over our spelling of "cough," "laugh," "enough," "though," &c., &c., &c. They have never knocked into our heads the simple fact that a letter saved in spelling is saved not once but millions of times every day.

I reflected on the number of plays Shakespear would have had time to write if he had written them in the phonetic alphabets of Pitman, Sweet, or Gregg, and on the staggering fact that Dickens, though a professional verbatim reporter, had to go through the drudgery of writing all his novels in Johnsonese longhand for the printer.

No author in his senses, having grasped the figures, would use the Phoenician alphabet if a British phonetic one were available. I wish some person with a mania for arithmetic would count the sounds in Shakespear's plays or Dickens's novels, and then count the letters these unfortunate scribes had to write to make readable manuscripts of them for the players and printers. I would burn all the commentaries and criticisms that have been wasted on their works for such a cast-up. It would prove that they in their short lives (I have lived nearly twenty years longer than either of them) could have written two or three more plays and novels than they had time to get through.

I always use the American termination *or* for *our*. Theater, somber, center, etc., I reject only because they are wantonly anti-phonetic: theatre, sombre, etc., being nearer the sound. Such abominable Frenchifications as programme, cigarette, etc., are quite revolting to me. Telegram, quartet, etc., deprive them of all excuse. I should like also to spell epilogue epilog, because people generally mispronounce it, just as they would mispronounce catalogue if the right sound were not so familiar. That is the worst of unphonetic spelling: in the long run people pronounce words as they are spelt; and so the language gets senselessly altered.

Multiple-Choice Test No. 4

Circle the correct spelling.

1. moitey   moity   moyety   moiety
(one half)

2. solfegio   sollfegio   solfeggio   sol'fegio
(singing sol-fa syllable)

3. parallelism   parralelism   parallellism   paralellism
(analogous direction, correspondence, resemblance)

4. manicle   manickle   manackle   manacle
(shackle or handcuff)

5. platelette   platelet   platalet   platalette
(flat body that is minute)

6. flibbertigibetty   flibbertigibbety   flibbertygibbety   flibbertigibbetty
(flighty)

7. stilleto   stilletoe   stiletto   stilettoe
(thin dagger)

8. tynitis   tinnitus   tinitus   tinitis
(ringing in the ears)

9. fraccasses   fracasses   fracases   fraccases
(brawls)

10. phouie   phooie   phooey   fooey
(expression of rejection)

11. scurrillous   scurilous   scurillous   scurrilous
(coarsely abusive)

12. dismennhorea   dismenorrea   dysmenhorea   dysmenorrhea
(painful menstruation)

13. acidophilos   asidophilus   asidophilos   acidophilus
(therapeutic bacteria-fermented milk)

14. senor   seignor   senore   senhor
(Portuguese man)

15. turniquette   turniquet   tourniquette   tourniquet
(bandage or binding to check bleeding)

16. falafell   felafal   fallafel   falafel
(fried patties of ground vegetables)

17. bisextile   bissestil   bisextille   bissextile
(pertaining to the added day in leap year)

18. trunchian   trunchion   trunchen   truncheon
(policeman's club)

19. guayot   guiot   gyot   guyot
(flat-topped seamount)

20. Hugeunot   Huegenot   Huguenot   Heugenot
(French Protestant of the sixteenth or seventeenth century)

a. chinziness   chinzyness   chintzyness   chintziness
(vulgar cheapness)

b. fuchia   fushia   fuchsia   fuschia
(shrub with reddish or purple flowers)

c. picayune   pickeyune   picyune   piccayune
(trivial)

d. agiorniamento   aggiorniamenta   aggiornamento   agiorrnamenta
(modernization)

e. easell   eazel   easal   easel
(painter's standing canvas support)

Before consulting the answers on page 288:
I think I spelled _____ words correctly on this test.
(If your estimate is correct, add one point to your score.)

Say It and Spell It Test No. 4

Write in the correct spelling.

1.	in tûr′kə lāt	_____	insert or introduce
2.	kol′ē flou ər	_____	cabbage-related vegetable
3.	jon′kwil	_____	fragrant flower
4.	swē′bak	_____	crispy egg-enriched baked bread
5.	hi bä′chē	_____	Japanese-style charcoal brazier
6.	kā′son	_____	artillery vehicle or watertight chamber
7.	rap rōsh män′	_____	cordial coming together
8.	ə pis′kə pit	_____	hierarchy of bishops
9.	gon də lēr′	_____	Venetian boatman
10.	skut′əl but	_____	rumor or gossip
11.	kap ar′ə sən	_____	colorful covering for a horse
12.	tə mol′ē	_____	Mexican cornmeal-wrapped meat

13.	shä′mən	_____	tribal priest and seer
14.	ō′lē ō	_____	miscellaneous mixture
15.	thal′ē ən	_____	bright fluorescent dye
16.	dal′yə	_____	ornamental flower
17.	ig′nis fach′o͞o əs	_____	deceptive or fatuous hope or purpose
18.	shib′ə leth	_____	distinguishing usage or criterion
19.	bel′ we<u>th</u> ər	_____	leader or initiator
20.	tho͝or′ə fər	_____	bearer of incense vessel in church
a.	əm bēr′ ə	_____	African wooden musical instrument that is plucked
b.	nem on′ik	_____	aiding memorization
c.	ten′oid	_____	toothed or comblike
d.	mär′shə nes	_____	wife of a marquess
e.	thon′ik	_____	infernal

Pronunciation key on page 10.

Before consulting the answers on page 288:
I think I spelled _____ words correctly on this test.
(If your estimate is correct, add one point to your score.)

AGGLUTINATION

Like the German language or a wondrous set of varied building blocks, English is a treasure-house of words and word parts that can be conveniently combined to make new and larger words. Take *land* and *lord* and you have *landlord.* Put together *clearing* and *house* and you have *clearinghouse,* if with a slightly changed meaning; in language, two plus two does not always equal four.

Agglutination—which is appropriately a mouthful of a word—is the linguistic term for such handy verbal piece-fitting. The vocabulary of English is enormous, and this is due not only to its constant absorbing of words from other languages but also to its welter of mateable, meaningful word parts (morphemes), from prefixes and suffixes to whole, ready-to-combine words.

Agglutination is so natural to English that we even conjure up wondrously agglutinative nonsense words, like *supercalifragilisticexpialidocious.*

But are long words, formed by agglutination, the hardest ones to spell? Not necessarily, and maybe not even usually. Judge for yourself. Following is part of a list of long words—sesquipedalians—compiled by Dmitri Borgmann in *Language on Vacation.* Would you find them tough to spell, or merely taxing on your syllable memory or writing-hand muscles?

anarchoindividualist
anthropomorphization
contrasuggestibility
philoprogenitiveness
ultrastandardization
anticonstitutionalist
indistinguishableness
phoneticohieroglyphic
hyperconscientiousness
omnirepresentativeness
pathologicohistological
transubstantiationalist

Words of One Syllable Test No. 4

Write in the correct spelling.

1.	gôt	_____	India riverbank stairway
2.	ko͞om	_____	steep bowllike basin on a mountain
3.	jour	_____	non-Muslim "infidel"
4.	thûrs	_____	flowering part
5.	gaf	_____	iron hook
6.	winz	_____	steep passageway in a mine
7.	mō	_____	unit of electrical conductance
8.	spo͝or	_____	plant reproductive body
9.	nīs	_____	metamorphic rock
10.	slīp	_____	narrow passage
11.	blok	_____	group of allied parties or nations
12.	nat	_____	small biting fly
13.	slo͞os	_____	water-controlling gate
14.	pyo͞och	_____	plotted overthrow of a government
15.	skweg	_____	oscillate unevenly electronically
16.	bät	_____	Thailand currency unit
17.	rum	_____	compass point

18. pelf   _____   money or goods

19. zhēg   _____   jig or lively dance movement

20. sīn   _____   Malayan wild ox; banteng

  a. silf   _____   slender and graceful girl

  b. spits   _____   northern heavy-coated, bushy-tailed dog

  c. klak   _____   hired or partisan group of applauders

  d. luf   _____   sailing near the wind

  e. dōj   _____   former Venetian or Genoese magistrate

Pronunciation key on page 10.

Before consulting the answers on page 288:
I think I spelled _____ words correctly on this test.
(If your estimate is correct, add one point to your score.)

Have Misspellings, Will Print

Wherever people write, they misspell. And wherever they put that writing into print, they misspell too, alas.

Our English language is so heterogeneous that it almost seems to breed misspellings, and the publishing business is not immune to the breeding, especially not these days.

Unfortunate but true, newspapers, magazines, and books today are rife with errant spellings. Astute readers and editorial people spot them daily and sigh or steam. How many readers don't detect them? How many editors not only don't detect them but are responsible—if often because of scheduling pressures and other mitigating circumstances—for letting them slip through?

The closest thing to an error-free publication traditionally has been *The New Yorker*. The copyeditors and fact checkers of this weekly magazine are renowned as editorial commandos who seek and destroy any mistakes in copy and take no prisoners. Not even *The New Yorker* is infallible; I won a bet several years back by finding a couple of slips. But if you're eagle-eyed and think you're better than the best, try to find a misspelling in an issue of this urbane periodical. It's sort of like a snipe hunt.

Even if you're a good speller, you

may not always notice misspellings when you're reading a publication. Take this book, for example. Show me a statement that published misspellings don't go back to well before daguerrotypes, nickelodions, mumble-teepeg, sassafrass sticks, and spitoons, and I'll show you a sentence you're now reading that contains several misspellings. But how many?

Spelling faux pas come at us daily from the left and the right, even politically speaking. One of my most memorable orthographic blooper finds occurred in the late 1960s, when I began working in publishing. Within the space of a week or two, I found the word *impostor* spelled *imposter* in both a Jules Feiffer strip in the *Village Voice* and in William F. Buckley, Jr.'s, magazine *National Review*. (This was a time of some polarization in American politics.)

Finding *imposter* twice delighted me. Was there some secret significance in this bipolar, almost simultaneous goof? Today I wouldn't be able to enjoy such a coincidence, as most dictionaries accept both spellings of the word. Indeed, even then Merriam-Webster's controversially liberal Third International included both, while its predecessor, the revered Second, was turning over in its grave. I still think *imposter* is an impostor for *impostor*.

Maybe I should have been attending more carefully to my own editorial work at the offices of the new American Heritage Dictionary. Only later did I learn that the AHD had pioneered a misspelled entry for *vichyssoise* (as *vichysoisse*) in the pages of its first printing. Which proves that while dictionaries are not supposed to be human, they unfortunately are.

It's important to note that misspellings in printed matter usually come under the rubric of typographical errors, or typos, these presumably being mechanical slipups rather than ignorant mistakes. Still, you can never be quite sure of the cause. The typesetter's haste or carelessness? Or was there a misspelling in the original manuscript copy that went unchallenged and lived happily ever after through galley and proof stages?

You don't have to work in publishing to see misspellings every day, but it helps. Copyeditors, who may catch hundreds of them in a single month but are sometimes drawn and quartered if one slips by into print, know this all too well. Having to read the same copy several times in its various stages doesn't make their job any easier: The critical eyes glaze over.

When I worked as a copyeditor for a magazine, I enjoyed the challenge of rooting out wrong spellings under deadline pressure. It was like finding dark little double agents on a board game, or sometimes like looking, bulge-eyed, for elusive or nonexistent needles in a haystack. When a colleague caught an error you had missed on your go-through, "Good catch!" was the standard compliment. But it's the no-catches that stay in the memory. I once let *dogie* (motherless calf) go through spelled *dogey*. Actually, large dictionaries give *dogey* as a variant spelling, but it's still a wart on my memory. The copyeditor and author of the magazine piece in question were one and the same: me.

If dictionaries are not infallible in spelling, not much else can be, including books specifically about the English language—like this one. One of my favorite books on unusual words, by an American, has *metotymy* for *metonymy*, *panagram* for *pangram*, *aeschrolgia* for *aeschrologia*, *opisthosgraphy* for *opisthography*, *pudenda* for *pudendum*, and *ertomania* for *erotomania* among its oversights (not the author's, I'm quite sure). Another word book, by an Englishman, has *tatoo* for *tattoo*, *acrolet* for *acrolect*, *langua franca* for *lingua franca*, and *volta face* for *volte-face*. Another language book of recent years is *Dictionary of Confusibles*. Shouldn't that be *Confusables?*

We all have our pet peeves, and misspellings—or particular misspellings— can make some people fume, especially writers or editors. For example, my hardworking writer friend Jim seethes poetic that a Scottish word *correi* in the Sir Walter Scott poem "Coronach" is not spelled *corrie;* that a character in a John Jakes historical saga is Phillipe, not Philipe; and that in Mario Puzo's novel *The Sicilian* the historically based protagonist's first name is spelled Guiliani, not Giuliani. Jim is great fun because he also seethes poetic about what he considers to be the noisome, meddling excesses of copyeditors.

You can have all the letters in the right sequence in a word and still misspell it. The misuse or omission of apostrophes is the pet peeve of my close friend Diane, who is a voracious reader and all-seeing editor and asserts that this "has to be one of the most common, if not *the* most common, class of spelling mistakes," exclamation point. I'm beginning to agree with her. Apart from examples of the ubiquitous *it's* for *its* (or vice versa) boo-boo, in the past year she's sent me other corpora delicti from various periodicals, including the *New York Times* op-ed page ("Shirley Conrans's 'Lace,' two Jacqueline Susann's"), *Newsweek* ("says the Cobra's Lou Green" [the team is the Cobras]), the *New York Press* (in a comic strip: "Right . . . lot's of fun . . ."), the *New York Times Magazine* ("Lot's of people"), *People* ("Burt Reynold's wedding" and "the Bush's pregnant English springer spaniel"), and a newsletter from Diane's own apartment building. And this is only local evidence.

Between her hectic job and time spent reading, Diane doesn't get to keep in shape as much as she'd like, but she does get to shake her head a lot. Recently a young job applicant at her office took a one-page circle-the-misspelling test and failed to catch the misspellings *definately, occurrance, repitition, drunkeness, superintendant, insistant, coroborate, occassion,* and *questionaire.* The young woman had recently graduated from Diane's own Seven Sisters alma mater, and the job she was applying for was proofreader.

I'm equally chagrined at the plague of misspelling (to say nothing of poor grammar) that afflicts current periodicals and books. But what is more sobering is the realization that there is so much of it around that keeping track or keepsakes of even some of the errors in print would be more than a full-time job—no longer an idle, rarity-collecting hobby for a language lover or guardian. Bloopers in such profusion are no longer so amusing.

Here, glaring or not, are just a few random items noted of late in newspapers and periodicals:

- "and a principle part of your neurosis" (ad by a British bookseller in the *New York Times Book Review*)
- "secretly maintains duel identities" (Sunday *Television* guide in the *New York Times*)
- "said Sylvia above her shining green sequines" (large-type pull-quote in the *New York Press*)
- "2 Rareties in New Jersey" (opera review headline in the *New York Times*)
- "fitness buff who accidently starts channeling" (*Doonesbury* comic strip)
- "BONO" (*New York Times* crossword puzzle answer for "Victor or Sonny" [it's Sonny Bono but Victor Buono])
- "this seering drama" ("Picks & Pans" in *People*)
- "A rare example of bouyantly irresponsible comedy . . ." (blurb for a book, large ad in the *New York Times Book Review*)
- Television commercial (fall 1988) for the New Jersey senatorial candidacy of Republican Pete Dawkins; the ad attacked opponent Frank Lautenberg—and misspelled his name as it appeared on the screen
- "and the apochryphal 'Let them eat cake'" (opening paragraph of book review in the *New York Times*)
- "Jacknife" (title of 1989 Robert De Niro movie, based on the Stephen Metcalfe play *Strange Snow*)
- "University of Wisconson" appears on the diplomas handed out to some 4,000 graduating seniors at the Madison, Wisconsin, university in 1988

To say nothing of increasing misspellings turning up in current fiction and nonfiction books. Well, almost nothing. In research for this book, I found on one page of a verbal workbook for the SAT, in a sample verbal test:

14. RADUIS: CIRCLE: :

(A) rubber : tire

(B) spoke : wheel
    etc.

So you have only to go to your nearest newsstand or library to see that misspelling continues apace and to test the acuity of your spelling eye. For more evidential jeremiads, there are plenty of articles and books around these days on America's creeping or leaping illiteracy.

This book, of course, is perfect and a marked exception.

> If a kid says, "Dad, how do you spell *fisickle?*" and Dad, hoping to teach self-reliance as well as spelling, says, "Look it up," he'll just be jamming a larger wedge into the generation gap.
>
> Thomas Middleton

Multiple-Choice Test No. 5

Circle the correct spelling.

1. catachumen   catechuman   catechumen   katachumin
   (one receiving Christian instruction)

2. mennorah   menorha   mennorha   menorah
   (candelabrum used in Judaism)

3. caniption   coniption   connyption   conniption
   (angry or hysterical fit)

4. scentilla   scintila   sintilla   scintilla
   (trace or bit)

5. fierier   firier   fireier   fieryer
   (having more flammatory power or spirit)

6. trichinosis   trychanosis   trichanosis   trychinosis
   (disease from undercooked pork)

7. malapropo   malappropo   malappropos   malapropos
   (inappropriate)

8. Milquitoast   Milquetoast   Milq'toast   Milktoast
   (meek person)

9. measily   measley   measly   measelly
   (despicably small)

10. quizling   quisling   quissling   quizzling
    (traitorous puppet leader)

11. bralle   breille   braille   brälle
    (raised-dot system for reading by the blind)

12. deboosh   debooch   debouche   debouch
    (emerge or issue out)

13. centinnary   centennary   centenary   centenery
    (one-hundredth anniversary; centennial)

14. boutonier   bouttonier   bouttoniere   boutonniere
    (buttonhole flower)

15. sequeli   sequelae   sequellae   sequelli
    (disease or injury aftereffects)

16. baccalaureat   bacchalaureate   baccalaureate   bacchalaureat
    (college bachelor's degree)

17. poultice   poltise   poltice   poultise
    (warm or medicated substance applied with a cloth)

18. glazeer   glasiere   glazier   glaziere
    (window fitter)

19. annyline   aniline   analine   anniline
    (amine used in dyes)

20. mearshaum   meershawm   meerschaum   mierschaum
    (white clayey silicate used for tobacco pipes)

 a. rebuttor   rebuter   rebutter   rebutor
    (one who counters another's reply)

 b. bacchanal   baccanale   bachanall   bachanale
    (drunken revelry)

 c. antidiluvian   antediluvian   antideluvian   antedeluvian
    (ancient)

 d. isoceles   isoscelles   isosceles   issoceles
    (of a triangle: having two sides equal)

 e. philipic   phillippic   phillipic   philippic
    (bitterly condemnatory speech)

Before consulting the answers on page 288:
I think I spelled _____ words correctly on this test.
(If your estimate is correct, add one point to your score.)

> One of the easy cases is that of the boy who said, "I can spell *banana* all right, only I don't know when to stop."
>
> Edna L. Furness

DOUBLE LETTER OR NOT

Remember these guys? Double your trouble, or single out your fun.

Double Letter or Not Test

Circle the correct spelling.

1.	misspelling	mispelling	14.	threshhold	threshold
2.	pasttime	pastime	15.	bookkeeper	bookeeper
3.	nighttime	nightime	16.	roommate	roomate
4.	poettaster	poetaster	17.	headdress	headress
5.	drunkenness	drunkeness	18.	musketteer	musketeer
6.	coattail	coatail	19.	teammate	teamate
7.	sonnetteer	sonneteer	20.	suddenness	suddeness
8.	occurrence	occurence	a.	accommodate	accomodate
9.	withhold	withold	b.	commemmorate	commemorate
10.	dumbbell	dumbell	c.	neccessity	necessity
11.	newsstand	newstand	d.	pusillanimous	pusilanimous
12.	durress	duress	e.	committment	commitment
13.	misshapen	mishapen			

> *Before consulting the answers on page 289:*
> I think I spelled _____ words correctly on this test.
> (If your estimate is correct, add one point to your score.)

STREPHOSYMBOLIA

Spelling aptitude differs from person to person because we all have slightly different ways of or capacities for perceiving—different cognitive equipment.

One handicap that some people

have with reading and spelling is a tendency to reverse the letters or symbols being read. This literally backward way of apprehending words is called strephosymbolia, a term meaning "twisted symbols" that was coined by neurologist Samuel T. Orton. (Not all psychologists accept his theory of cerebral-hemisphere dominance and laterality in relation to dyslexia.) A person with strephosymbolia on confronting the word *reservable* might see *reversible*, for example (or *reversable*). Or he or she might see not *denigrate* but *degenerate*, not *look* but *kool*, not *satisfy* but *safety*— or so spell these words. In some cases the perceptual transposition will even be of an upside down or mirroring nature: *boom* will be read or written as *woog*.

Strephosymbolia is usually a serious learning disability. But most of us may have a slight touch of it spellingwise, now and then, as when we're writing in haste or overly anticipating a coming syllable in a long word. Haven't you ever mistakenly scribbled or typed, say, *tevelision* instead of *television*?

Say It and Spell It Test No. 5

Write in the correct spelling.

1.	shik ā′nə rē	_____ trickery
2.	sim pä ti kō	_____ likable as a person
3.	pal′ing	_____ becoming comrades
4.	kyoō lot′	_____ divided pantslike skirt
5.	dəp′il āt	_____ remove hair
6.	koŏl də sak′	_____ dead-end street
7.	pol ē an′ə	_____ overly optimistic person
8.	ak roō′əl	_____ increase or accumulation
9.	hoŏk′ə	_____ water pipe, for smoking
10.	vī′ing	_____ contesting
11.	pat rə lin′ ē əl	_____ descending from the father
12.	bib lē ol′ ə tər	_____ book or books devotee
13.	hâr′ bredth	_____ very narrow margin
14.	ef ər ves′əz	_____ bubbles
15.	kûr′ və chər	_____ state of being curved
16.	kro shā′ər	_____ needlework (with looped stitches) practitioner
17.	tē lē ol′ə jē	_____ study of ultimate purposes or final causes

18.	pan′tē wāst	_____	sissy
19.	və nē rē ol′ə jē	_____	study of sexual diseases
20.	tē′tō təm	_____	small letter-inscribed top used in game
a.	par′ə fin	_____	waxy substance used in candles
b.	sûr plis	_____	priest's loose white vestment
c.	mä yō′	_____	tights or one-piece bathing suit
d.	ab hör′ənt	_____	repellent
e.	rou′əl	_____	disk part of a rider's spur

Pronunciation key on page 10.

Before consulting the answers on page 289:
I think I spelled _____ words correctly on this test.
(If your estimate is correct, add one point to your score.)

Dissipating at the Soda Fountain

(A Brief History of the Spelling Bee)

For many Americans, the spelling bee is no mere rote schoolroom exercise. It is a sort of institution, socially as well as educationally, as the eminent linguistic scholar Allen Walker Read has certified in his researches into the subject (and to whom I am greatly indebted here). The octogenarian Mr. Read is, among other things, the world's foremost authority on the all-American term *O.K.*

Spelling bees, Read notes in an article written for the Modern Language Association, "take rank among the conservative influences in American speech. They are a factor that helps to account for the prevalence of spelling pronunciations [careful, syllabic pronunciations of words based on the written rather than the heard word—see page 92] in the United States and for a central body of speech that does not yield to passing fashions."

Many educators today see little point in old-fashioned oral spelling exercises. They feel that having pupils vocalize letters ("w-o-r-d") detracts from the more important matter of the sounds that those letters represent, and insist that we properly use spelling for writing, not for pronouncing aloud. But others argue that while the spelling bee seems only a competitive exercise in alphabetic recall, there's no getting away from another fact: It motivates children—and adults, for that matter—to improve their spelling.

Bees have been in and out of fashion over the years since the first "trials in spelling" musters were held in American schoolrooms in the late eighteenth century. Such "matches" or "schools" or "spell-downs"—they were not commonly called bees until about 1875—were an established practice before the American Revolution. We owe the British some acknowledgment here, for two centuries earlier Elizabethan schools sometimes had pupils "opposing" one another in a spelling-improvement exercise. As Allen Walker Read points out, it was important then, as it is today for our National Spelling Bee entrants, that the pupil carefully syllabify in spelling the words aloud:

> Teach the childe, in spelling his syllabes, to leaue the consonant, that commeth before a vowel, to the syllabe following, exampe: in this word, manifold, Let him spell, for the first syllabe *m* and *a* onely, for he may not take but *n* and *i*, for *f* hath *o*, the vowel next after him. To the third syllabe he must take the foure letters that remaine, *f, o, l,* and *d.* In this order than let him spell it, saying: *m, a,* ma: *n, i,* ni: *f, o, l, d,* fold, manifold. And like wise of all other words.

But spelling matches, except for a brief period in the late nineteenth century, never found much favor in Great Britain—although the British press often reported on the phenomenon in America (and seemed to think that "bee" referred to a single spelling contestant). Perhaps this was due to the fact that England didn't possess a Benjamin Franklin, whose urgings regarding the importance of orthography (and of dividing words into syllables) gave impetus to competitive spelling in our country. Franklin recommended pairing students off, with one giving the other ten words to be spelled each day. He was also wise enough to know that the winner should have a reward, "a pretty neat Book of some Kind useful in their future Studies."

In subsequent years, in Connecticut, Rhode Island, Maine, New Hampshire, and other states, the victor's prize was more often than not the classic act of moving ahead a place in line or classroom desk or to the head of the class, or a certificate of good scholarship. For preparation, pupils used special spelling books (like those of Noah Webster, which were so enormously successful). Spell-downs, Edna Furness notes in *Spelling for the Millions*, were often a special treat on Friday afternoons that pupils looked forward to all week. Sometimes they were a reward for good performance in studies or for good conduct. "And sometimes spelling competition was 'the program' at parent-teacher get-togethers to demonstrate the teacher's ability and the pupils' progress. The spelling bees, however, were not limited to the schoolroom. At frontier functions, many a person won prestige and position in the community by spelling down the others. At a box [lunch] social the crowning event was often a spelling bee."

Bees thus became a community social occasion, with champions from different schools assembling for a showdown at a given schoolhouse or church in the evening. In New Hampshire, the astoundingly precocious Horace Greeley, later a renowned journalist and political figure, attended such matches at the age of four —and even at that age was sometimes the winner. Particularly during the first quarter of the nineteenth century, citizens flocked to these—for the time —almost glamorous events. American pupils discovered the giddy thrill and pride of accomplishment in spelling down a rival classmate or challenger from another school in the area.

Great passions could be—and still are—aroused in the conducting of spelling bees. Evidently, officiating schoolmasters were sometimes less than fair to the contestants, especially when spellers were in top form, things

were running late, and a loser had to be found. Read cites an 1832 diary of a Maine woman teaching in Indiana who reported how the spelling-master would use trickery when desperate: " 'Bay' will perhaps be the sound; one scholar spells it 'bey,' another 'bay,' while the master all the times means 'ba,' which comes within the rule, being *in the spelling book*."

Edward Eggleston's 1871 novel called *The Hoosier Schoolmaster*, which did much to popularize bees in the Frontier West, had the superspelling hero meet defeat only when Squire Hawkins pulled out of his pocket "a list of words just coming into use in those days—words not in the spelling-book"; and the hero was unable to spell *daguerreotype*. More often than not, too, we might remember, words given to pupils to spell were not defined or explained back then and back when.

Fair or not, spelling bees were once socially spirited and even cozy occasions, worthy of an illustration by Norman Rockwell. Read quotes the following observations of a New Englander in 1848, memories that evoke a rural and small-town America now pretty much lost to us:

As soon as the stars began to glisten, boisterous lads and modest misses came from all the neighborhood within two miles. For it is deemed fine amusement to engage in such spelling matches.

They are attractive in the coldest weather. A huge pile of fuel lay on the broad hearth; another, torching and crackling, gleamed from the wide fire-place, lighting up a sweet boquet [sic] of happy faces. The teacher's ringing bell brought in throngs of blithe boys from noisy snowball contests, puffing as if they would crack their ruddy cheeks. All became suddenly silent and two leaders began choosing their favorite champions. But the prettiest were called first—a pardonable partiality. It was diverting to see the rosy girls flirt bashfully round to their places, holding spelling-books up before their sparkling eyes, more to avoid our glances than the fire's bright glare. Directly the instructor, standing in front, commenced giving out alternative words to the rival parties. Not one in a hundred was misspelled. It is the best time of life, and the best method of learning that indispensable art, orthography. After an hour's sharp contention, the side having a majority of girls, of course, came out victorious. To relieve the monotony of this exercise, many curious lessons in geography were chanted by the whole school, with beautiful precision and harmony. As the clock struck nine, our delighted company vanished, the bravest youths politely offering to escort their favorite lasses home through the bitter air.

Even then, it seems, girls generally did better than boys as spellers.

When spelling bees fell out of fashion or became too "social" in the somewhat puritanical East, they went—with frontier-minded schoolteachers—west, to Illinois, Iowa, Indiana, even California, where they became esteemed as "cultural" events. The hero of the above-mentioned *The Hoosier Schoolmaster* was based on an actual Indianan named Jim Phillips. The success of Eggleston's novel made Phillips something of a celebrity, as, Read tells us, the author later reported. "As time passed on, Phillips found himself a lion. Strangers desired an introduction to him as a notability, and invited the champion to dissipate with them at the soda fountain in the village drug store."

But spelling bees were too much a part of culture in the East to be completely forgotten there, and it was in Philadelphia, on March 25, 1875, that the bee of all bees was held. Eighty competitors looked word after word in the eye before an unruly crowd of some four thousand people at the grand Academy of Music. (The words that defeated five of the final six contestants were *purview, testacious* [sic], *distension, infinitessimal* [sic], and (misspelled by the runner-up) *hauser* [sic]. Two months later, a match staged at a Hartford, Connecticut, church was introduced by none other than Mark Twain, who had his inimitable doubts about the sanity of the occasion (see page 86).

The spelling bee did not remain quite so fashionable, though it never left the American schoolroom for good. Bees languished in the early 1900s, then enjoyed a revival in the 1920s and 1930s, when for a while they became features on radio programs.

Today bees are no more the warmly communal events they once were, and as we've noted, many educators deplore the practice. (The question of how best to teach English spelling remains a matter of some controversy.) But for many Americans the spelling bee is an indispensable part of our national cultural heritage. Bees continue to be held in classrooms all over the United States, and each year a single, remarkable American schoolgirl or schoolboy is crowned our national orthographic champion (see page 136).

> It is a pity that Chawcer, who had geneyus, was so unedicated. He's the wuss speller I know of.
>
> Artemus Ward

Multiple-Choice Test No. 6

Circle the correct spelling.

1. pallazzo   palazzo   palazo   pallazo
   (imposing palacelike building)
2. mullato   mulato   mulatto   mullatoe
   (person of Negro-Caucasian parentage)
3. espadrille   espedrille   espodrille   espedrill
   (flat shoe with a cloth upper)
4. narcissist   narscissist   narsissist   narscisist
   (self-enamored person)
5. pariquot   paraquot   paraquat   pariquat
   (type of weed killer)
6. Nawgahide   Naugahide   Naugahyde   Nawgahyde
   (vinyl-coated fabric)
7. encription   incryption   encryption   encrypsion
   (encoding)
8. chlamydia   clamidia   chlamidia   clahamidia
   (venereal disease)
9. Sechzuan   Szechuan   Seczhuan   Sczechuan
   (peppery and spicy type of Chinese cooking)
10. abcize   abcise   abbscise   abscise
    (to cut off)

11. salaam   salahm   saalam   sallahm
    (Eastern bow with the hand held to the forehead)

12. habeas corpos   habeas corpus   habeus corpus
    habeus corpos
    (writ challenging the detention of a person)

13. commissery   commiserry   comissary   commissary
    (movie studio lunchroom)

14. Methuselah   Mathusalah   Methusela   Methuselha
    (Noah's long-living ancestor)

15. Africanss   Afrikans   Afrikaans   Afrikkans
    (language of South Africa)

16. paramountcy   parimountcey   paramountcey   parimouncy
    (supremacy)

17. génerallisimo   générallisimo   generalissimo   generalisimo
    (army commander in chief)

18. balistrade   balustrade   ballistrade   ballustrade
    (railing with upright curved supports)

19. pasell   pa'cel   passel   passle
    (large number)

20. herculian   herculeian   herculaean   herculean
    (powerful or extraordinary)

a. cicitrix   cicatrix   ciccitrix   ciccatrix
    (scar)

b. discumbobbulate   discombobbulate   discumbobulate   discombobulate
    (to confuse)

c. oleander   oliandor   olliander   olleander
    (shrub with fragrant red, pink, or white flowers)

d. divvigation   divvagation   divagation   divigation
    (wandering or digressing)

e. hebdommidal   hebbdomidal   hebdomadal   hebdomidal
    (weekly)

> *Before consulting the answers on page 289:*
> I think I spelled _____ words correctly on this test.
> (If your estimate is correct, add one point to your score.)

OUR SPELLING IS A MUESS!

Although this comment may be tright,
Our English spelling is a fright!
We should develop some technique
That wouldn't make it quite so blique.
If only we could make some rules
That children, when they go to skules,
Could learn, and wouldn't have to guess,
We might see more effectiveness.
The words would roll right off their tongue,
And they might learn to read quite yongue.
If we would spell with some technique,
They'd learn to read in just one wique!
Yet many people take to heart
The problems that such change would steart.
American printers from ocean to ocean
Would all protest with great commocean;
While changing, adjustment would have to be made—
Teachers would want to be doubly pade.
It might cause a great amount of trouble
To burst this awful spelling bouble.
How did our spelling get in this muess?
There are several reasons why, I guess.
Some borrowed words retained their signs
To show their etymological ligns.
The problem of spelling began to weigh
When words got easier to seigh
And spelling stayed the same as before
This caused a problem, or three or fore.
Printers, spelling's greatest friends,
Started several spelling triends.
Foreign printers printed words
With spellings that were "for the bords."
They changed the spelling of words like ghost;
Then left some words, but altered mhost.
They added letters to save their rows,
Or subtracted some—this caused more wows.
Uneducated printers would
Misspell some words—This wasn't gould.

We owe these printers quite a debt—
Our spelling hasn't recovered yebt!
The vowel shift in men's dialogue
Also helped to make a fogue;
The spelling differences came because
Vowels shifted, and spelling stayed as it wause.
Other spellings also came through
Scholars who wanted to show what they nough
Where words came from (though we doubt
That they were thorough in checking some oubt).
Etymologies often were shown—
This causes modern spellers to grown!
These are some reasons, just a few,
Why spelling may be hard for yew.
But why let old spelling be taught
Instead of changing them, as we aught?
One reason why our spelling's a trial
Is that standard spelling is the stial.
One who from standard spelling is turned
Is classified as being unlurned.
A person who hopes to own a yacht
Must learn to spell, like it or nacht.
Reform would affect a great many people,
From the base of the hill to the top of the steople.
The first reaction will be "No!"
For change is sometimes very slo.
Perhaps someday we'll open our eyes
And maybe we will realyes
The need for change, but until then
We'll have to spell the way we've ben.
But as long as present spelling reigns,
Reading and writing will cause us peigns.

Sandra Leman

Say It and Spell It Test No. 6

Write in the correct spelling.

1. bûr′dē ing   _____   achieving one under par in
                                                golf

2. kan′ē nes   _____   shrewdness

3.	stip'tik	_____	to check bleeding
4.	kar ə vel'	_____	sailing ship
5.	ev ə nes'ing	_____	dissipating
6.	pär'səns ta'bəl	_____	simple rectangular table
7.	biv'oō wak ing; biv'wak ing	_____	encamping
8.	yōō'lə lāt, ul'yə lāt	_____	howl or wail
9.	gran'it	_____	rock containing quartz
10.	bil'it	_____	military lodging
11.	kon kwis'tə dōr	_____	sixteenth century Spanish military leader
12.	dum'dum	_____	hollow-point bullet
13.	dum'dum	_____	stupid person
14.	tō'paz	_____	yellowish gem
15.	ō'lē o	_____	hodgepodge
16.	tin'ē nes	_____	a quality like that of tin
17.	ôld' lang zīn'	_____	good old times
18.	ter ə kot'ə	_____	fired clay used in art and architecture
19.	lap fōol	_____	enough to be cradled against the loins
20.	dûr es'	_____	forcible restraint
a.	ə nol'ing	_____	abrogating
b.	kuv'ē	_____	small flock of birds
c.	sī səl	_____	strong fiber
d.	dou'sing rod	_____	water-locating stick
e.	sod'ər	_____	meltable metal alloy

Pronunciation key on page 10.

Before consulting the answers on page 289:
I think I spelled _____ words correctly on this test.
(If your estimate is correct, add one point to your score.)

MARK TWAIN'S INTRODUCTION TO A SPELLING BEE

The following introductory remarks were tendered by Mark Twain in Hartford, Connecticut, in 1875, as a prelude to a spelling bee held at the Asylum Hill Congregational Church. They are preserved because they were taken down stenographically.

Ladies and Gentlemen: I have been honored with the office of introducing these approaching orthographical solemnities with a few remarks. The temperance crusade swept the land some time ago—that is, that vast portion of the land where it was needed—but it skipped Hartford. Now comes this new spelling epidemic, and this time *we* are stricken. So I suppose we needed the affliction. I don't say we needed it, for I don't see any use in spelling a word right, and never did. I mean I don't see any use in having a uniform and arbitrary way of spelling words. We might as well make all clothes alike and cook all dishes alike. Sameness is tiresome, variety is pleasing. I have a correspondent whose letters are always a refreshment to me; there is such a breezy, unfettered originality about his orthography. He always spells Kow with a large K. Now that is just as good as to spell it with a small one. It is better. It gives the imagination a broader field, a wider scope. It suggests to the mind a grand, vague, impressive, new kind of cow. Superb effects can be produced by variegated spelling. Now, there is Blind Tom, the musical prodigy. He always spells a word according to the sound that is carried to his ear. And he is an enthusiast in orthography. When you give him a word he shouts it out—puts all his soul into it. I once heard him called up to spell orang-outang before an audience. He said, "O, r-a-n-g, orang, g-e-r, ger oranger, t-a-n-g, tang, orranggertang!" Now, a body can respect an orang-outang that spells his name in a vigorous way like that. But the feeble dictionary makes a mere kitten of him. In the old times people spelled just as they pleased. That was the right idea. You had two chances at a stranger then. You knew a strong man from a weak one by his iron-clad spelling, and his handwriting helped you to verify your verdict. Some people have an idea that correct spelling can be taught, and taught to anybody. That is a mistake. The spelling faculty is born in man, like poetry, music and art. It is a gift; it is a talent. People who have this gift in a high degree need only to see a word once in print and it is forever photographed upon their memory. They cannot forget it. People who haven't it must be content to spell more or less like—like thunder —and expect to splinter the dictionary wherever their orthographical lightning happens to strike. There are 114,000 words in the unabridged dictionary. I know a lady who can spell only 180 of them right. She steers clear of all the rest. She can't learn any more. So her letters always consist of those constantly-recurring 180 words. Now and then, when she finds herself obliged to write upon a subject which necessitates the use of some other words, she— well, she don't write on that subject. I have a relative in New York who is almost sublimely gifted. She can't spell any word right. There is a game called Verbarium. A dozen people are each provided with a sheet of paper, across the top of which is written a long word like kaleidoscopical, or something like that, and the game is to see who can make up the most words out of that in three minutes, always beginning with the initial letter of the word. Upon one occasion the word was cofferdam. When time was called everybody had built from five to twenty words except this young lady. She had only one word—calf. We all studied a moment and then said: "Why, there is no 'l' in cofferdam!" Then we examined her paper. To the eternal honor of that inspired, unconscious, sublimely independent soul be it said, she had spelled the word 'caff'! If anybody here can spell calf any more sensibly than that let him step to the front and take his milk. The insurrection will now begin.

Multiple-Choice Test No. 7

Circle the correct spelling.

1. ciceronne   cicerrone   ciccerone   cicerone
   (tourists' guide)

2. inamorata   inamouratta   enamorata   inamoratta
   (woman one loves)

3. sebbaceous   sebaceous   sebbhaceous   sebacious
   (fatty)

4. crannie   cranny   cranney   craney
   (small crevice)

5. collosal   collossal   colossal   colossall
   (gigantic)

6. veteranarian   veternarian   vetrinarian   veterinarian
   (animal doctor)

7. gutta-percha   gutta-pertcha   guta-purcha   gutta-purcha
   (rubberlike substance used in dentistry)

8. tittilate   titilate   tittillate   titillate
   (excite or stimulate)

9. silouhette   sillouhette   sillhouette   silhouette
   (outline or shaped likeness)

10. gluttenous   gluttinous   glutenous   glutinous
    (containing doughy protein substance found in wheat flour)

11. brumagemm   brummagem   brummegem   brumagem
    (cheap or counterfeit)

12. pennicilin   peniccilin   penicillin   penicilin
    (mold-produced antibiotic)

13. hors d'oeuvres   hor d'ouvres   hor d'oeuvres   hors d'ouvres
    (appetizers)

14. skivies   skivvies   scivies   skivees
    (T-shirts and shorts)

15. gallosches   galloshes   galoshes   galosches
    (high rubber overshoes)

16. piccallo   piccollo   picollo   piccolo
    (small flute)

17. iscicle   iciccle   icycle   icicle
    (shaft of ice formed by dripping)

18. tam-o'-shanter   tamm-o'-shanter   tam'-o-shanter
    tam-o-shantur
    (Scottish flat woolen cap with a pompon atop)

19. tryvette   trivet   trivette   tryvet
    (metal support for a hot dish)

20. succotache   sucotash   succotash   succotasch
    (dish of cooked beans and corn)

 a. euchalyptus   eucalyptis   eucalyptus   euchalyptus
    (tree with aromatic leaves used medicinally)

 b. chichi   shi-shi   chic-chic   chi-chi
    (frilliness or affectation)

 c. battalion   batallion   battallion   bataillon
    (military unit)

 d. drommadary   drommedary   dromedary   dromidary
    (swift type of camel)

 e. astrakkan   astrekkan   astrakan   astrakhan
    (Russian type of curly-wool hat)

Before consulting the answers on page 290:
I think I spelled ____ words correctly on this test.
(If your estimate is correct, add one point to your score.)

BUSINESS SPELLING

However, the contributions of business to the health of the language have not been outstanding. Spelling has been assaulted by Duz, and E-Z Off, and Fantastik, and Kool and Arrid and Kleen, and the tiny containers of milk and cream catchily called the Pour Shun, and by products that make you briter, so that you will not be left hi and dri at a parti, but made welkom.

This book was originally typed on paper drawn from a "slide-out pak."

"You're saked," the angry Amtrak chief said. "I caught on to you in the nik of time. I don't know what it was, but something cliked.

If it hadn't, an entire trainload of knikknaks would have been lost. You make me sik," he went on. "There has been no lak of understanding of you here. You've carried on like a high muky-muk, with assistants at your bek and call, but you're driving us to rak and ruin. You'd have us in hok up to our neks. You were hoping that I'd blow my stak and crak under the strain, but I won't. Pik up your money, pak your things, and go. I want you cheked out in an hour, by four. You thought that you could duk responsibility, that you were dealing with a bunch of hiks, and that we were stuk with you. You were playing with a staked dek. Well, in sixty minutes, I want you out of here, lok, stok and barrel."

"Sok it to him, boss," a Uriah-Heep-like character among the employes murmured. "He has no kik coming. He just couldn't hak it." He gave a quaklike laugh and fed himself from a tube of Squeez-a-snak.

Dik Windingstad (for it was indeed he) hardly knew how to respond, so shoked was he, so taken abak by the Amtrak chief's attak, so roked bak on his heels. He felt like a hokey goalie hit in the face by a puk off the stik of Bobby Hull, and the tik-tik-tok of the stately clok as it stood against the wall sounded in his ears like the sharp reports of ak-ak guns. His heartbeat quikened. Then he thought sardonically to himself, "The buk stops here," and his mood changed. "We've had some yaks," he thought. "I must have upset the peking order."

He glanced down at his finely tailored slaks, never again to be worn in these precincts. "I'll go," he said finally. "But not with my tail tuked between my legs, as you'd like. Hek, no. Lok me out, if you want to. Mok me. Someday you'll take a different tak. Someday I'll get in the last lik. All I can say now is good-by and—for some of you, anyway—good luk. Please forward my mail to Hamtramk."

Dik spun on his heel and made traks. Amtraks.

In many such monstrosities, the companies involved know what they are doing. In others they often do not, especially when it is a matter of grammar.

Edwin Newman
Strictly Speaking

Words of One Syllable Test No. 5

Write in the correct spelling.

1. mak ⎯⎯⎯⎯⎯⎯ high-velocity number
2. skrē ⎯⎯⎯⎯⎯⎯ rocky debris at the base of a slope
3. kōnt ⎯⎯⎯⎯⎯⎯ adventure tale or long short story
4. lēch ⎯⎯⎯⎯⎯⎯ dissolve out by percolation
5. yŏŏrt ⎯⎯⎯⎯⎯⎯ nomad's domed tent
6. skōl ⎯⎯⎯⎯⎯⎯ Danish word used as a toast
7. brōōch ⎯⎯⎯⎯⎯⎯ pin or dress ornament
8. yät ⎯⎯⎯⎯⎯⎯ pleasure-cruising ship
9. velt ⎯⎯⎯⎯⎯⎯ African grassland
10. mōō ⎯⎯⎯⎯⎯⎯ grimacing or pouting expression
11. les ⎯⎯⎯⎯⎯⎯ yellowish brown loamy deposit
12. swoch ⎯⎯⎯⎯⎯⎯ fabric sample
13. yeg ⎯⎯⎯⎯⎯⎯ safecracker
14. rāth ⎯⎯⎯⎯⎯⎯ specter or ghost
15. mēn ⎯⎯⎯⎯⎯⎯ appearance or demeanor
16. vān ⎯⎯⎯⎯⎯⎯ wind direction indicator
17. skûrj ⎯⎯⎯⎯⎯⎯ whip or punish
18. brev ⎯⎯⎯⎯⎯⎯ mark indicating a vowel is short
19. mēt ⎯⎯⎯⎯⎯⎯ dispense or dole
20. gar ⎯⎯⎯⎯⎯⎯ pikelike fish
a. klōsh ⎯⎯⎯⎯⎯⎯ close-fitting woman's hat
b. dān ⎯⎯⎯⎯⎯⎯ condescend superciliously
c. bāəl ⎯⎯⎯⎯⎯⎯ false god or idol
d. grēb ⎯⎯⎯⎯⎯⎯ loonlike diving bird
e. jōōl; joul ⎯⎯⎯⎯⎯⎯ unit of work or energy

Pronunciation key on page 10.

> *Before consulting the answers on page 290:*
> I think I spelled ⎯⎯ words correctly on this test.
> (If your estimate is correct, add one point to your score.)

You Say CARE-FLEE And I Say CARE-FULL-EE

(Spelling Pronunciations)

Do you pronounce *dour* DOER or DOWER? *Thyme* as TIME or THIME? Is *pulpit* PULL-PIT or PUHL-PIT?

If the latter, in all three cases, you are uttering what is known as a spelling pronunciation.

For correct spellings we all betimes refer to the dictionary. We also flip open our handy home or school lexicon to be sure of a pronunciation, which we ascertain (or puzzle out) from those parenthetical phonetics following the word in question.

But dictionaries can have a third effect on (or power over) readers. The words' spellings themselves—appearing in print as they do in an "authoritative" reference—often affect the way readers pronounce those words.

The word *waistcoat*, for example, has traditionally been pronounced WES-KUT, but it may also be pronounced WAYST-KOTE. Similarly, the people of one town named Worcester call their place of residence WOOS-TER while those living in a different Worcester, in a different state, know that they are from WER-SES-TER.

Spelling pronunciations, then, are pronunciations that endure not because of seasoned usage among speakers but rather because of the way certain readers—or schoolteachers—

construe them to sound from their spellings. In the examples just given, WAYST-KOTE and WER-SES-TER are spelling pronunciations. Another, more American example is the word *sophomore*. Most people pronounce it SOF-MORE, but you've undoubtedly also heard (or favored) SOF-O-MORE, a spelling pronunciation.

The "more American" example is not inappropriate, as spelling pronunciations are more prevalent in American than in British English—for several reasons, perhaps. We are a younger country, and one with a population far less homogeneous than that of Great Britain (where *Happisburgh* is traditionally pronounced HEZ-BRUH). Many words in the extraordinary vocabulary of English tend to be somewhat unfamiliar to many Americans, and not only in rural areas. How does one pronounce a word just seen in print for the first time, that one has never heard used in conversation? By piecing together its written syllables, as it were—and often thereby pronouncing elements that are unstressed or silent in the word's customary or natural pronunciation. We thereby pronounce *catsup* or *charivari* or *sarsaparilla* the way they *look* like they should be pronounced. We do this, consciously or not, by making implicit analogies or comparisons with other words that we do know. And we leave no syllable unturned.

Thus, while heated debate concerning spelling usually centers on why we don't spell words as we pronounce them, there is this curious flip side: the tendency to pronounce words as we spell them.

In place names the phenomenon of spelling pronunciation—or local usage—can clearly be detected. Think only of the different ways that such words as *Greenwich*, *Leicester*, *Houston*, and *Warwick* are pronounced, or of the numerous French-derived names of American cities and towns pronounced in a midwestern rather than Gallic way. Furthermore, as you've probably noted, local pronunciations of place names differ from those of other people who have only encountered the names in writing or on maps.

But spelling pronunciations are peculiarly American also because of the reverence most of us have for the primacy of the dictionary, because of the force of popular education here. If a word is plainly printed and spelled in such a way in the Ultimate Verbal Authority, isn't it clear enough that it should be *carefully* pronounced that way?

The English, for better or worse, generally take dictionaries less seriously. (Paradoxically, Americans who took the dictionary more seriously by checking the phonetics, indicating a more natural pronunciation as preferred, would be less prone to spelling pronunciations.) British speakers often glide over or leave out syllables in words that we think we are being more precise about pronunciationally. Possibly we're being more precise without being more correct. Thousands and thousands of English words have never been pronounced the way they "look" (hence the challenge of spelling bees and tests), and it is generally agreed that oral usage is law in matters of language.

Linguistic scholars today tend to speak ill of spelling pronunciations, if only because they are strained anomalies to actual, time-tested pronunciation that come of fluent utterance; and, most important, because natural pronunciation should preferably develop from the *context* in which a single word finds itself. Pedantic "overpronunciations"—spelling pronunciations—are all the more deplorable, they feel, when perpetuated by teachers and dignified by dictionaries. "When spellings lead to the revival of a pronunciation long since given up," writes Dwight Bolinger, "their force is not conservative but reactionary. In Southern Britain the word *often* is coming more to be pronounced with a (t) and with the *o* of *odd*. When a spelling leads to a pronunciation that never existed, its influence is neither conservative nor reactionary but subversive."

Early in the nineteenth century, Dennis Baron notes in *Grammar and Good Taste: Reforming the American Language,* James Fenimore Cooper argued that the New England accent was the result of spelling pronunciation; and Noah Webster felt it imperative that American orthography be reformed because of the dangers of spelling pronunciation.

But spelling pronunciations are here to stay in our language, and consequently have their own odd authority as part of everyday usage. The influence of writing on the spoken language, according to Bolinger, "is a condition of literate societies. Universal literacy is too recent a phenomenon to reveal long-range effects, but it seems reasonable to suppose that one such effect will be to stabilize language to a certain extent. Reading is more widely shared over a longer period of time than any form of listening: we 'hear' an author of a hundred years ago as clearly as we hear one today, if we read him, and the cultivation of classics insures that we will."

Whether we use them or refuse them, we should at least be aware of spelling pronunciations. They remind us of the curious gulf in language between eye and ear, the kind of twilight zone in which we encounter a word seen but never before heard. Like the ominously articulating Rod Serling, with a twilight word we are often inclined to be slow and deliberate, to give each printed syllable its vocal due.

> You must remember that it is permiss*ible* for spelling to drive you crazy. Spelling had this effect on Andrew Jackson, who once blew his stack while trying to write a Presidential paper. "It's a damn poor mind that can think of only one way to spell a word!" the President cried.
>
> John Irving

Multiple-Choice Test No. 8

Circle the correct spelling.

1. kolrabbe   kolrabi   kohlrabi   kohlrabe
   (type of cabbage)

2. philogeny   philogyny   phylogyny   phylogeny
   (evolution of related organisms)

3. rickitty   ricketty   rickkity   rickety
   (run-down or shaky)

4. semaphore   semmiphore   semiphore   semmaphor
   (system for signaling by waving of flags)

5. particapitory   participatory   participitory   particapatory
   (with direct involvement)

6. habilliments   habilements   habiliments   habilaments
   (dress or clothes)

7. Drammamine   Dramamin   Dramamine   Drammamin
   (anti-nausea medication)

8. doilie   doily   doilly   doillie
   (decorative napkinlike mat)

9. callomine   calimine   calamine   callimine
   (healing ointment)

10. tergiversate   turgiversate   turgyversate   terrgiversate
    (to desert a cause or be evasive)

11. talcy   talcky   talcey   talckey
    (having or like a soft silicate used in powder)

12. ippicac   ipicac   ipecac   ipeccac
    (root used medicinally)

13. bludgen   bludgion   bluddgen   bludgeon
    (to strike in a heavy or brutal way)

14. poinsetta   poyntsetta   pointsettia   poinsettia
    (Mexican plant having bright red or white bracts)

15. crochety   crotchetty   crotchitty   crotchety
    (irritable)

16. afidavit   affidavid   afidavitt   affidavit
    (legalized sworn statement)

17. hemmorage   hemorrhage   hemmhorage   hemorhage
    (extreme bleeding)

18. capuccino   cappucino   cappuccino   capucino
    (espresso coffee with milk)

19. Capouchin   Cappuchin   Capuchin   Caputchin
    (member of an austere monastic order)

20. obelisk   obbelisk   obelisque   obbelisque
    (squared and tapering pillarlike monument)

 a. inveigle   inveigel   invaigle   invaygle
    (to entice)

 b. molassas   molasas   mollasses   molasses
    (sugary brown syrup)

 c. complaysant   complacent   complaisant   complacant
    (obliging or accommodating)

 d. pasteurize   pasturise   pastorize   pasturize
    (to sterilize partially through heat)

 e. toopelo   tupelo   toupelo   tupello
    (North American tree; black gum)

Before consulting the answers on page 290:
I think I spelled _____ words correctly on this test.
(If your estimate is correct, add one point to your score.)

À COUPS DE DICTIONNAIRE

The word *coup* in French means "blow," of the punching or striking variety, and English has borrowed several phrases using that word. A coup d'état is a group's violent overthrow or rearrangement of the existing government (or "stroke of state"). In English we also use coup de grace (a death blow or finishing-off), coup de théâtre (a theatrical success or something sensationally dramatic), and coup de main (a forceful attack).

You may also strike or beleaguer somebody with a dictionary, unliterally, in the sense of constantly checking or referring to a lexicon. If while in a discussion or argument you harp on the precise dictionary definition of this or that, you're expatiating *à coups de dictionnaire.*

Spellers, too, may be inclined to invoke what the dictionary says orthographically. Is this a sign of pedantic arrogance or of educational insecurity? Whichever, *à coups de dictionnaire* is a good phrase for a student of correct spelling to know, if only to stop the conversation dead.

Say It and Spell It Test No. 7

Write in the correct spelling.

1.	is′məs	_____	connecting strip of land
2.	pol′ē klin ik	_____	outpatient department
3.	hī men′ē əl	_____	nuptial
4.	tiz′ik	_____	tubercular
5.	vē ə lən chel′ō; vī ə lin chel′ō	_____	large stringed instrument
6.	bā′tid	_____	reduced or restrained
7.	kafēn′	_____	coffee ingredient
8.	ək roo′ment	_____	increase or accumulation
9.	stā tol′ə trē	_____	belief in powerful central government
10.	zom′bē iz əm	_____	cult of the living dead
11.	shoo′flī	_____	(~ pie) molasses-brown sugar mixture
12.	ə but′mənt	_____	projection or architectural support
13.	ak′nēd	_____	having inflamed skin
14.	disk′har ō	_____	farmer's land-plowing implement
15.	ga loot′	_____	odd fellow
16.	non′sked′	_____	nonscheduled airline or flight

17. wej'wood   —————————   English ceramic
                                                        manufacturer

18. mis'əl rē   —————————   arsenal of projectiles
19. dā kəl täzh'   —————————   low neckline
20. hô'zər   —————————   thick nautical rope
  a. kra vat'   —————————   neck scarf
  b. han'səl   —————————   good-luck gift
  c. kur'ē ər ēs   —————————   leather finishing or
                                                        softening shops
  d. yo͞o'nək   —————————   castrated male
  e. pom ād'   —————————   hair dressing

Pronunciation key on page 10.

> *Before consulting the answers on page 290:*
> I think I spelled ____ words correctly on this test.
> (If your estimate is correct, add one point to your score.)

RESTAURANT SPELLING

Claims to superiority are common. The restaurants that say that they are best might also fill a stadia, probably the Sugar Bowl, but the wise person has his own favorites. When my mind turns to food—an untoward development, since the legs usually go first, turning, in times of stress, to jelly—I think of smorgasborg, and then omelete assorti. I think next of an 8 per cent fillet mignion served in Amarillo, Texas—8 per cent is as much of that as I want to eat at a sitting; of Lindy's Crab and Seafood Market in Linden, New Jersey, which is open seven days a week and Sundays and holidays; of a restaurant in Buffalo, New York, that specializes in eye rib of beef, lean and succulant, cooked to your indiscriminant taste; and then of a stay at the Hollenden House, in Cleveland, where the restaurant listed appetite provacateurs, among them shrimp scampies, a mischievous but endearing crustacean. I long to go to a restaurant called La Diplemat, in Nashville, Tennessee, and I wonder what is on its menu. Perhaps Kitsch Lorraine, chicken en brochay, and two Irish dishes, O'Grattan potatoes and lemon moran pie.

A mad hunger takes possession of me and I am unindated by memories of the Granada Royale Hometel in Omaha, where a light and airy courtyard lends a sidewalk cafe affect to meals. I remember a roast beefe sandwich I had at the Red Lion Restaurant of the Beverly Hilton Hotel. Ah! Ye roast beefe of Olde England. Alors! Le petit strip sirloin at the Hyatt Regency Hotel at O'Hare Airport in Chicago, served with the Frenchman's favorite wine, Beaujolias. My mind skips to the Chez Bon Dining Lounge near L'Aéroport de Detroit; to the Board Room Restaurant in New York, which serves Les Asparagus de France, though not Les Tomatoes or La Lettuce; and to a plate du jour at a country club in North Carolina, where I saw a woman carrying a L'Tote cosmetics bag by Lancome. Her carriage suggested that her girdle was a Fleur d'Lace.

The French should be gratified that their cuisine is enjoyed across the United States. Stouffer's Denver Inn, where Brian and Liz were congradulated, serves French Dip, consisting of sliced Colorado beef on a roll with savory au jus so good it sets you humming. A cup of coffee, a sandwich and au jus. Au jus is turning up in many places. I was offered a cup of it on an airplane. It appears to be a case of the wandering au jus. At Lake Tahoe, Shrimp Provenciale is presented as evidence of one restaurant's Continental flare, and the DELInclineTESSEN restaurant features Escargot Cognac and a galantina sandwich. I thought that anybody who would drink Escargot Cognac must be galantina indeed, but a preoccupation with food can lead you astray. When Mario Merola, the Bronx District Attorney, made some comments about a superseder by Governor Hugh Carey, he proved to be talking about the possibility that Carey would remove one prosecutor from office in favor of another. I had assumed that the Governor was giving an unusually large Passover feast for his Jewish friends. This seemed not out of the question in New York politics.

My mind drifts back to the best, and only, baked lasange I've ever had, in Hudson Falls, New York. It skips to a motel in Charlotte, North Carolina, where it was possible to begin a meal with anti-pasto, a dish popular with those who dislike Italian cooking (I am pro-pasto myself), and then, for those unable to make up their minds about sauces, go on to Veal Parmigiana Milanese. All roads lead to Rome, or elsewhere.

Edwin Newman
A Civil Tongue

Words of One Syllable Test No. 6

Write in the correct spelling.

1. fī′(ə)l _____ close-woven fabric with slight ribs in the weft
2. nil _____ nothing, zero
3. serk _____ steep mountain basin
4. dīt _____ *archaic:* to dress or adorn
5. kwäf _____ to arrange or brush hair
6. sfeks _____ type of wasp
7. ras _____ brightly colored spiny-finned fish
8. gīl _____ beer from one brewing
9. dōb _____ braised meat stew
10. sist _____ sac or fluid-filled pouch in the body
11. strep _____ septic sore throat
12. kongk _____ mollusk or its spirallike shell
13. tōk _____ woman's tight brimless hat
14. näsh _____ to munch or snack
15. gôlt _____ thick clay soil
16. dalz _____ river rapids in a gorge
17. swä<u>th</u> _____ to bind or wrap
18. sklaf _____ in golf: to scrape the ground on one's swing
19. plās _____ European flounder
20. dun _____ a demanding of payment
a. sān _____ vertically hanging, floating fishnet
b. wûrt _____ fermented-mash liquid used in making beer
c. zekt _____ German champagne
d. fras _____ insect excrement
e. rē<u>th</u> _____ to make or shape to coil around

Pronunciation key on page 10.

Before consulting the answers on page 291:
I think I spelled _____ words correctly on this test.
(If your estimate is correct, add one point to your score.)

WHY SOUND MUST RUN, AND SPELLING LAG BEHIND

The Bee its spelling carefully arranged,
But looked around, and found the Sound had changed:
For Etymology stuffs such a trove
Down Spelling's throat, the creature scarce can move,
While Sound's a hopper of a speed so rare
That when you see him he's no longer there.

One bygone aeon, Spelling dared Pronun-
Ciation to a race, and might have won—
Pronunciation, as a handicap,
Reclining in mid-race to take a nap.
But when the Bee approached, Sound oped his eyes,
Resumed the race, and hopped off with the prize.

Orthography since then prefers to stop
At home, and let Pronunciation hop.

Willard Espy

Multiple-Choice Test No. 9

Circle the correct spelling.

1. cinnammon   cinamon   cinammon   cinnamon
   (spice from the bark of a tree)
2. tinntinnabulation   tintinabulation   tinntinabulation
   tintinnabulation
   (ringing or chiming)
3. placket   plaquet   plackette   plackit
   (slit in a garment)
4. daguerreotype   daguerotype   dageurrotype   daguerriotype
   (old photograph on a silver or copper plate)
5. rutabaga   rootabaga   rootibaga   rutibaga
   (type of turnip)
6. dingies   dinghies   dingees   dingys
   (small boats carried on ships)
7. aquious   aqueous   acqueous   acquious
   (watery)

8. geniollogically   geneologically   genealogically   geniologically
   (in terms of family or heredity)

9. panagyric   panigyric   pannagyric   panegyric
   (speech of praise)

10. solsticial   sollsticial   sollstitial   solstitial
    (occurring around June twenty-second or December twenty-second)

11. bicentennary   bicenntenary   bicentinary   bicentenary
    (two hundredth anniversary; bicentennial)

12. mallette   mallet   malette   mallett
    (hammer with a wooden head)

13. abbacuses   abbaccuses   abacusses   abacuses
    (beads-on-rods calculating instruments)

14. rimy   rhimy   rhimey   rimey
    (frosty)

15. napftha   nopftha   naphptha   naphtha
    (hydrocarbon mixture used in solvents)

16. Antiaen   Antean   Antaean   Anteian
    (having superhuman strength)

17. litoral   litteral   littoral   litorral
    (coastline)

18. acetyleen   ascetylene   accetylene   acetylene
    (hydrocarbon used in welding)

19. catanary   katanary   katenary   catenary
    (chainlike)

20. phadorra   fadora   fadorra   fedora
    (man's low felt hat)

 a. mareschino   marraschino   marreschino   maraschino
    (large fermented-liqueur cherry)

 b. geoddysey   geodecy   geodosy   geodesy
    (science of determining the earth's dimensions)

 c. phantesmagoria   phantasmagoria   fantesmagoria
    fantasmagoria
    (series of bizarre or shifting visual impressions)

d. Taggalog   Tagalog   Tagalogg   Taggalogue
   (language of the Philippines)
e. giggalo   gigolo   giggolo   gigollo
   (woman's supported male escort)

> *Before consulting the answers on page 291:*
> I think I spelled _____ words correctly on this test.
> (If your estimate is correct, add one point to your score.)

EYE WORDS

Some words, you may have noticed, you see in print but rarely, if ever, hear in conversation. Words like *nonpareil, eleemosynary, exiguous, autarky, phthisis,* and *maillot.*

Such visual vocables are known, unmysteriously, as eye words. What makes a word an eye word? The answer may be in the eye of the beholder. The word's meaning may be rather special, less than indispensable for purposes of everyday conversation, a quality that would be true of more than just technical terms. The word's meaning might be fairly simple—*eleemosynary,* for example, means charitable—but oral (or aural) use is scant because there are simpler or briefer synonyms. Length alone would not seem to be the determining factor—most of us do not shy away from uttering *prestidigitation, recalcitrant,* or *superheterodyne.*

Pronounceability definitely is a factor in making a word an eye word—pronounceability or spelling. When a word is learned from hearing it repeatedly, it obviously doesn't present a pronunciation problem. But when it is encountered only in print and the spelling seems odd or perplexing, the tongue may tie at the thought of using it in speech; or it will be uttered hesitantly, self-consciously, with almost apologetic uncertainty. Another eye word is perpetuated.

But like spelling bugbears, eye words are individual. One man's eye word is another woman's conversational staple.

Eye words (paradoxically, perhaps) usually make excellent spelling test words. You might say they're often seen but rarely spelled.

Say It and Spell It Test No. 8

Write in the correct spelling

1.	sem′ə nəl	_____	centrally indispensable, creative
2.	hâr′əs; hə ras′	_____	vex
3.	kə mem′ə rāt	_____	honor in memory
4.	plā′rīt	_____	dramatist
5.	ə noint′	_____	bedaub with oil or consecrate
6.	də fer′mənt	_____	postponement
7.	stoop′ə fī	_____	bewilder
8.	fôr′ôr dān′	_____	predestinate
9.	sul′kē	_____	carriage
10.	kon sen tā′nē əs	_____	in agreement, unanimous
11.	vit′rē əl	_____	acid, caustic antipathy
12.	kən fûr′əl	_____	bestowal or consultation
13.	riv′yoo let	_____	small stream
14.	lin′təl	_____	horizontal span or support
15.	ə pyoon′	_____	assail
16.	wôl′les	_____	lacking a vertical enclosure or partition
17.	gut′ə rəl	_____	from the throat
18.	ou′lit	_____	small owl
19.	är′mə chər	_____	framework
20.	fresh′ət	_____	stream overflowed
a.	ek′stûr pāt	_____	root out
b.	kas′tiz əm	_____	Hindu hereditary class system
c.	râr′i tēs	_____	uncommon events or things
d.	pab′ləm	_____	easily absorbed food
e.	jen tēl′ē	_____	with propriety or elegance

Pronunciation key on page 10.

Before consulting the answers on page 291:
I think I spelled _____ words correctly on this test.
(If your estimate is correct, add one point to your score.)

SPELLING YIFFNIFF

My father used to offer an array of prizes for anyone who could spell yiffniff. That's not how to spell it, of course—yiffniff. I'm just trying to let you know what it sounds like, in case you'd like to take a crack at it yourself. Don't get your hopes up: this is a spelling word that once defied some of the finest twelve-year-old minds Kansas City had to offer.

The prizes were up for grabs any time my father drove us to a Boy Scout meeting. After a while, all he had to say to start the yiffniff attempts was "Well?"

"Y-i . . ." some particularly brave kid like Dogbite Davis would say.

"Wrong," my father would say, in a way that somehow made it sound like "Wrong, dummy."

"How could I be wrong already?" Dogbite would say.

"Wrong," my father would repeat. "Next."

Sometimes he would begin the ride by calling out the prizes he was offering: ". . . a new Schwinn three-speed, a trip to California, a lifetime pass to Kansas City Blues baseball games, free piano lessons for a year, a new pair of shoes." No matter what the other prizes were, the list always ended with "a new pair of shoes."

Some of the prizes were not tempting to us. We weren't interested in shoes. We would have done anything to avoid free piano lessons for a year. Still, we were desperate to spell yiffniff.

"L-l . . ." Eddie Williams began one day.

"Wrong," my father said. "Next."

"That's Spanish," Eddie said, "the double *L* that sounds like a *y*."

"This is English," my father said. "Next."

Sometimes someone would ask what yiffniff meant.

"You don't have to give the definition to get the prizes," my father would say. "Just spell it."

As far as I could gather, yiffniff didn't have a definition. It was a word that existed solely to be spelled. My father had invented it for that purpose.

Occasionally some kid in the car would make an issue out of yiffniff's origins. "But you made it up!" he'd tell my father, in an accusing tone.

"Of course I made it up," my father would reply. "That's why I know how to spell it."

"But it could be spelled a million ways."

"All of them are wrong except my way," my father would say. "It's my word."

If you're thinking that my father, who had never shared the secret of how to spell his word, could have simply called any spelling we came up with wrong and thus avoided handing out the prizes, you never knew my father. His views on honesty made the Boy Scout position on that subject seem wishy-washy. There was no doubt among us that my father knew how to spell yiffniff and would award the prizes to anyone who spelled it that way. But nobody seemed able to do it.

Finally, we brought in a ringer—my cousin Keith, from Salina, who had reached the finals of the Kansas State Spelling Bee. (Although Keith's memory has always differed from mine on this point, I'm sure I was saying even then that the word he missed in the finals was "hayseed.") We told my father that Keith, who was visiting Kansas City, wanted to go to a Scout meeting with us to brush up on some of his knots.

"Well?" my father said, when the car was loaded.

"Yiffniff," my cousin Keith said clearly, announcing the assigned word in the spelling bee style. "Y-y . . ."

Y-y! Using *y* both as a consonant and as a vowel! What a move! We looked at my father for a response. He said nothing. Emboldened, Keith picked up the pace: "Y-y-g-h-k-n-i-p-h."

For a few moments the car was silent. Then my father said, "Wrong. Next."

Suddenly the car was bedlam as we began arguing about where our plans had gone wrong. "Maybe we should have got the guy who knew how to spell 'hayseed,' " Dogbite said. We argued all the way to the Scout meeting, but it was the sort of argument that erupts on a team that has already lost the game. We knew Keith had been our best shot.

Keith now teaches English to college students. He presumably has scholarly credentials that go beyond spelling, but he still worries about yiffniff. Not long ago, while we were talking about something else, he suddenly said, "Maybe I should have put a hyphen between yiff and niff."

"No, it doesn't have a hyphen," I said.

"How do you know?"

"Because the other day one of my kids spelled it your way except with a hyphen, and I had to tell her she was wrong," I said. "It's a shame. She's really had her eye on winning that new pair of shoes."

Calvin Trillin
If You Can't Say Something Nice

Multiple-Choice Test No. 10

Circle the correct spelling.

1. de rigor de rigeur de rigueur de rigeure
   (proper and essential)
2. adinoidal adynoidal adenoidal adynnoidal
   (pertaining to tissue at the back of the pharynx)
3. chameleon camelion camellion chamellion
   (lizard whose skin changes color)
4. phillately phyllately philatelly philately
   (stamp collecting)
5. bougainvillea bouganvillea bougainvillia bougaenvillia
   (colorful American tropical woody vine)
6. prestidigitater prestodigitator prestodigitater
   prestidigitator
   (sleight-of-hand artist)
7. spinate spinet spinette spinnet
   (small upright piano)
8. octorroon oktoroon octoroon octtoroon
   (person one-eighth Negro in ancestry)
9. brisket briskette brisquet brisquette
   (breast cut of beef)
10. demurrhal demural demurral demerral
    (hesitation or objection)
11. mineret minerette minaret minarette
    (slender mosque tower)
12. homburg hamborg hamburg homborg
    (type of man's felt hat)

13. cabbalero   cabalero   cabballero   caballero
    (cavalier or horseman)

14. passamentery   passementerie   passimenterie   passimentery
    (fancy trimming or edging)

15. chatawqua   chautaqua   chautauqua   chatauqua
    (old American tradition of outdoor lectures, concerts, etc.)

16. dillatation   dilitation   dilatation   dillitation
    (widening)

17. garret   garrette   garette   garrett
    (room just beneath the roof)

18. collophon   colophon   collofon   coliphon
    (printer's inscription or emblem in a book)

19. tomaine   ptomaine   ptomain   phtomaine
    (food poisoning)

20. trekkor   treckor   treker   trekker   ,
    (one who makes a difficult journey)

a. antimaccasar   antimaccassar   antemaccasar   antimacassar
    (small covering on the back or arms of a piece of furniture)

b. betel   beatle   beatel   beetel
    (Asian pepper whose leaves are chewed)

c. revetment   rivetment   revettment   rivetement
    (embankment support or barricade)

d. chrysalis   crysalis   chrysallis   chrysalice
    (butterfly pupa)

e. anise   anice   annice   annise
    (aromatic herb)

Before consulting the answers on page 291:
I think I spelled ____ words correctly on this test.
(If your estimate is correct, add one point to your score.)

Say It and Spell It Test No. 9

Write in the correct spelling.

1. də zûrts'   _____   deserved reward or rewards
2. mə rid′ē ə nəl   _____   southern

3.	grip	_____	influenza
4.	ob strep′er əs	_____	unruly
5.	kon sen′ shoo əl	_____	by agreement
6.	in ten′dəns	_____	management or supervision
7.	pit′əns	_____	small amount
8.	ploo′mē	_____	like a plume
9.	shood	_____	driven or scared away
10.	av′ə lanch	_____	mountain downslide
11.	prō tem′	_____	for the time being
12.	div′ēd	_____	divided
13.	in fin i tes′ə məl	_____	minute in size
14.	sə rôr′əl	_____	sisterly
15.	fā′ə ten	_____	carriage or touring car
16.	lenz′les	_____	lacking a piece of curved optical glass
17.	fyoo nē′rē əl	_____	somber
18.	pâr′i sīd	_____	killing of one's father
19.	hâr′brānd	_____	stupid
20.	sin′jer	_____	one who singes
a.	sach′əl	_____	small bag
b.	lē ā′zon	_____	relationship or illicit meeting
c.	en chə lä′də	_____	filled tortilla
d.	sôlt′sel ər	_____	salt dispenser
e.	em bar′əs	_____	make uncomfortable

Pronunciation key on page 10.

Before consulting the answers on page 292:
I think I spelled _____ words correctly on this test.
(If your estimate is correct, add one point to your score.)

GOOD SPELLING: YOU CAN TAKE IT TO THE BANK

In the customer-service line at Marine Midland:

Woman: Look at this stupid bank, they don't even know how to spell their own stupid forms. Look how they made "supersede"—with a *c*.

Man: *C* is right.

Woman: It most certainly is not.

Man: How much?

Woman: Five dollars.

Man: Miss, can you get us a dictionary? She says you spell "supersede" with an *s*, not a *c*.

Customer Service Woman: With a *c* is right.

Woman: That's what you say.

(Customer Service Woman produces dictionary, looks up "supersede.")

Customer Service Woman: Uh-oh, we're in trouble here.

Man: Let me see that. Well, what do you know? (Hands over $5.)

Woman: Thank you very much.

Man: I'm glad you didn't say a hundred. Miss?

Customer Service Woman: Yes?

Man: I think this bank owes me five dollars.

Rhoda Koenig
New York magazine

POOR SPELLER JAILED 3 YEARS FOR BANK HEIST

An illiterate bank robber with more than 40 criminal convictions in the past 11 years has been sentenced to three years in prison.

"This is a up," Wayne John Kennedy wrote in his holdup note, according to prosecutor Faye McWatt.

She said when police asked Kennedy to write "This is a holdup," he wrote "This is a up," 10 times in a row.

Defence counsel Ken Danson called the situation "pathetic."

One of 22 children, Kennedy did not finish Grade 4 and constantly breaks the law because of his feelings of frustration and being unloved by his parents, his sister said.

"As long as he's been able to talk he's had a problem" getting into trouble, the sister told the court last week.

Kennedy, 28, of 9th St., Etobicoke, was found guilty by Judge C. S. Lazier in Toronto District Court of robbing a Toronto-Dominion Bank branch on Lake Shore Blvd. W., in Etobicoke, in his own neighborhood, of $1,800 on Aug. 14 last year.

Toronto Star

MISSPELLED HOLDUP NOTE LEADS POLICE TO ARREST

A spelling error has led police to charge a woman with robbing a bank just two weeks after they charged her sister with the same offence.

Yesterday a note given to a teller at a Toronto Dominion Bank branch said: "Give me the money. I'm armed and dangerouse." The robbers got $600 but detectives remembered a note given to a teller in a July 21 robbery also had the extra letter "e."

Police yesterday arrested Marie Connolly, 29, and Gary Michael O'Dell, 35, at a Hamilton apartment. Connolly's sister, Carolyn Connolly, 34, was charged in the July 21 robbery.

Toronto Star

Multiple-Choice Test No. 11

Circle the correct spelling.

1. pommagranate   pomegranite   pommegranite   pomegranate
   (large reddish berry)
2. nimiety   nemiety   nimmiety   numiety
   (excess)
3. descenary   decenary   decennery   decennary
   (period of ten years)
4. bruskerie   brusquery   bruskery   brusquerie
   (brusqueness of manner)

5. bitummenous bytumenous bitumenous bituminous
   (pertaining to soft coal)

6. anuroid aneroid anaroid annaroid
   (using no liquid)

7. rehntgen roentgen rentgen roentgon
   (unit of radiation)

8. Armmagedon Armageddon Armagedon Armaggedon
   (final battle between good and evil)

9. parillogism parallogism paralogism parilogism
   (logically false argument)

10. velleity veliety veleity velliety
    (slight wish)

11. cautchuc couchouc caoutchouc coutchouc
    (rubber)

12. monodnok monodnoc monadnock monadnoc
    (isolated hill or mountain of rock)

13. vermeill vermiell vermiel vermeil
    (gilded silver)

14. pharoah pharoh pharaoh pharho
    (ancient Egyptian ruler)

15. veruccose verucose verrucose verruccose
    (warty)

16. papilionacious papillionaceous papilionaceous
    papillionacious
    (like a butterfly)

17. florescent fleurescent flourescent fluorescent
    (absorbing and emitting radiation or light)

18. rhadamanthine rhadimanthine radhamanthine
    radamanthine
    (strict but just)

19. nickolic nicolic niccollic niccolic
    (containing nickel)

20. shekkel shekell shekel schekel
    (Israeli coin)

 a. beelzebubb beelzebbub bielzebub beelzebub
    (the Devil)

b. mistletoe   misteltoe   mistletow   mistleto
    (green, berried shrub popular at Christmastime)

c. gouwache   gouasche   g'washe   gouache
    (opaque watercolor)

d. propaedeutic   propedeutic   propideutic   propodeutic
    (involving preparatory learning)

e. murrh   murrhe   myrrh   myrre
    (aromatic gum resin)

Before consulting the answers on page 292:
I think I spelled _____ words correctly on this test.
(If your estimate is correct, add one point to your score.)

THE SPELL AGAINST SPELLING

(a poem to be inscribed in dark places and never to be spoken aloud)

My favorite student lately is the one who wrote about feeling clumbsy.
I mean if he wanted to say how it feels to be all thumbs he
Certainly picked the write language to right in in the first place.
I mean better to clutter a word up like the old Hearst place
Than to just walk off the job and not give a dam.

Another student gave me a diagragm.
"The Diagragm of the Plot in Henry the VIIIth."

Those, though, were instances of the sublime.
The wonder is in the wonders they can come up with every time.

Why do they all say heighth, but never weighth?
If chrystal can look like English to them, how come chryptic can't?
I guess cwm, chthonic, qanz, or quattrocento
Always gets looked up. But never momento.
Momento they know. Like wierd. Like differant.

It is a part of their deep deep-structure vocabulary:
Their stone axe, their dark bent-offering to the gods:
Their protoCro-Magnon pre-pre-sapient survival-against-cultural-odds.

You won't get *me* deputized in some Spelling Constabulary.
I'd sooner abandon the bag-roke-whiff system and go decimal.
I'm on their side. I better be, after my brush with "infinitessimal."

There it was, right where I put it, in my brand-new book.
And my friend Peter Davison read it, and he gave me this look,
And he held the look for a little while and said, "George . . ."

I needed my students at that moment. I, their Scourge.
I needed them. Needed their sympathy. Needed their care.
"Their their," I needed to hear them say, "their their."

You see, there are *Spellers* in this world, I mean mean ones too.
They shadow us around like a posse of Joe Btfsplks
Waiting for us to sit down at our study-desks and go shrdlu
So they can pop in at the windows saying "tsk tsk."

I know they're there. I know where the beggars are,
With their flash cards looking like prescriptions for the catarrh
And their mnemnmonics, blast 'em. They go too farrh.
I do not stoop to impugn, indict, or condemn;
But I know how to get back at the likes of thegm.

For a long time, I keep mumb.
I let 'em wait, while a preternatural calmn
Rises to me from the depths of my upwardly opened palmb.
Then I raise my eyes like some wizened-and-wisened gnolmbn,
Stranger to scissors, stranger to razor and coslmbn,
And I fix those birds with my gaze till my gaze strikes hoslgmbn,
And I say one word, and the word that I say is "Oslgmbnh."

"Om?" they inquire. "No, not exactly. *Oslgmbnh.*
Watch me carefully while I pronounce it because you've got only two more
    guesses

And you only get one more hint: there's an odd number of esses,
And you only get ten more seconds no nine more seconds no eight
And a right answer doesn't count if it comes in late
And a wrong answer bumps you out of the losers' bracket
And disqualifies you for the National Spellathon Contestant jacket
And that's all the time extension you're going to gebt
So go pick up your consolation prizes from the usherebt
And don't be surprised if it's the bowdlerized regularized paperback abridgment
     of Pepys
Because around here, gentlemen, we play for kepys."

Then I drive off in my chauffeured Cadillac Fleetwood Brougham
Like something out of the last days of Fellini's Rougham
And leave them smiting their brows and exclaiming to each other "Ougham!
O-U-G-H-A-M Ougham!" and tearing their hair.

Intricate are the compoundments of despair.

Well, brevity must be the soul of something-or-other.

Not, certainly, of spelling, in the good old mother
Tongue of Shakespeare, Raleigh, Marvell, and Vaughan.
But something. One finds out as one goes aughan.

George Starbuck
From *The Argot Merchant Disaster*

BRITISH SPELLINGS

To our American eyes, those old-fashioned British spellings of certain words look like they should be Yanked. But remember that the people in that island kingdom started the language, before we vastly improved it. If you went to work as an editor in London, could you translate U.S. English into English English? If you were a secret American agent over there, would your spelling betray you?

British Spellings Test

	American	British		American	British
1.	eon	_____	16.	dullness	_____
2.	hemorrhage	_____	17.	siphon	_____
3.	curb	_____	18.	pajamas	_____
4.	carburetor	_____	19.	fecal	_____
5.	specialty	_____	20.	naught	_____
6.	wagon	_____	21.	vise	_____
7.	artifact	_____	22.	pretense	_____
8.	connection	_____	23.	maneuver	_____
9.	homeopathy	_____	24.	anemic	_____
10.	apologize	_____	25.	harbor	_____
11.	enroll	_____	a.	biased	_____
12.	cider	_____	b.	worshiper	_____
13.	tomorrow	_____	c.	behoove	_____
14.	jail	_____	d.	diarrhea	_____
15.	enthrallment	_____	e.	medieval	_____

> *Before consulting the answers on page 292:*
> I think I spelled _____ words correctly on this test.
> (If your estimate is correct, add one point to your score.)

HOBSON-JOBSONS

One of the more familiar scenes in movies is the caught-in-the-act confrontation with that same classic line. The gangster or husband bursts into a room to find the girlfriend or wife enjoying a close body-hold with a third party. The startled woman disengages quickly from her partner and sputters but always manages to get the cliché out: "Wait . . . please . . . I can explain . . . it's not what it looks like!"

There are words and phrases that aren't what they look like, either.

Our word *bully* comes not from *bull* but from a Dutch word for lover, *boel.* *Fakir,* now part of our language, has nothing to do with faking or being an impostor but refers to a Muslim beggar or Hindu ascetic and derives from an Arabic word meaning "poor." The section of London called Rotten Row is actually named from a major bending of the French *route de roi,* or king's highway. Greyhounds aren't grey (or gray) for a good reason: The first syllable is an Anglicization of a Norse word for "dog."

English is chock-full of such deceptions, most of them due to a kind of natural distorting of foreign borrowings. The result is a tendency of native speakers of English to see in loanwords English word elements where in fact none exist—and often thereby to mistake the meaning.

Such "nativized" words are called Hobson-Jobsons. The linguistic term *Hobson-Jobson* is itself, appropriately, a Hobson-Jobson, as it comes from the Arabic *ya Hasan, ya Hosain,* an Islamic mourning cry that the British rounded off into two common English surnames.

Meaning can easily be misconstrued when a word is a Hobson-Jobson, either because of its sound or because of its written form. The word niggardly, meaning stingy or cheap, has Scandinavian origins (and is akin to an Old Norse word for "stingy") and has nothing to do with the offensive racial epithet familiar to all black people. *Humble pie,* similarly, comes not from *humble* but from Middle English *umbles* or *noumbles,* meaning animal entrails.

But one's spelling, too, can be affected by the Hobson-Jobsons phenomenon. If you are uncertain about the spelling of a word, you may wrongly (if quite logically) associate it with another English word and consequently misspell it.

The only antidote to this pitfall is to check your dictionary now and then for word derivations. Etymology can become a fascinating hobby.

Meanwhile, beware of Hobson-Jobson goblins.

Multiple-Choice Test No. 12

Circle the correct spelling.

1. hazenpfeffer   hasenfeffer   hazenfeffer   hasenpfeffer
   (rabbit stew)

2. loup   loupe   louppe   loope
   (jeweler's magnifying glass)

3. kiosk   quiosque   kyosque   qioske
   (newsstand structure)

4. pallette   palette   pallet   pallatte
   (painter's hand-held pigment board)

5. cocquettry   coquettry   coquetterie   coquetry
   (flirtatiousness)

6. inards   innerds   innards   innerdes
   (animal's internal parts)

7. opalescent   opulescent   opallescent   opellescent
   (reflecting light iridescently)

8. sarsparella   sarsaparilla   sasparella   sassaparella
   (flavorful root used in a soft drink)

9. buccanneer   bucaneer   bucanneer   buccaneer
   (freebooter or pirate)

10. napery   naperie   napperie   nappery
    (table linen)

11. paregoric   paragoric   parigoric   parragoric
    (pain-relieving camphorated tincture of opium)

12. aperitif   apperitif   appertif   aperitiv
    (pre-meal cocktail)

13. compasse mentice   compus mentis   compass mentis
    compos mentis
    (sound of mind)

14. revellie   reveille   revvely   revveille
    (military wake-up call)

15. schnappse   shnapps   schnapps   shnaps
    (strong Dutch gin)

16. psychedelic   psychodelic   psychadelic   psychadellic
    (pertaining to abnormal mental or visual effects, hallucinatory)

17. eleemosynery   eleymosynary   eleymosinary   eleemosynary
    (charitable)
18. Demmeral   Demerol   Demmerol   Demoral
    (drug: meperidine)
19. hermineutics   hermaneutics   hermeneutics   hermanutics
    (scholarly interpretation)
20. piranha   pirannah   pirana   piranah
    (carnivorous South American fish)
 a. chickel   chicel   chickle   chicle
    (chewing gum ingredient)
 b. schrapnel   shrapnell   schrapnell   shrapnel
    (grenade fragments)
 c. siphyllis   siphylis   syphillis   syphilis
    (venereal disease)
 d. adscititious   adcititious   adsititious   adsciticious
    (additional or extrinsic)
 e. plankten   planckton   planckten   plankton
    (minute floating aquatic animal and plant life)

Before consulting the answers on page 292:
I think I spelled ＿＿＿ words correctly on this test.
(If your estimate is correct, add one point to your score.)

Multiple-Choice Test No. 13

Circle the correct spelling.

1. lineament   linnement   liniment   linament
   (salve)

2. ophthalmology   ohpthalmology   opthalmology   oppthalmology
   (medical field pertaining to the eyes)

3. bouillibaisse   bouillabaisse   bouillebaisse   bouillabaise
   (fish stew)

4. caduceous   caduceus   cadutious   caducious
   (symbol of entwined snakes on a staff; physician's symbol)

5. Shaeol   Sheol   Sheole   Sheoll
   (Hebrews' realm of the dead)

6. camillia   chamelia   camellia   chamellia
   (ornamental shrub with roselike flowers)

7. sibilant   sibillant   syballant   sybillant
   (making an *s* or *sh* sound)

8. smorrgasbord   smorgasboard   smorgesboard   smorgasbord
   (buffet meal)

9. cameraderie   camaradery   camaraderie   cameradery
   (comradeship)

10. jittney   jitney   gitney   djittney
    (small bus)

11. censer   scenser   senser   sensor
    (incense burner)

12. maggety   maggoty   maggotty   maggotie
    (infested with legless grubs)

13. chuka   chukah   chukkah   chukka
    (ankle-high boot)

14. peccadilo   peccadillo   pecadillo   peccidillo
    (minor sin)

15. chapleted   chapletted   chappletted   chappleted
    (wearing a head wreath)

16. zeppillin   zeppolinn   zepellin   zeppelin
    (football-shaped airship)
17. mumu   mumuu   muumuu   moomoo
    (loose and long colorful dress)
18. nickleodion   nickelodeon   nickelodion   nickleodeon
    (early movie theater)
19. cirhosis   cirhossis   cirrhosis   scirhossis
    (liver disease)
20. macaroon   maccarroon   macarroon   maccaroon
    (small coconut or almond cookie)
 a. cemateries   cemmiteries   cemeteries   cemmeteries
    (burial yards)
 b. quinquennium   quintquennium   quinquenium
       quinnquennium
    (period of five years)
 c. empirean   empyrian   empyrean   empiraen
    (celestial)
 d. piccador   picadore   picador   piccadore
    (bullfighting lancer on horseback)
 e. gyper   gipper   gypper   gyppor
    (swindler)

> *Before consulting the answers on page 293:*
> I think I spelled _____ words correctly on this test.
> (If your estimate is correct, add one point to your score.)

Multiple-Choice Test No. 14

Circle the correct spelling.

1. jelignite   gelignite   gellignite   jellignite
   (type of dynamite)

2. vacqueros   vaqueroes   vaqueros   vacquéros
   (cowboys)

3. dacquerie   daiquiri   daiqueri   daiquerie
   (rum and lime juice cocktail)

4. balilaikah   ballilaikah   balilaika   balalaika
   (Russian stringed musical instrument)

5. topsy-turviness   topsi-turvyness   topsi-turviness
   topsy-turvyness
   (upside-downness or confusion)

6. topsi-turvidom   topsi-turvydom   topsy-turvydom
   topsy-turvidom
   (upside-downness or confusion)

7. luauh   luau   luaue   louau
   (Hawaiian banquet)

8. spinacker   spinaker   spinnackor   spinnaker
   (large triangular sail)

9. derndal   derndl   dirnndl   dirndl
   (tight-bodiced peasant-style dress)

10. finagle   phenagle   phinagle   finnagle
    (to scheme or acquire deviously)

11. treliss   trellace   trellis   trelliss
    (latticework frame)

12. lhamasery   lamasery   llamasary   llamasery
    (Buddhist monastery)

13. kindergardener   kindergartner   kindergardner
    kindergardenner
    (pupil usually four to six years old)

14. jodhpurs   jodpurs   johdpurs   jodphurs
    (riding breeches)

15. barret   barrette   barette   barrete
    (woman's hair clip)

16. mannicoti   mannicotte   manicotti   mannicotti
(Italian pasta dish)

17. paene   paeane   peane   paean
(tribute or hymn of praise)

18. slavies   slaveys   slavees   slavveys
(female servants)

19. fricassee   friccisee   fricissee   friccasee
(stewed chicken dish)

20. marquis   markee   markey   marquee
(theater entrance canopy)

a. Sisuphian   Sisyfian   Sisyphean   Sissyphean
(arduous or futile)

b. nigretude   negretude   nigritude   negritude
(extreme darkness or blackness, as at night)

c. carusel   carousel   carrusel   carousell
(merry-go-round)

d. kich   kitch   kittch   kitsch
(tasteless articles)

e. stevadore   steevadore   stevedore   stevador
(port cargo worker)

> *Before consulting the answers on page 293:*
> I think I spelled ____ words correctly on this test.
> (If your estimate is correct, add one point to your score.)

Multiple-Choice Test No. 15

Circle the correct spelling.

1. odyssies   oddysseys   odysseys   oddyseys
(travels)

2. shillala   shilally   shillelagh   shellelagh
(Irish cudgel)

3. whippoorwill   whipporwill   whipoorwill   whipoorwyl
(nocturnal bird, goatsucker)

4. vichisoise   vichysoisse   vichyssoise   vichysoise
(pureed cold soup)

5. para-mutual   pari-mutual   parimutual   pari-mutuel
(betting pool)

6. sassifrass   sasifrass   sasafrass   sassafras
(flavorful root bark)

7. Appaloosa   Apaloossa   Apalloosa   Appalloosa
(Western saddle horse)

8. castinettes   castanets   castanettes   castinets
(hand-held musical percussion shells)

9. diosiscan   diocisan   dioscesan   diocesan
(pertaining to a bishop's jurisdiction)

10. Philipinos   Filipinos   Philippinos   Filippinos
(citizens of the Pacific nation whose capital is Manila)

11. granary   grainary   granery   grainery
(grain storehouse)

12. hulliballoo   hullibaloo   hullabaloo   hulleballo
(ruckus)

13. Cupie   Kewpee   Kewpie   Cupee
(chubby doll)

14. millenneum   millennium   millenium   milennium
(thousand years)

15. byalis   byallies   bialys   bialies
(flat breakfast rolls)

16. obeyescence   obeisance   obeisence   obeiscence
(deference or submission)

17. Weimarinor   Weimaraner   Whymariner   Weimariner
(short-haired German dog breed)

18. tinsellerie   tinselerie   tinnsillry   tinselry
    (ornamentation)

19. symoleon   simolion   simoleon   simolleon
    (dollar)

20. babbushka   babuschka   babbuschka   babushka
    (head kerchief)

a. spermiceti   spermecetti   spermaceti   spermicetti
   (waxy substance from whales)

b. winable   winnible   winible   winnable
   (capable of being won)

c. dihptheria   diphtheria   diptheria   dyptheria
   (contagious disease usually first affecting the throat)

d. antehistamine   antihistimine   antehistimine   antihistamine
   (allergy-countering)

e. spitoon   spittoon   spittoone   spitoone
   (receptacle in which to spit)

Before consulting the answers on page 293:
I think I spelled _____ words correctly on this test.
(If your estimate is correct, add one point to your score.)

TEN REASONS WHY ENGLISH SPELLING IS SO CONFUSED

After taking four multiple-choice tests in a row, you may be a little orthographically punch-drunk and need some reassurance about how tough English spelling is. Here's a handy review of reasons for our language's being a mare's nest, drawn from the brief history of our language provided on page 13.

- English is a rich but mongrel language, drawn from other languages having different pronunciation and spelling systems. Alphabetically, it possesses too many sounds (more than forty) for too few letters (twenty-six) in its Roman alphabet.
- The written word could not keep up with the spoken word. Pronunciation over the centuries underwent many periods of

change too rapidly for a truly phonetic spelling to keep abreast. Sometimes, even as a spelling was becoming standard in print, the word's pronunciation was changing.

- Authoritative opinions regarding proper spelling have often differed, with some favoring simplified, phonetically appropriate orthography but others maintaining that spellings should above all manifest etymology—that is, a word's derivation.

- At times letters were inserted in words (by analogy with other words) to make them more etymologically sound, a detraction from actual pronunciation; in many instances the supposed etymology (until modern times a science based very much on guesswork) was erroneous.

- The Norman Conquest, and French as a new language of court and government, ultimately enriched the language but profoundly disrupted the basis (Old English) for a stabilized spelling in Britain. (To the Norman influence English owes the letters *j, q, v,* and *z,* but now *c* was written for *s, o* for *u,* and *ou* for *ū,* or long *u.*

- The advent of printing and proliferation of books brought with it some orthographic stability but also much confusion. Early compositors were often German or Dutch, and different printing houses followed different spelling practices.

- For many years spelling was arbitrary and thought to be of little importance.

- The spellings in Samuel Johnson's influential dictionary, which became a world-famous model for lexicographers, were based largely on etymology, not on actual pronunciation.

- In America, Noah Webster's legendary American dictionary greatly simplified and standardized U.S. spelling. But to foster better sale of his dictionaries in England, Webster sometimes left less simple British spellings untouched.

- Proposals over the centuries for reform of English spelling have never won sustained support. To most people it seems impracticable to overhaul an entire language and its history. Proposed systems of phonetic spelling seem either too simplistic or too complicated. The most eminent proposers and scholars have found themselves in violent disagreement. And the idea of devising a spelling system based on actual pronunciation always founders on the most problematical of all questions related to spelling reform: Based on whose pronunciation?

"SPELLING" (COMIC STRIP BY LYNDA BARRY)

DITTOGRAPHS AND HAPLOGRAPHS

When you're engaged in writing and misspell a word, it's not always because you don't know the correct spelling. Sometimes you miswrite out of haste or carelessness. Your pen or typewriter tries to pass your mind at the turn and has a slight orthographic blackout. Such a momentary bad spell is called a lapsus calami or lapsus pennae, or slip of the pen.

Two of the most common types of inadvertent misspellings are the dittograph and the haplograph. A dittograph (or dittography) is what you get when you unwittingly double a letter, syllable, or word. Instead of writing "Never express something in two words when it can be expressed in one," you find, on rereading, that you have written, "Never express something in two two words when it can be expressed in one." On the other hand, you may commit a haplograph (or haplography) by leaving something out of a sentence. Meaning to write "I can't wait to finish penning this sentence," you write, "I can't wait finish penning this sentence."

People don't usually make such graphological goofs at the beginnings or ends of sentences, it seems. Your occasional dittograph or haplograph probably occurs in the middle of a sentence, and probably involves a short word—typically an article, pronoun, or preposition—rather than a long one, or a part of a word.

When can one encounter dittographs and haplographs in speech as well as in writing? In spelling bees, of course, when nervous competitors double or leave out elements of words whose correct spelling they in fact know. This is why bee contestants are always advised to spell carefully and slowly.

One broad problem was never solved, and it has plagued English spelling to this day. The Greeks had supplied too few vowels, and nobody with power enough tried to overhaul the vowels in the Western vernaculars. Scribes made some attempts (apparently they understood the desirability of letters representing sounds), but they had troubles. English was much fractured by dialect, and the transcribing was further confused by Norman copyists trying to write it with alphabetic traditions that had grown in Continental languages.

Charlton Laird

A TEST—COURTESY OF A SPELLING CHAMPION—FOR YOU TO GIVE

Rageshree Ramachandran

Tired of taking tests and eager to give one yourself? For this book, Rageshree Ramachandran, the 1988 Scripps Howard National Spelling Bee Champion, was invited to choose ten of her favorite words that would make a good spelling test. She graciously replied with the following ten, which she finds "quite interesting because of their etymology." Here Rageshree's words have been supplied with brief definitions.

1. humuhumunukunukuapuaa
   (small Hawaiian pig-snouted triggerfish)
2. Andalusian
   (pertaining to a region of southern Spain)
3. caoutchouc
   (India rubber)
4. mho
   (electrical practical unit of conductance)
5. moue
   (small grimace or pout)
6. wildebeest
   (African oxlike antelope; gnu)
7. chthonic
   (pertaining to underworld deities or spirits; infernal)
8. stollen
   (German form of sweetened bread)
9. meshuggener
   (foolish or crazy person)
10. infundibulum
    (funnel-shaped or conical part or organ)

(Note: Coincidentally, a number of Rageshree's ten words appear on other tests elsewhere in this book.)

TWO SPELLINGS ALLOWED TESTS

This is a compassionate book, in places. Here are three tests in which not one but two possible answers are correct.

The author would like to point out that some of these words used to have only one correct spelling, and that many still have a particular single spelling preferred by most writers and editors. But the dictionary is the dictionary is the dictionary. With two shots here, you shouldn't get any wrong, right?

Two Spellings Allowed Test No. 1

Write in the correct spelling.

1.	an'yə riz əm	_____	abnormal dilation of a blood vessel
2.	bôrn	_____	*archaic:* boundary or goal
3.	kar ə van'sə rē	_____	inn
4.	in eks pun'ji bəl	_____	not obliterable
5.	kē'stər	_____	*slang:* fanny, behind
6.	shtet'əl	_____	European Jewish village
7.	tum'brəl	_____	French Revolution execution cart
8.	wān'skot ing; wān'skō ting	_____	wall paneling material
9.	mə vŏor nēn	_____	*Irish:* my darling
10.	per snik'itē	_____	fussy
11.	ə sof'ə gəs	_____	tubal passage from the throat
12.	kē ə rə skyŏor'ō	_____	artistic shading technique
13.	wī'zən hī mər	_____	smark aleck
14.	jen yŏo flek'shən	_____	bending the knee in worship
15.	hŏop'lä	_____	commotion
16.	koun'slər	_____	adviser
17.	lē je nârs' də zēz'	_____	type of pneumonia
18.	tē'tōt lər	_____	abstainer from alcohol
19.	kok'ə mā mē	_____	senseless or crazy
20.	kə put'	_____	broken
a.	bark	_____	small sailing ship
b.	wād'ə bəl	_____	able to be waded in

c. ep ə let′   _____   shoulder pad or ornament

d. mon′i kər   _____   nickname

e. par′ə lel ē   _____   in an analogous or similar way

Pronunciation key on page 10.

> *Before consulting the answers on page 293:*
> I think I spelled _____ words correctly on this test.
> (If your estimate is correct, add one point to your score.)

Two Spellings Allowed Test No. 2

Write in the correct spelling.

1. gônt′let   _____   armored glove
2. chôk′lə tē   _____   tasting like cacao
3. kal ə mär′ē   _____   squid
4. ling wē′nē   _____   thin flat pasta
5. hoo dun′it   _____   mystery novel
6. sil′ə bub   _____   sweetened cream-based wine or cider drink
7. kal′ə pər   _____   pincerlike measuring instrument
8. loo′fə   _____   plant skeleton used as a sponge
9. man ə kē′ən   _____   dualistic philosophically
10. bōn′ə mē′   _____   geniality
11. lan′yûrd   _____   cord
12. om′let   _____   eggs beaten and fried
13. kē   _____   waterway landing place
14. grom′it   _____   flexible loop or eyelet
15. sloo   _____   large number
16. ab′sinth   _____   strong green aromatic liqueur
17. brī′ər   _____   prickly bush
18. stī   _____   eyelid swelling
19. klar ə net′ist   _____   woodwind instrument player
20. bär kə rōl′   _____   Venetian boat song

a. eks'trə vert _____ outwardly oriented person
b. kôk _____ make watertight
c. trī'kôrn _____ cocked hat
d. dred'nôt _____ British battleship
e. jan'ə ser ē _____ loyal soldier or follower

Pronunciation key on page 10.

Before consulting the answers on page 294:
I think I spelled _____ words correctly on this test.
(If your estimate is correct, add one point to your score.)

Two Spellings Allowed Test No. 3

1. nī trə glis'ə rin _____ dynamite ingredient
2. kôr net'ist _____ player of trumpetlike instrument
3. en'voi _____ concluding stanza
4. bel'dəm; bel'dam _____ hag
5. môr'tis _____ rectangular hole in construction
6. gran'dam' _____ grandmother
7. grō tesk ə rē' _____ bizarre unnaturalness
8. en jam'ment _____ line running over in verse
9. blōō'ing _____ laundering anti-yellowing
     substance
10. ap'ə nij _____ rightful property
11. gä'nē ən _____ citizen of West African country
12. lech _____ sexual desire
13. klôr'ə fil _____ plant coloring substance
14. om'i kron'; ō'mik ron' _____ Greek alphabet letter
15. sat ēn' _____ satinlike fabric
16. mī'nə _____ crested Asian bird
17. bri ket _____ brick-shaped mass
18. ban da'nə _____ large patterned kerchief
19. wil'fəl _____ perverse or stubborn

20. kə sē′nō   ———————— card game
 a. âr ə gram   ———————— airmail folding sheet envelope
 b. kris′tē   ———————— type of skiing turn
 c. kris′mə sē   ———————— suggestive of Noel
 d. krēm pas′ yo nel′   ———————— sexually motivated crime
 e. ôt′ō gī′rō   ———————— rotor-powered aircraft

Pronunciation key on page 10.

Before consulting the answers on page 294:
I think I spelled ____ words correctly on this test.
(If your estimate is correct, add one point to your score.)

THE SPELLING BEE AT ANGELS

(Reported by Truthful James)
Waltz in, waltz in, ye little kids, and gather round my knee,
And drop them books and first pot-hooks, and hear a yarn from me.
I kin not sling a fairy tale of Jinnys[1] fierce and wild,
For I hold it is unchristian to deceive a simple child;
But as from school yer driftin' by, I thowt ye'd like to hear
Of a "Spelling Bee" at Angels that we organized last year.

It warn't made up of gentle kids, or pretty kids, like you,
But gents ez hed their reg'lar growth, and some enough for two.
There woz Lanky Jim of Sutter's Fork and Bilson of Lagrange,
And "Pistol Bob," who wore that day a knife by way of change.
You start, you little kids, you think these are not pretty names,
But each had a man behind it, and—my name is Truthful James.

There was Poker Dick from Whisky Flat, and Smith of Shooter's Bend,
And Brown of Calaveras—which I want no better friend;
Three-fingered Jack—yes, pretty dears, three fingers—*you* have five.
Clapp cut off two—it's sing'lar, too, that Clapp ain't now alive.
'T was very wrong indeed, my dears, and Clapp was much to blame;
Likewise was Jack, in after-years, for shootin' off that same.

Qy. Genii.

The nights was kinder lengthenin' out, the rains had jest begun,
When all the camp came up to Pete's to have their usual fun;
But we all sot kinder sad-like around the bar-room stove
Till Smith got up, permiskiss-like, and this remark he hove:
"Thar's a new game down in Frisco, that ez far ez I can see
Beats euchre, poker, and van-toon, they calls the 'Spellin' Bee.'"

Then Brown of Calaveras simply hitched his chair and spake,
"Poker is good enough for me," and Lanky Jim sez, "Shake!"
And Bob allowed he warn't proud, but he "must say right thar
That the man who tackled euchre hed his education squar."
This brought up Lenny Fairchild, the schoolmaster, who said
He knew the game, and he would give instructions on that head.

"For instance, take some simple word," sez he, "like 'separate:'
Now who can spell it?" Dog my skin, ef thar was one in eight.
This set the boys all wild at once. The chairs was put in row,
And at the head was Lanky Jim, and at the foot was Joe,
And high upon the bar itself the schoolmaster was raised,
And the bar-keep put his glasses down, and sat and silent gazed.

The first word out was "parallel," and seven let it be,
Till Joe waltzed in his "double l" betwixt the "a" and "e;"
For since he drilled them Mexicans in San Jacinto's fight
Thar warn't no prouder man got up than Pistol Joe that night—
Till "rhythm" came! He tried to smile, then said "they had him there,"
And Lanky Jim, with one long strike, got up and took his chair.

O little kids, my pretty kids, 't was touchin' to survey
These bearded men, with weppings on, like schoolboys at their play.
They'd laugh with glee, and shout to see each other lead the van,
And Bob sat up as monitor with a cue for a rattan,
Till the Chair gave out "incinerate," and Brown said he'd be durned
If any such blamed word as that in school was ever learned.

When "phthisis" came they all sprang up, and vowed the man who rung
Another blamed Greek word on them be taken out and hung.
As they sat down again I saw in Bilson's eye a flash,
And Brown of Calaveras was a-twistin' his mustache,

And when at last Brown slipped on "gneiss," and Bilson took his chair,
He dropped some casual words about some folks who dyed their hair.

And then the Chair grew very white, and the Chair said he'd adjourn,
But Poker Dick remarked that *he* would wait and get his turn;
Then with a tremblin' voice and hand, and with a wanderin' eye,
The Chair next offered "eider-duck," and Dick began with "I,"
And Bilson smiled—then Bilson shrieked! Just how the fight begun
I never knowed, for Bilson dropped, and Dick, he moved up one.

Then certain gents arose and said "they'd business down in camp,"
And "ez the road was rather dark, and ez the night was damp,
They'd"—here got up Three-fingered Jack and locked the door and
    yelled:
"No, not one mother's son goes out till that thar word is spelled!"
But while the words were on his lips, he groaned and sank in pain,
And sank with Webster on his chest and Worcester on his brain.

Below the bar dodged Poker Dick, and tried to look ez he
Was huntin' up authorities thet no one else could see;
And Brown got down behind the stove, allowin' he "was cold,"
Till it upsot and down his legs the cinders freely rolled,
And several gents called "Order!" till in his simple way
Poor Smith began with "O-r"—"Or"—and he was dragged away.

O little kids, my pretty kids, down on your knees and pray!
You've got your eddication in a peaceful sort of way;
And bear in mind thar may be sharps ez slings their spellin' square,
But likewise slings their bowie-knives without a thought or care.
You wants to know the rest, my dears? Thet's all! In me you see
The only gent that lived to tell about the Spellin' Bee!

———

He ceased and passed, that truthful man; the children went their way
With downcast heads and downcast hearts—but not to sport or play.
For when at eve the lamps were lit, and supperless to bed
Each child was sent, with tasks undone and lessons all unsaid,
No man might know the awful woe that thrilled their youthful frames,
As they dreamed of Angels Spelling Bee and thought of Truthful
    James.

Bret Harte

Of Course You Know What *Epyllion* Means, but Can You Spell It?

(The Scripps Howard National Spelling Bee)

Whether you're fifteen years old or in your seventies, if you grew up and went to school in this country, chances are you have a memory or two of a spelling bee.

Ever since rules for spelling competitions were invented by—who else?—Benjamin Franklin in 1750, this heady educational ritual has been a cornerstone of American verbal education. Granted that many spellers or nervous competitors would just as soon forget such preadolescent and adolescent showdowns, many others value them as an almost patriotic tradition. Language scholars and historians have claimed that at least one reason Americans have continually resented attempts to reform or simplify English orthography is that we love the right-or-wrong, stand-or-fall challenge of our spelling bees.

We needn't invent a science of psycho-orthography to see the appeal of this little-red-schoolhouse exercise, both to teachers and to pupils. It helps, even inspires, young people to learn to spell correctly. Being a miss-and-you're-out game, it cannot help but instill in grammar schoolers the fact that there are—usually—no two ways about the correct letters forming a word: It's right or it's wrong. Such good, old-fashioned absoluteness seems special in our increasingly relativistic world (and educational curricula). Not only American elementary schools but corporations and civic groups are sponsoring spelling bees nowadays. Giving a boost to the cause of literacy is one impetus, but it's also the realization that bees make people buzz together, that bees can liven things up. Among the buzzers are senior citizens, who have been organizing annual bees in Florida, Oklahoma, Texas, and other states. A bee held at a Bronx juvenile detention center was recently described in the *New York Times.* Can spelling become a new rehabilitative tool?

In short, bees are great competitive fun, and can give any English class the drama of a sudden-death overtime. For schoolchildren who excel at a local or regional level, the fun may diminish and the pressures grow keener as they find themselves on the way to the bee of all bees, in Washington, D.C.

Every spring the Scripps Howard National Spelling Bee, to determine a national l-i-t-e-r-a-t-i-o-n champion, is held in our nation's capital under the sponsorship of the Scripps Howard newspaper syndicate. The competition dates back to 1925, when the first such orthographic tournament was promoted by the Louisville *Courier-Journal.* One of the biggest boosters of the event was the FBI's J. Edgar Hoover, who annually congratulated the winner. In recent years the *Seattle Times* and the Seattle Mariners major league baseball team have been staunch supporters.

Contestants—they must not have passed beyond the eighth grade at the time of their individual school finals, and they must not have reached their sixteenth birthday on or before the date of the National Spelling Bee (in 1988, one finalist was an eight-year-old girl in the third grade)—are sponsored by newspapers around the United States. Previous winners may not compete again. Scripps Howard, which has owned the sponsoring rights since 1941, estimates that some eight or nine million American schoolchildren participate in the school, district, city, and regional bees from which the national contenders are drawn. The National Spelling Bee is thus not simply a once-a-year event in Washington. It is, according to Scripps Howard, "an educational program designed to help students improve their spelling, increase their vocabularies, acquire concepts, learn language development, and improve reading skills that will benefit them all their lives."

The finals merely represent the climax to all this competitive, coast-to-coast spelling and misspelling. In recent years young spellers par excellence, each sponsored by a newspaper and accompanied by an escort, have arrived in Washington for two days of empyrean-level spelling. They come from private and parochial as well as public schools. In 1925 there were nine sponsored contestants. Now there are more than two hundred, representing most of our states and the District of Columbia, the Virgin Islands, Puerto Rico, Guam, and Mexico.

One dictionary is the *sanctum sanctorum* for all National Spelling Bees. It is more than 2,500 fine-print pages of Merriam-Webster's *Third New International Dictionary* and its Addenda Section, published by Merriam-Webster, Inc.

Sponsors of ultimate national champions over the years have included newspapers in Des Moines, El Paso, Winston-Salem, Syracuse, Omaha, Harrisburg, Tulsa, Birmingham, San Juan, Houston, and Topeka. Of the sixty-five champions to date (no championships were held during the war years 1943, 1944, and 1945, and there were ties in 1950, 1957, and 1962), thirty-five have been girls and thirty, boys; the boys, according to Scripps Howard, have been "catching up" of late.

How does a ten- to fifteen-year-old (or younger) spelling whiz get into verbal shape for the World Series of spelling?

By reading dictionaries, of course. But potential contestants should also study Latin and Greek roots, a bit of etymology, and various word lists made up locally for spelling bee students in city and regional contests. And they should also absorb *Words of the Champions,* a handy and most intimidating booklet of several thousand practice words published annually by Scripps Howard and distributed to students all over the country.

Under the National Spelling Bee program, spelling competitions prior to the finals may be written as well as oral. But the nationals in Washington are solely oral and aural, with each contestant standing at a microphone, listening to the word given by the official "pronouncer," and going for it, letter by letter.

Over two days in a hotel ballroom at the 1989 championship (the sixty-second), 222 spellers, wearing numbered placards, went through thirteen rounds of elimination. After the first day, 170 contestants were left. On the final day, all four spellers in the ninth round made it to the tenth round, but only three were left at the eleventh and only two at the twelfth. Words are not necessarily progressively difficult; and though Scripps Howard tries hard to be equitable, the luck of the draw— which word one gets—is a definite factor. In 1989 it took 903 spelled and misspelled words to determine a champion: fourteen-year-old Scott Isaacs of Littleton, Colorado.

At the end, after twelve-year-old Ojas Tejani of Hixson, Tennessee, went down on *senescing,* Isaacs spelled it correctly and won the title by spelling *spoliator.* First prize brought Isaacs, besides a trophy and a plaque for his school, $1,500. It also won him an invitation to spell a few words on Johnny Carson's "The Tonight Show."

How well would you do as a National Spelling Bee contestant?

Possibly not so well as you'd think. Webster's Third, the source for all words chosen, is a very large dictionary. English is a daunting language. Many of the practice words found in

Words of the Champions—like *epyllion, takkanah, natte, peirastic,* and *appetitost*—would dumbfound anybody regarding meaning as well as spelling, much more so the average fifth- to eighth-grader. National Spelling Bee finalists are definitely not average. (Many teachers and administrators—and students—involved believe that too many of the words chosen are unfairly rare or exotic, and according to Sondra Austin of Scripps Howard there is a "new age" movement afoot to make the words chosen appropriately challenging but less recherché.)

Are you primed and ready?

If you want to organize your own spelling bee, you'll find after this discussion the official rules that govern the National Spelling Bee championship. You'll also need access to a copy of Webster's Third for spellings, pronunciations, and definitions, and you should have in reserve sentence examples using the words in case requested. If you want to be NSB-tested yourself, have somebody else devise a bee using these rules.

Or maybe you don't want to venture such an undertaking but would just like to get an idea of exactly what sort of words prodigious young spellers face once a year in Washington. Following, from a recent *Words of the Champions* booklet, is a sampling of First Round words, Intermediate words, and Final words, followed by a finalists' Waterloo list—the specific words that knocked out finalists in the 1987 event.

Preceding the NSB rules and those lists, here is a veritable in-a-word capsule history of the National Spelling Bee for your perusal: twenty-four different words on which championships have been won since the contest was first held, most of them, curiously, easier than those that follow this list:

abbacy	milieu
acquiesced	narcolepsy
asceticism	odontalgia
brethren	onerous
cambist	propitiatory
condominium	propylaeum
croissant	purim
deification	sarcophagus
elucubrate	staphylococci
hydrophyte	transept
incisor	vouchsafe
maculature	psoriasis

NATIONAL SPELLING BEE CONTEST RULES

1. City and regional champions participating in the championship finals of the Scripps Howard National Spelling Bee in Washington, D.C., must qualify under two basic requirements: (a) they must not have passed beyond the eighth grade at the time of their individual school finals; and (b) they must

not have reached their sixteenth birthday on or before the date of the national finals.

2. Contests for classroom, school, district, city or regional championships may be conducted either in writing or orally, or a combination of the two. The national championship finals, however, shall be an oral competition, with eliminations on a "miss-and-out" basis in the traditional Spelling Bee manner.

3. Words used in the national finals shall be selected from the *Words of the Champions* book, from the lists used in the various city and regional contests, and from *Webster's Third New International Dictionary*, copyright 1986 Merriam-Webster, Inc., and its Addenda Section.

4. Words shall be pronounced according to the diacritical markings in *Webster's Third New International Dictionary*, copyright 1986 Merriam-Webster Inc., and its Addenda Section, from which the pronouncer shall select the definition or definitions that he/she gives. With the approval of the judges, he/she may give a fuller explanation of the meaning of a word to supplement the dictionary definition or definitions quoted.

5. In competition, after the pronouncer gives the contestant a word, the contestant may also pronounce the word before spelling it and after spelling it. However, no contestant will be eliminated for failing to pronounce a word.

6. The contestant may request the pronouncer to repronounce the word, define it, or use it in a sentence. The contestant may ask for the language origin of a word. No other information about the etymology or history of a word will be given. If the contestant has a *specific* root word in mind, the contestant may ask if the dictionary lists that word as the root of the word to be spelled. The pronouncer shall grant all such requests until the judges agree that the word has been made reasonably clear to the contestant. JUDGES MAY DISQUALIFY ANY CONTESTANT WHO IGNORES A REQUEST TO START SPELLING.

7. Having started to spell a word, a contestant may stop and start over, retracing the spelling from the beginning, but in the retracing there can be no change of letters or their sequence from those first pronounced. If letters or their sequence are changed in the respelling, the speller will be eliminated.

8. Upon missing the spelling of a word, the contestant immediately drops out of the contest. The next word on the pronouncer's list is given to the next contestant.

9. When the contestants are reduced to two, the elimination procedure changes. At that point, when one contestant misspells a word, the other contestant shall be given an opportunity to spell that same word. If the second contestant spells that word correctly, plus the next word on the pronouncer's list, then the second contestant shall be declared the champion.

10. If one of the last two spellers misses and the other, after correcting the error, misspells the new word submitted to him/her, then the misspelled new word shall be referred to the first speller. If the first speller then succeeds in correcting the error and correctly spells the next word on the pronouncer's list, then he/she shall be declared the champion.

11. If both spellers misspell the same word, both shall continue in the contest, and the one who first misspelled the word shall be given a new word to spell. The contest shall then continue under Rules 9, 10, and 11.

12. *Webster's Third New International Dictionary,* copyright 1986 Merriam-Webster, Inc., and its Addenda Section shall serve as the final authority for the spellings of words in the national finals. If more than one spelling is listed for a word, any of these spellings will be accepted as correct if the word either matches the pronunciation and definition provided by the pronouncer, or if it is clearly identified as being a standard variant of the word that the contestant has been asked to spell.

Spellings at other locations having *archaic, obsolete* or *regional labels* (such as North, Midland, South, Brit(ish), Irish) that are different from those at the main entry will not be accepted as correct.

13. Any question relating to the spelling of a word should be referred to the judges immediately. The deadline for making a protest is before the contestant affected would have received his/her next word had he/she stayed in the contest. No protest will be entertained after that word has been given another speller. When only two spellers remain, a protest must be made immediately, that is, before the second speller has started to spell the word given him/her, or, if both have missed the same word, before the correct spelling is given the audience.

14. The judges are in complete control of the Bee. Their decision shall be final on all questions.

15. Any child having once won a Scripps Howard National Spelling Bee championship is ineligible for future competition in the Scripps Howard National Spelling Bee.

FIRST ROUND WORDS (PRACTICE)

accrue	dulcet	ligature	snippet
anoint	effluent	mallet	stodgily
argosy	fiasco	phonics	weevil
baboon	grammar	proclivity	zodiac
caress	hideous	riffraff	
clique	hopscotch	shoddiness	
confetti	juror	shovellike	

INTERMEDIATE WORDS (PRACTICE)

arboret
auricular
blas
bradawl
bulliform
campanology
cark

culgee
drakelet
foraminate
grapnel
immund
mozzarella
pisco

ptosis
roleo
sangaree
shigellosis
simnel
strepitous
tiralee

trochlea
vinculum
washin
xerosis

FINAL WORDS (PRACTICE)

alegar
amertoy
anaqua
apiculus
arachin
argillaceous
arrasene
bamboche
barrabora
bhabar
brankursine
cacuminal
ceraceous
chistka
chough
coaration
conquian
couac
coutil
cupressineous
decalage
dipsas
discigierous

esconson
exedent
ferraiolone
fjeld
fughetta
granophyre
greffier
gruine
hexafoos
iliacus
impofo
incienso
intertriginous
jacal
lebbek
leggieramente
miljee
mistassini
mofussil
neossology
opodeldoc
panettone
persillade

phrenicectomy
piloncillo
projicient
psammophile
quatenus
quokka
radzimir
rhytidome
roussette
saffian
salsilla
scytodepsic
shaganappi
shillibeer
shubunkin
solvolysis
spacistor
spiedino
stolkjaerre
strisciando
stromuhr
svabite
tabetisol

taiaha
taraxein
tarogato
thymiaterion
tichorrhine
tripelennamine
trochiline
truttaceous
tydie
umbellulone
vespetro
vindaloo
viuva
weddellite
whally
wickawee
wiikite
wiliwili
wirrah
wokas
xanthism

FINALIST'S WATERLOO (1987): WORDS THAT KNOCKED OUT CONTESTANTS

apocynthion	guyot	menat	torrone
boson	haylage	mugient	urceole
cassioberry	huarizo	psittacine	xylitol
circumforaneous	jarrah	puli	zucchetto
concrescence	kalanchoe	rhodochrosite	
decistere	lorcha	tacan	
euryene	macfarlane	targhee	

> So long as the effective use of language is a matter of memorising and applying rules, there is no scope for the outstanding achievement that demands outstanding effort. We do not congratulate a man on the excellence of his spelling.
>
> G. L. Brook

Death by Spelling College

Welcome to Death by Spelling College, where you can test yourself with some truly curricular spelling.

Spelling tests are usually assortments of words in relatively common usage but from different areas of life; they are generally general. But each of us has interests or expertise in special fields, from cooking to bird-watching to nuclear physics. Maybe you've occasionally thought while taking some of *Death by Spelling*'s general tests, "I may not know all these words, but I sure know how to spell words having to do with my own job and my own hobbies."

Here's your chance to matriculate in the spelling test of your (subject) choice. It's also a test of your familiarity with specific terminologies. If you don't know one or two of the terms in the field you know or are learning about, well, maybe you should. You can learn vocabulary as well as spelling here.

You have fifty-five subjects to spell your way through.

Welcome, speller, to the orthography of orismology.*

* technical terminology

American Cities

1. Talahasee   Tallahassie   Tallihassie   Tallahassee
   (Florida)
2. Albaquerque   Albuqerque   Albuquerque   Albequerque
   (New Mexico)
3. Ypsalanti   Ypsilante   Ypsilanti   Ypselanti
   (Michigan)
4. Wapiton   Wahpiton   Wapeton   Wahpeton
   (North Dakota)
5. Corvalis   Corvalliss   Corvallas   Corvallis
   (Oregon)
6. Oskallousa   Oskaloosa   Oscilloosa   Oskilloosa
   (Iowa)
7. Chattennoga   Chattanooga   Chattinooga   Chattannooga
   (Tennessee)
8. Schenechtedy   Schenectedy   Schenecttedy   Schenectady
   (New York)
9. Wilkes-Bare   Wilkes-Barre   Wilkes-Barrie   Wilks-Barre
   (Pennsylvania)
10. Chillicoth   Chilicothe   Chillecothe   Chillicothe
    (Ohio)
11. Ammarilo   Ammarrilo   Amarillo   Amarrillo
    (Texas)
12. Champaign   Champain   Champagne   Champaigne
    (Illinois)
13. Boguloosa   Bogaloosa   Bogalusa   Bogulusa
    (Louisiana)
14. Casper   Caspor   Caspur   Caspere
    (Wyoming)
15. Manasquan   Mannasquan   Manasquon   Mannisquan
    (New Jersey)
16. Elkharte   Elkheart   Elkhart   Elkhard
    (Indiana)
17. Meriden   Meridan   Merriden   Merridan
    (Connecticut)

18. Fredericksburg   Fredericsburg   Fredericsberg
      Fredericksberg
      (Virginia)

19. Montpellier   Montpellior   Montpelier   Montpelior
      (Vermont)

20. Savanna   Savvannah   Savanah   Savannah
      (Georgia)

21. Scheboygun   Scheboygan   Sheboygun   Sheboygan
      (Wisconsin)

22. Misoulla   Missula   Missoulla   Missoula
      (Montana)

23. Parigould   Parragould   Paragould   Parrigould
      (Arkansas)

24. Phenixe City   Phenix City   Phoenixe City   Phoenix City
      (Alabama)

25. Brainerd   Brainerde   Brainard   Brainarde
      (Minnesota)

26. Atcheson   Atchison   Atchesson   Atchisson
      (Kansas)

27. McAllister   McAlester   McAllester   MacAlister
      (Oklahoma)

28. Toule   Toole   Toulle   Tooele
      (Utah)

29. Petaluma   Pettaluma   Petiluma   Petalluma
      (California)

30. Pocatelo   Pocotelo   Pocotello   Pocatello
      (Idaho)

31. Spartenberg   Spartanberg   Spartenburg   Spartanburg
      (South Carolina)

32. Paducah   Paduccah   Padducah   Padukah
      (Kentucky)

33. Vermilion   Vermileon   Vermillion   Vermilleon
      (South Dakota)

34. Woonsocket   Woonsokette   Woonsockett   Woonsockette
      (Rhode Island)

35. Buckhannon   Buckhanan   Buckhanon   Buckhannan
      (West Virginia)

36. Chickopie   Chickopee   Chicopie   Chicopee
    (Massachusetts)

37. Winachee   Winache   Wenache   Wenatchee
    (Washington)

38. Kechikan   Ketchikan   Kechekan   Ketchekan
    (Alaska)

39. Wiluku   Waillukoo   Wailluku   Wailuku
    (Hawaii)

40. Hattiesburg   Hattysburg   Hatteesburg   Hattiesberg
    (Mississippi)

41. Walsenburg   Wallsenburg   Walsinburg   Walsunburg
    (Colorado)

42. Plastow   Plaisto   Plaistow   Playsto
    (New Hampshire)

43. Millinockit   Millinockett   Millinockitt   Millinocket
    (Maine)

44. Sedalia   Sidalia   Sedallia   Sidallia
    (Missouri)

45. Winnimuca   Winnemucca   Winnemuca   Winnimucca
    (Nevada)

46. Dundalk   Dundalke   Dundolk   Dundaulk
    (Maryland)

47. Smyrrna   Smyrna   Smyrnna   Smirna
    (Delaware)

48. Canapolis   Kanapolis   Cannapolis   Kannapolis
    (North Carolina)

49. Holldridge   Holdridge   Holdrege   Holdrige
    (Nebraska)

50. Bisby   Bisbe   Bisbee   Bisbie
    (Arizona)

Before consulting the answers on page 295:
I think I spelled _____ words correctly on this test.
(If your estimate is correct, add one point to your score.)

Anatomy

1. malliolus   maleolus   maliolus   malleolus
   (ankle bone protuberance)

2. gracilis   graccilus   grassilus   gracillis
   (inner thigh muscle)

3. pereostium   pereosteum   periostium   periosteum
   (bone tissue and its layers)

4. gastroknemius   gastrocniemius   gastrocnemius
      gastrocneemius
   (large calf muscle)

5. apophysis   apophisis   apophusis   apophesis
   (protuberance or outgrowth)

6. triquietrum   tryquetrum   triquetrum   trychwetrum
   (wrist bone)

7. ischium   ysscheum   iskium   ischeum
   (bone in pelvis)

8. massieter   mussieter   masseter   mascieter
   (muscle in cheek)

9. suprispynatus   supraspinatus   supraspeinatus   supraspynaitus
   (muscle near shoulder)

10. ziphoid   xiphoid   zyphoid   xyphoid
    (part of the sternum)

11. gemmelus   gimmelus   gemellus   gimellus
    (one of two small hip muscles)

12. teries   terres   terries   teres
    (one of two small muscles behind shoulder)

13. seraitus   serratis   seratis   serratus
    (rib or vertebral muscle)

14. sternocleidomastoid   sternokleidomastoid
       sturnokleidomastoid   sturnoclydomastoid
    (one of two thick neck muscles)

15. philanges   phylanges   phalanges   phillanges
    (finger or toe bones)

16. obteurator   obtiorator   obterater   obturator
    (one of two upper leg muscles)

17. breghma   bregma   breggma   braegma
    (skull suture junction)

18. hypothinar   hypothanar   hypothenar   hypothinare
    (part of palm below little finger)
19. coricobrachialis   corricobrachialis   coracobrachialis
    corocobrachialis
    (upper arm muscle)
20. sessimoid   sesamoid   sessamoid   sescimoid
    (nodule of bone or cartilage at a tendon)
21. illiopsoas   iliopscoas   ileopsoas   iliopsoas
    (thigh-pelvis muscle)
22. pterygoideus   teragoideus   teragoidius   terragoidius
    (one of two lower jaw muscles)
23. interosius   interoseus   interosseus   interoscius
    (muscle in the hand)
24. trochanter   troekanter   troechanter   trochantor
    (one of two thigh-pelvis muscles)
25. piriformis   pirriformis   piraformis   pireformis
    (pelvic muscle)

Alternative Words

a. psoas major   psois major   pscoas major   psous major
   (one of two thigh-pelvis muscles)
b. epykondyle   epykondil   epicondyle   epicondile
   (protuberance at end of a bone)
c. platysma   platisma   plattisma   plattysma
   (one of two neck muscles)
d. callcaneus   callcanius   calcanius   calcaneus
   (heel bone)
e. humerous   humerus   heumerus   humeris
   (upper arm bone)

> *Before consulting the answers on page 295:*
> I think I spelled ____ words correctly on this test.
> (If your estimate is correct, add one point to your score.)

Animals and Dinosaurs

1. pecary   peccary   peckarie   peccarrie
   (hoofed piglike animal)

2. dourmous   dourmouse   doormouse   dormouse
   (squirrellike rodent)

3. terridactyl   pterodactyl   terrodactyl   pterridactyl
   (prehistoric flying reptile)

4. ocelot   occelot   ocellot   occellot
   (leopardlike cat)

5. hartibeast   hartibeest   hartebeest   harrtibeest
   (African antelope)

6. hipopotamous   hippopotamous   hippopatamous
      hippopotamus
   (large hairless African mammal)

7. walabee   wallaby   wallabee   wallabby
   (kangaroolike marsupial)

8. lhama   llama   lama   lhamma
   (South American camellike but humpless animal)

9. maccaque   mackaque   maccak   macaque
   (monkey)

10. megithere   megathere   megathyr   megithyr
    (prehistoric slothlike animal)

11. gemsbock   gemmsbock   gemsbok   gemmsbok
    (African antelope)

12. tryceritops   tryceratops   triceratops   triceritops
    (dinosaur with a neck crest and three horns)

13. orryx   orix   oryx   aurix
    (African antelope)

14. cappibara   capobara   capybarra   capybara
    (large tailless South American rodent)

15. platipuss   platypuss   platypus   platipus
    (aquatic mammal with a bill and webbed feet)

16. terripin   terrapin   terapin   terrepin
    (North American turtle)

17. okapi   okkapi   okappi   okape
    (African mammal like short-necked giraffe)

18. agouti   aggooti   agooti   agoutee
(South and Central American rodent)

19. coatimundi   koatimundi   coatamundi   koatamundi
(raccoonlike omnivore)

20. mannatee   manatee   mannattee   mannitee
(aquatic mammal with flippers and a wide tail)

21. dymetrodon   dimetrodon   dymetridon   dimetridon
(dinosaur with a dorsal tail)

22. Kommodo dragon   Comodo dragon   Komodo dragon
Komoddo dragon
(monitor lizard)

23. kayman   quayman   caymann   caiman
(crocodilian)

24. Hela monster   Gila monster   Gilla monster   Giela monster
(venomous lizard)

25. archiopterix   archiopteryx   archaeopteryx   archeopteryx
(prehistoric reptilelike bird)

Alternative Words

a. tyrannosaur   tyrannisaur   tyrranisaur   tyranisaur
(carnivorous erect-walking dinosaur)

b. kinkijoo   kinkajou   kinkijou   kinkajoo
(arboreal animal with a prehensile tail)

c. marmut   marrmot   marmot   marmet
(heavy rodent; woodchuck)

d. quockuh   quokka   kwokkuh   kwokka
(Australian marsupial like a large rat)

e. nutria   noutria   nuttria   nutrea
(aquatic South American rodent; coypu)

Before consulting the answers on page 295:
I think I spelled ____ words correctly on this test.
(If your estimate is correct, add one point to your score.)

Anthropology

1. shamminism   shammanism   shamanism   shaminism
(tribal belief in spirits and person who can influence them)

2. cromlech   cromleck   crommlek   crommlech
(megalithic chamber tomb)

3. Austrailopithicus   Australopithecus   Australopithicus
Austrailopithocus
(hominid genus)

4. ethnogeny   ethnogyny   ethnogony   ethnageny
(study of evolution of races)

5. Nilotic   Nilottic   Nylotic   Nileotic
(pertaining to peoples of the Nile River region)

6. mythapeia   mythopeia   mythopoeia   mythopaeia
(creation of myth)

7. adellphic   addelphic   adelphic   adelephic
(of marriages in which wives are sisters or husbands are brothers)

8. dollicocephalic   dolicocephalic   dolikocephalic
dolichocephalic
(long-headed)

9. labrett   labbret   labret   labrette
(lip ornament)

10. Melonesian   Melanesian   Mellinesian   Mellanesian
(of the islands northeast of Australia)

11. technonymy   tecnonomy   teknonomy   tecnanomy
(renaming a parent after a child)

12. poligeny   polygeny   polygony   polygyny
(marriage to two or more wives at the same time)

13. quadroumenous   quadrumenous   quadrumanous
quadrumainous
(having four handlike feet)

14. Kulturkryse   Kulturkreis   Kulturkreise   Kulturkrise
(related cultural traits spreading from a centrum)

15. totumism   totemism   tottemism   tottumism
(veneration of an object by members of a group)

16. Ollduvai Gorge   Olduvai Gorge   Olduvi Gorge
Ollduvi Gorge
(famed Tanzania site of humanlike fossils)

17. cymotrichous   cimotrichous   ceimotrichous   chymotrichous
    (curly-haired)
18. infibulation   enfibulation   infybulation   infibbulation
    (fastening together of the vulval lips)
19. euhiemerism   euhemerism   euheimerism   euhymerism
    (theory that gods derive from dead heroes)
20. Sicladic   Cycladic   Cykladic   Psycladic
    (of a Greek Bronze Age culture)
21. Boscopoid   Bosquipoid   Boskopoid   Boskipoid
    (of a particular human fossil found in South Africa)
22. zilomancy   zylomancy   xylomancy   xeilomancy
    (divination by means of twigs and bits of wood)
23. caterine   catarine   catarrhine   caterhine
    (of a group including humans, apes, and monkeys)
24. Chukutien   Choukutien   Choukoutien   Chukoutien
    (Peking or Beijing fossil site)
25. corroberee   corroboree   coroberie   corroborie
    (Aborigine ritual gathering)

Alternative Words

a. baelism   baalism   baallism   balism
   (ancient Semitic worship of a local deity)
b. Caucasoid   Caukusoid   Caucusoid   Cauccusoid
   (pertaining to the white race)
c. Elleusinean mysteries   Eleusinean mysteries
   Eleusinian mysteries   Eleusinaean mysteries
   (ancient Greek mysteries that were celebrated)
d. hennotheism   henitheism   henytheism   henotheism
   (worship of one god while allowing for other gods)
e. apitropaism   appitropaism   apotropaism   appotropaism
   (use of ritual to ward off evil)

> *Before consulting the answers on page 296:*
> I think I spelled _____ words correctly on this test.
> (If your estimate is correct, add one point to your score.)

Archeology

1. skewomorph   skiuomorph   skeuomorph   skaeuomorph
   (utensillike design or ornament on an object)

2. callumet   calumet   callumette   calumette
   (long ceremonial Indian pipe)

3. mydden   midden   myden   miden
   (refuse heap)

4. Ascheulian   Acheulean   Achoulian   Ascheulean
   (of a lower Paleolithic culture characterized by large axes)

5. värv dating   varrv dating   varve dating   vahrv dating
   (dating through study of lake sediments)

6. sgrafitto   sgraffitto   sgraffito   sgrafito
   (pottery ornamentation technique)

7. buhrin   burin   buerin   byoorin
   (engraving tool)

8. Mycenean   Mycenaean   Meicenean   Mycennean
   (of the ancient Greek civilization 2000–1100 B.C.)

9. ocullis   ocullus   oculis   oculus
   (eye design, as on pottery)

10. souterrain   souturrain   souterraine   souterane
    (grotto)

11. Pliestoscene   Pleistoscene   Pleistocene   Pliestocene
    (epoch of geologic time)

12. aribalos   arybalos   ariballos   aryballos
    (type of oil jar in antiquity)

13. Ninnevah   Ninneveh   Nineveh   Niniveh
    (site of Assyrian ruins)

14. cranug   cranog   kranog   crannog
    (islandlike lake dwelling)

15. fybula   fibula   fybbula   fibbula
    (ancient brooch or clasp)

16. Shlieman   Schlieman   Schliemann   Shliemann
    (German archeologist and excavator of Troy)

17. homeotaxis   homitaxis   homotaxis   homotachsis
    (similarity in content or arrangement of fossils)

18. sillabary   silabary   syllabary   syllubary
    (code of written symbols)

19. cist   cyst   ciste   cyste
    (Neolithic slab-lined grave)

20. Chiczén Itsá   Chichén Itzá   Chichzén Itzá   Chichzún Itsá
    (site of Mayan ruins)

21. paleolimology   paleolimnology   paliolymnology
    paleolemnology
    (study of ancient lakes)

22. canopic jar   cannopic jar   kanoppic jar   kanopic jar
    (ancient Egyptian jar containing parts of an embalmed body)

23. palietiology   palaetiology   palae-etiology   palyetiology
    (study of the causes of past events)

24. teramarra   terramara   teramara   terramarra
    (lake dwelling of northern Italy)

25. Tiahuanaco   Tiajuanaco   Tiahuanoco   Tiajuanoco
    (of a pre-Incan culture)

Alternative Words

a. Sollutrian   Sollutrean   Sollutraean   Solutrean
    (of an Upper Paleolithic European arrowhead culture)

b. fluveatile   fluvveatile   fluviatile   fluvviatile
    (produced by or found in rivers)

c. matock   mattock   matok   mattok
    (pickaxlike digging implement)

d. senitaph   senotapf   cenotaph   cenitaph
    (memorial tomb for one whose body is elsewhere)

e. caranation   carranation   carrination   carination
    (keellike formation)

> *Before consulting the answers on page 296:*
> I think I spelled ____ words correctly on this test.
> (If your estimate is correct, add one point to your score.)

Architecture History

1. clairstory   clairestory   clerestory   clarestory
   (windowed church interior wall above adjacent rooftop)

2. phinial   finial   phinnial   finnial
   (ornamental top piece)

3. timpanum   tympinum   timpinum   tympanum
   (recessed triangular face of a pediment)

4. grimmthorp   grimthorpe   grimm-thorp   grimmthorpe
   (to remodel in an ugly way)

5. voussoir   voussoire   vousoire   veusoire
   (wedgelike piece of an arch)

6. cartouche   carrtouche   carteuch   kartooch
   (oval or round piece bordered by ornamental scrollwork)

7. stilobate   stylobat   stilobat   stylobate
   (foundation of a temple colonnade)

8. montin   muntin   munntin   monntin
   (window sash bar)

9. gallilee   galillee   gallillee   galilee
   (English church tower vestibule)

10. introdos   intrados   intradoss   introdoss
    (inner curve of a vault or arch)

11. urrhythmy   eurhythmi   eurrhythmy   eurythmy
    (harmony of proportion)

12. cinquefoille   cinqfoyl   cinquefoil   cinquefoyl
    (five-lobed ornament)

13. acquiduct   aquiduct   acqueduct   aqueduct
    (ancient stone erection to conduct water)

14. Brunneleschi   Brunelleschi   Bruneleschi   Brunnellschi
    (Florentine architect)

15. guilloch   guilloche   guillosch   guillosche
    (ornamental ribbon-patterned border)

16. Coloseum   Collosseum   Colosseum   Colloseum
    (famed Roman amphitheater)

17. mettope   metopie   mettopie   metope
    (square space in a Doric frieze)

18. valute   volute   vallute   vollute
(scroll-like ornament on a capital)

19. tyrceron   tierceron   thyrceron   tiereceron
(diagonal rib)

20. plaiteresque   platoresque   plateresque   platteresque
(sixteenth-century Spanish architectural style)

21. lancet   lancette   lanncet   lanncette
(high and narrow window)

22. reliquery   relequery   reliquary   relequary
(container for relics)

23. campenile   campennile   campanile   companile
(bell tower)

24. balddachin   baldachine   baldachin   balddachine
(ornamental canopy)

25. pilaster   pilastor   pillaster   pillastor
(columnlike projection from a wall)

Alternative Words

a. logie   loggia   loggie   logia
(arcade or gallery open on one side)

b. Palladean   Paladean   Paladian   Palladian
(in the style of the famed sixteenth-century Italian architect)

c. Bauehous   Bauehause   Bauhaus   Bauhous
(Weimar school of design)

d. accanthis   acanthus   acanthis   accanthus
(leaflike ornament)

e. koffered   coffered   koffored   coffored
(having a pattern of sunken panels, as a ceiling)

Before consulting the answers on page 296:
I think I spelled _____ words correctly on this test.
(If your estimate is correct, add one point to your score.)

Art History

1. Phydeus   Phydeas   Phideus   Phidias
   (Greek sculptor)

2. gliptic   glyptic   gliptich   glyptich
   (carved)

3. de Stil   de Stihl   de Stijl   de Stihll
   (twentieth-century Dutch school of art)

4. crackelure   craquelure   craqueleur   craquelor
   (cracks on the surface of a painting)

5. Botticelli   Boticelli   Botticeli   Boticcelli
   (Italian Renaissance painter)

6. sfuemato   sffumatoe   sfumato   sfummato
   (painter's subtle blending or blurring of color)

7. carryatid   karryatid   caryatid   karyatid
   (sculpted female figure used as a support)

8. Ruault   Rouolt   Rualt   Rouault
   (French painter)

9. pouto   puto   putto   poutto
   (cherub or winged cherub)

10. tromp l'oile   tromp l'oeil   trompe l'oeil   trompe l'oeile
    (painting effect visually or realistically deceptive)

11. Breugel   Breugell   Brueghel   Braughel
    (Flemish painter)

12. tescelated   teselated   tesselated   tescellated
    (mosaiclike)

13. marrmorial   marmorial   marrmoreal   marmoreal
    (marblelike)

14. Beaus-Art   Beaux-Arts   Beaux-Arte   Beaux-Artes
    (Parisian architectural style)

15. quatroccento   quattrocento   quattroccento   quatrecento
    (fifteenth century)

16. tryptich   tryptych   triptych   triptitch
    (three side-by-side paintings)

17. Kokaschka   Kokkoshka   Kokoshka   Kokoschka
    (Austrian painter)

18. churigeuresque   churrigeuresque   churrigueresque churigueresque
    (of a florid style of Spanish baroque architecture)
19. tenibrism   tennibrism   tenebrism   tennebrism
    (Caravaggian shadow-and-light painting style)
20. Velászques   Velázquez   Velásques   Velázques
    (Spanish painter)
21. controposto   contraposto   contropposto   contrapposto
    (asymmetrical or curved depiction of the human body)
22. Pissarro   Pizzarro   Pissaro   Pisarro
    (French painter)
23. Ghirlondaio   Ghirlandio   Ghirlondio   Ghirlandajo
    (Italian painter)
24. plainaireism   pleinaireism   plainairism   pleinairism
    (French painting style accenting natural light)
25. Caniletto   Canaletto   Canilletto   Canalletto
    (Italian painter)

Alternative Words

a. Buonarotti   Buonaroti   Buonnaroti   Buonarroti
   (Michelangelo)
b. grisail   grizail   grisaille   grizaille
   (painting style using shades of gray)
c. limbner   limner   limbnor   limmer
   (medieval manuscript illuminator)
d. synthetism   synethetism   sinthetism   sinnthetism
   (French painting theory associated with Gauguin)
e. nobi   nabi   nabbi   nobbi
   (member of circa 1890 group of French artists emphasizing graphic arts)

> *Before consulting the answers on page 297:*
> I think I spelled ____ words correctly on this test.
> (If your estimate is correct, add one point to your score.)

Astronomy

1. gibus   gibous   gibbus   gibbous
   (more than half full, as the moon)

2. Pleades   Pleides   Pleiades   Plieades
   (star cluster in Taurus)

3. aphelion   appheleon   apphelion   apheleon
   (orbital point of a body farthest from the sun)

4. selinodyssey   selenodesy   selinodesy   sellinodyssey
   (study of the moon's surface)

5. deforent   deferent   deforrent   deferrint
   (Ptolemaic orbital circle around the earth)

6. Kassigraine   Cassigraine   Kassegraine   Cassegrain
   (type of reflecting telescope)

7. interpherometry   interferometry   interphorometry
   interforometry
   (measurement of angular separation of double stars)

8. areocentric   ariocentric   aryocentric   araeocentric
   (centered on Mars)

9. parilax   paralax   parillax   parallax
   (apparent changed position of a celestial body)

10. Dimos   Deimos   Diemos   Demos
    (one of two moons of Mars)

11. gegendschein   gegenschein   gegendshein   gegenshein
    (night-sky light from sun reflected by meteoric matter)

12. collimator   collimater   colimator   colimater
    (converging lens of a spectroscope)

13. Betelguse   Betelgueuse   Betelgeuse   Betelgues
    (bright star in Orion)

14. faculla   feculla   facula   fecula
    (bright patch on the surface of the sun)

15. astrolob   astrolobe   astrolab   astrolabe
    (ancient astronomical altitude instrument)

16. allmucantor   almucantar   almukantar   almukanter
    (celestial-sphere circle paralleling the horizon)

17. Cepheid variable   Cephaeid variable   Cephid variable
    Cephead variable
    (star with varying brightness)

18. Magellanic cloud   Magilanic cloud   Magelanic cloud
    Magillanic cloud
    (either of two galactic clusters in the southern sky)

19. ippact   ipact   epact   y-pact
    (difference between solar and lunar year)

20. celostat   cielostat   coelostat   ceolostat
    (timed mirror apparatus used with a telescope)

21. cilunar   cylunar   cislunar   cyelunar
    (of the region between earth and the moon's orbit)

22. auraura borialis   aurora borealis   arora borealis
    aurora borrialis
    (northern lights)

23. kiloparsec   kilaparsec   kiliparsec   kiloparsek
    (distance unit: 1,000 × 3.26 light-years)

24. telluric   telleuric   tellurik   teluric
    (terrestrial)

25. szygy   zysygy   syzygy   zysogy
    (alignment of three celestial bodies)

Alternative Words

a. Foucoult pendulum   Foucault pendulum   Faucalt pendulum
   Faucault pendulum
   (pendulum indicating earth's rotation)

b. Boëtes   Boütes   Boötes   Bötes
   (northern constellation, the Herdsman)

c. syderial   siderial   seiderial   sidereal
   (determined by the stars)

d. Chondrasekhar limit   Chondrasekhor limit   Chandrasekhar limit
   Chandrasekhor limit
   (mass limit preventing a star from becoming a white dwarf)

e. Casseopia   Casseopeia   Cassiopia   Cassiopeia
   (northern constellation, the Lady in the Chair)

> *Before consulting the answers on page 297:*
> I think I spelled _____ words correctly on this test.
> (If your estimate is correct, add one point to your score.)

Automobiles

1. magnito   magneto   magnitto   magnetto
   (small generator providing ignition current)

2. landau   landow   landaue   landaugh
   (auto with a closed body but rear folding-top compartment)

3. Peninfarina   Penninfarina   Pininfarina   Pinninfarina
   (Italian auto designer)

4. ommeter   ohmmeter   ometer   ohmeter
   (instrument measuring electric resistance)

5. Peugot   Puegot   Peugeot   Peugaut
   (French automobile)

6. coollent   coollant   coolent   coolant
   (temperature-reducing substance)

7. sollinoid unit   solenoid unit   sollenoid unit   solinoid unit
   (electrical conducting switch used in starting system)

8. cowl   caul   cowle   cowel
   (frontal part to which windshield and instrument panel are attached)

9. Indiannapolis 500   Indianappolis 500   Indianapolis 500
   Indiannappolis 500
   (annual race)

10. fliver   flivver   flivor   flivvor
    (old automobile)

11. Lambhorgini   Lamborgini   Lamborghini   Lammbhorgini
    (Italian automobile)

12. checane   chicane   checcane   chiccane
    (planned deviation in a racetrack layout)

13. tachometer   takometer   tacometer   tachommeter
    (instrument measuring velocity)

14. macadam   maccadam   McCaddam   macaddam
    (roadway with broken-stone layer)

15. tapit   tappet   tappit   tapet
    (sliding rod attached to a valve)

16. etholene glycol   ethelene glycol   ethylene glycol
    ethylene glycole
    (antifreeze)

17. Astin-Martin   Aston Martin   Aston Marten   Astin Martin
    (British automobile)

18. tuneau   toneau   tonneau   tunneau
    (waterproof cover for convertible; rear part of auto body)
19. ahmeter   ahmmeter   ameter   ammeter
    (current-measuring instrument)
20. taillight   tail light   taillite   tail lite
    (rear red light)
21. Reaux   Rio   Reo   Reaux
    (classic car)
22. Grahame-Paige   Graham-Paige   Graham-Page
    Graham-Payge
    (classic car in some models)
23. Carddin joint   Carddan joint   Cardin joint   Cardan joint
    (type of universal joint)
24. catylytic converter   catalytic converter   catylitic converter
    catalitic converter
    (antipollution exhaust device)
25. pinyin   pinion   pinyan   pinian
    (type of gear)

Alternative Words

a. shims   shimms   schims   schimms
   (thin metal strips used as spacers between parts)
b. Darracq   Darraque   Darac   Darrac
   (classic car)
c. synkromesh   syncromesh   synchromesh   synchromeshe
   (synchronized shifting mechanism)
d. gasket   gasquet   gaskit   gasquette
   (watertight piston housing)
e. cambeur   cambore   camber   cambor
   (bottom tilted-in setting of front wheels)

Before consulting the answers on page 297:
I think I spelled _____ words correctly on this test.
(If your estimate is correct, add one point to your score.)

Barfly

1. bacchanalianism   bachanalianism   baccanalianism
   bachannalianism
   (drunken revelry)

2. julip   julipp   julep   julepp
   (bourbon with sugar, and a sprig of mint, on crushed ice)

3. amarretto   amaretto   ammareto   ammarretto
   (almond-flavored liqueur)

4. Camparri   Comparri   Campari   Compari
   (Italian dry aperitif)

5. mei-tei   mai-tai   mai-tais   mai-thai
   (rum cocktail with *word no. 14 below*, brandy, grenadine, and lime)

6. Kalúah   Kalúa   Kahlúa   Kahlúah
   (Mexican coffee-flavored liqueur)

7. ouso   ouzzo   ouzot   ouzo
   (unsweetened anise-flavored Greek liqueur)

8. Mickey Finn   Mickey Fin   Micky Finn   Mickie Finn
   (drugged drink)

9. Galliano   Galleano   Galleonno   Galiano
   (Italian anise-flavored sweet yellow liqueur)

10. pous-café   poussé-caffé   pousse-café   Pous-caffé
    (after-dinner drink of layers of liqueurs)

11. acquavit   aquavit   aquavite   aquaviet
    (clear Scandinavian liquor)

12. Tzingtau   Tsingtao   Tzingtao   Tsingtau
    (brand of Chinese beer)

13. marguerita   margarita   marguarita   margeurita
    (tequila, orange-flavored liqueur, and lime or lemon juice)

14. curiçau   curaçau   cureçao   curaçao
    (liqueur from sour orange peel)

15. siedel   seidel   siedle   seidle
    (large beer glass)

16. glügg   glögg   glöeg   glöegg
    (Swedish hot punch)

17. kirsh   kirsch   kirshe   kirsche
    (colorless cherry brandy)

18. crème de cacau   crème de caccao   crème de cocao
    crème de cacao
    (liqueur flavored with chocolate)
19. Drambouie   Drambuie   Drambooie   Drambeuie
    (herbal liqueur made with honey)
20. Calvados   Calvodos   Calvodas   Calvadas
    (French applejack)
21. annisette   anisette   anissette   annissette
    (aniseed-flavored liqueur)
22. kümel   kümell   kümmel   kümmell
    (caraway-seed-flavored aromatic liqueur)
23. cassise   cassis   kassis   casisse
    (black-currant liqueur)
24. sammbucca   sambucca   sambucha   sambuca
    (Italian licorice-flavored liqueur)
25. Du Bonné   Dubonné   Dubonnet   Dubonnett
    (aromatic French aperitif)

Alternative Words

a. Rob Roy   Robb Roy   Rob Roi   Robb Roi
   (manhattan made with scotch)
b. shandygaffe   shandiegaff   shandygaff   shandiegaffe
   (beer with ginger beer)
c. peña collada   piña collada   piña colada   peña colada
   (rum drink with cream of coconut and pineapple juice)
d. pillsner   pilsner   pilzner   pilzener
   (light beer)
e. Duos Eqis   Dos Equis   Dos Ecquis   D'os Equise
   (brand of Mexican beer)

> *Before consulting the answers on page 298:*
> I think I spelled ____ words correctly on this test.
> (If your estimate is correct, add one point to your score.)

Bible

1. Doay Bible   Douay Bible   Doai Bible   Douai Bible
   (Roman Catholic translation)

2. Pentiteuch   Penteteuch   Pentateuch   Pentetuch
   (first five Old Testament books)

3. Collosseans   Collossians   Colosseans   Colossians
   (book of the New Testament)

4. Balum   Baalum   Balaam   Baalam
   (diviner or an ass who blessed the Israelites)

5. Giliad   Gilead   Gileade   Gillead
   (area of Palestine)

6. Niccodemus   Nicodemus   Nicoddemus   Nicodeimos
   (pharisee who secretly followed Jesus)

7. Annannias   Anannias   Ananias   Annanias
   (man who lied and was struck dead)

8. diateseron   diatessoran   diatesseron   diatessaron
   (narrative synthesizing the four Gospels)

9. Gommora   Gommorah   Gomorra   Gomorrah
   (city destroyed for its wickedness)

10. Elohist   Ellohist   Elluhist   Eluhist
    (writer from whom the Hexateuch is drawn)

11. Capernum   Capernaum   Cappernaum   Cappernam
    (where Jesus ministered, in northern Israel)

12. Philipians   Phillipians   Philippians   Philipaeans
    (Epistle by Paul)

13. Gallilian   Gallilean   Galilean   Galilian
    (inhabitant of region of northern Palestine)

14. Septeugint   Septuigint   Septuagint   Septuagent
    (oldest Greek version of the Old Testament)

15. Jehashophat   Jihoshiphat   Jehoshephat   Jehoshaphat
    (king of Judah)

16. Golguthah   Golgothah   Golgotha   Golgetha
    (site of Jesus' crucifixion)

17. Zadock   Zadok   Zaddok   Zaadok
    (priest in I Samuel)

18. canonical   cannonicle   cannonical   canonicle
(pertaining to authoritative and authentic holy scripture)

19. Gaedite   Gadite   Gaeddite   Gaddite
(member of tribe descended from son of Zilpah)

20. Johanan   Johanine   Johannine   Johannan
(pertaining to John or to his New Testament writings)

21. Parilipomenon   Paralipomenon   Paralippomenon
    Parilippomenon
(Chronicles in no. 1 above)

22. Ecclesiastus   Ecclesiasties   Ecclesiastes   Ecclessiastes
(book of the Old Testament)

23. Judas Macabeus   Judas Maccabaeus   Judas Macabbaeus
    Judas Macabaeus
(Judean patriot)

24. Naihem   Nahem   Naihum   Nahum
(a Minor Prophet; book of the Old Testament)

25. Knostic   Gnostic   Knostik   Gnostik
(member of early Christian sect)

Alternative Words

a. ecsagetics   exagetics   ecsogetics   exegetics
(Biblical interpretation)

b. Sadducean   Sadducian   Saduccian   Saduccean
(member of a Palestinian sect)

c. Torrah   Torhah   Torah   Toraah
(Jewish scripture)

d. Kumran   Qumran   Quomran   Koumran
(name applied to texts of Dead Sea Scrolls)

e. Gallatians   Galatians   Galaitians   Gallaitians
(book of the New Testament)

Before consulting the answers on page 298:
I think I spelled _____ words correctly on this test.
(If your estimate is correct, add one point to your score.)

Biology

1. Linean   Linnian   Linaean   Linnaean
   (pertaining to established binomial nomenclature)

2. eccesis   ecesis   ecciesis   ecsesis
   (plant or animal becoming established in a new environment)

3. procarryate   prokarryote   prokaryote   procaryate
   (cellular organism with a nuclear membrane)

4. tranceferaze   transferaze   transferrase   transferase
   (type of enzyme)

5. mytochondrion   mitochondrion   mitochondreon
   mytochondrian
   (cytoplasmic element used in energy production)

6. anelid   annelid   anilid   annilid
   (type of worm)

7. deoxirybonucleic acid   deoxyribonucleic acid
   deoxiribonucleic acid   deoxyrybonucleic acid
   (DNA)

8. phylogeny   philogeny   phylogony   philogyny
   (evolution or developmental history of a group of organisms)

9. gnatobiotic   natobiotic   notobiotic   gnotobiotic
   (inoculated with certain microorganisms)

10. Ceilenterata   Coelenterata   Celenterata   Ceolenterata
    (invertebrate phylum including hydras and jellyfishes)

11. occellus   ocellus   occelus   occellis
    (type of eye in invertebrates)

12. cytolysis   citolysis   cytalysis   cytalisis
    (cell degeneration)

13. axesis   auxesis   aucsesis   acsesis
    (growth, as from increased cell size)

14. nifridium   niphridium   nefridium   nephridium
    (invertebrate excretory organ)

15. alleel   alele   allele   allelle
    (type of gene)

16. organell   organelle   organel   orgonelle
    (specialized part of a cell)

17. Lycencoism   Lysencoism   Lysenkoism   Lysanckoism
    (genetic belief that acquired characteristics can be inherited)

18. crustacean   crustacaean   crustacian   crustasion
    (arthropod with a hard shell)
19. mesintery   mesintary   mesentery   mesentary
    (intestinal membrane)
20. testacious   testaceous   testatious   tessitacious
    (partaining to or having a shell)
21. allantoice   allanttois   alantoice   allantois
    (vascular membrane in reptiles and birds)
22. phytaplankton   phytoplanckton   phytoplankton
    phitoplanckton
    (tiny plants and plantlike animals)
23. skolex   scolecks   scolex   scollex
    (head of a tapeworm)
24. miosis   miossis   meosis   meiosis
    (stage of gamete formation)
25. thirology   therology   thyrology   thurology
    (mammalogy)

Alternative Words

a. nucliolus   nucleolus   nucleollus   nucleolis
   (round body within a cell nucleus)
b. vacuol   vaccuol   vacuole   vaccuole
   (cavity within a cell)
c. cledistics   cladistics   kledistics   kladistics
   (organism classification system)
d. gammatophyte   gamatophyte   gametophyte   gametophite
   (sexual form of a plant)
e. centriole   centriolle   sentriol   sentriolle
   (cylindrical part of a cell)

> *Before consulting the answers on page 298:*
> I think I spelled _____ words correctly on this test.
> (If your estimate is correct, add one point to your score.)

Birds

1. taucan   tucan   toucan   toukan
   (fruit-eating tropical bird)

2. grosbeak   grosbeek   grossbeek   grossbeak
   (stout-billed finch)

3. curleyou   curlew   curlieu   curlewe
   (long-legged migratory bird)

4. guirefalcon   girefalcon   gyrefalcon   gyrfalcon
   (arctic and largest falcon)

5. bobalink   bobolink   bobbolink   bobbilink
   (migratory songbird)

6. tanager   tanageur   tannager   taniger
   (American woodland bird)

7. kookibura   kookabura   kookaburra   kookiburra
   (Australian kingfisher)

8. niddifugous   nittifugous   nidifugous   nitifugous
   (departing the nest soon after hatching)

9. barbett   barbet   barbete   barbette
   (tropical bird with a stout and bristled bill)

10. phalerope   phalarope   fallarope   falarope
    (sandpiperlike shorebird that swims well)

11. ratite   wratite   rattite   wrattite
    (ostrich or similar bird having a flat breastbone)

12. eegret   egret   egritte   eigret
    (heron having long plumes in breeding season)

13. chafinch   chaufinch   chauffinch   chaffinch
    (European finch)

14. lammergeier   lammargeier   lamergeier   lamargeier
    (Eurasian vulture)

15. pileated   pyleated   pilleated   pylleated
    (having a crest atop the head)

16. whiduh   whidah   whyduh   whydah
    (African weaverbird)

17. neossology   neoseology   neosology   neosseology
    (study of young birds)

18. dicksissel   dickcissel   dicksisal   diksissal
    (migratory American black-throated finch)
19. psitticosis   psittikosis   psittacosis   psitacossis
    (bird disease transmissible to man)
20. altricial   alitricial   allitricial   alatricial
    (immature and helpless when hatched)
21. pipet   pipit   pippet   pippit
    (larklike singing bird)
22. guilemot   guilamot   guillemot   guillimot
    (narrow-billed auk of northern seas)
23. cignet   cygnet   cignette   cygnette
    (young swan)
24. murganser   merganser   mergansor   murgansor
    (fish-eating, slender-billed diving duck)
25. avocet   avicet   avicett   avocett
    (long-legged, web-footed shorebird)

Alternative Words

a. jager   jaeger   jaguer   jaeguer
   (strong-flying, dark-colored bird of northern seas)
b. passerine   passorine   paserine   pasorine
   (pertaining to the largest order of birds)
c. coramorant   cormorent   cormorant   coramorent
   (long-necked, web-footed seabird)
d. petrell   petrul   petrel   pettrel
   (small, long-winged seabird that flies far from land)
e. verio   vireo   virio   vereo
   (small American bird that feeds on insects)

> *Before consulting the answers on page 299:*
> I think I spelled ____ words correctly on this test.
> (If your estimate is correct, add one point to your score.)

Botany

1. zylem   zylum   xylum   xylem
(water- and nutrient-conducting tissue in vascular plant)

2. dichotyledon   dichotyledan   dicotyledon   dicotyledan
(class of angiospermous plants)

3. saprophitic   sapriphytic   saprophytic   saprephitic
(feeding on dead organic matter)

4. brachteol   brachteole   bracteol   bracteole
(small leaf or leaflike part)

5. batalogy   battology   batology   batylogy
(study of brambles)

6. lenticell   lenticel   lentacell   lentacel
(lens-shaped spot or pore on a plant stem)

7. anthyr   anther   anthor   anthyre
(part of a stamen bearing pollen)

8. connivent   conivent   connivant   conivant
(converging)

9. phlome   phloem   phloam   phyloem
(food-conducting plant tissue)

10. brakky   brakey   brakkey   braky
(abounding in bushes or brambles)

11. rizome   rhyzome   rhizome   rhyzzome
(rootlike stem underground)

12. cesspitose   scesspitose   caespitose   coespitose
(forming tufts or matlike clusters)

13. abbcissic acid   abscisic acid   absisic acid   abcisic acid
(growth-regulating hormone)

14. paeduncle   pedduncle   paedoncle   peduncle
(flower stalk)

15. involuchre   involucher   involucre   involucer
(grouping of bracts beneath a flower cluster)

16. pomalogy   pomology   pommalogy   pommology
(study of fruits)

17. legule   ligule   legulle   ligulle
(grass blade outgrowth)

18. effluorescence   efluorescence   eflorescence
    efflorescence
    (flowering)
19. callix   calix   callyx   calyx
    (outermost floral parts; the sepals)
20. deciduous   desciduous   disiduous   disciduous
    (shedding leaves annually)
21. corimb   corumb   corymb   corromb
    (flat-topped flower cluster)
22. Cycidofilicales   Cycidofillicales   Cycadofilicales
    Cicydofilicales
    (order of fossil trees or climbing plants)
23. Gnetum   Gnietum   Gnytum   Gneitum
    (genus of tropical shrubs or small trees)
24. briophite   bryophite   briophyte   bryophyte
    (true moss or liverwort)
25. calamite   calimite   callamite   callimite
    (fossil plant from the Carboniferous period)

Alternative Words

a. lichin   lichen   lychin   lychen
   (fungal-algal plants)
b. thalis   thalus   thallis   thallus
   (simple vegetative body)
c. micology   mycology   mychology   meicology
   (study of fungi)
d. pheitology   phitology   phaitology   phytology
   (botany)
e. Ginkgoales   Gingkoales   Gingkhoales   Ginkhoales
   (order of gymnospermous trees having one surviving species today)

Before consulting the answers on page 299:
I think I spelled ____ words correctly on this test.
(If your estimate is correct, add one point to your score.)

Brand Name Shopper

1. Jaccuzi   Jacuzzi   Jacuzi   Jaccuzzi
   (whirlpool bath)
2. Sweet and Low   Sweet n' Low   Sweet 'n' Lo   Sweet 'n Low
   (sugar substitute)
3. Dr. Pepper   Doctor Pepper   Dr Pepper   Doctor Peppor
   (soft drink)
4. Chap Stick   Chappstick   Chap Stik   Chap-Stick
   (salve for chapped lips)
5. Proctor & Gamble   Procter and Gambol   Procter & Gamble
   Procter and Gambel
   (manufacturer)
6. Handiwipes   Handy Wipes   Handi Wipes   Handywipes
   (towelettes)
7. Tinkertoy   Tink-r-toy   Tinker Toy   Tinker-Toy
   (child's building toy)
8. K-Mart   K mart   K Mart   k mart
   (department store)
9. Nutri-sweet   Nutra-Sweet   NutraSweet   Nutri-Sweet
   (sugar substitute)
10. Ty-D-bol   Tidi-Bol   Ty-Dy-Bol   Ty-dee-Bol
    (toilet bowl cleaner)
11. Juijy Fruits   Jujee-Froots   Jujyfruits   Jujy-Fruits
    (candy)
12. Levis   Levys   Levis'   Levi's
    (jeans)
13. Brylcream   Bryllcream   Brylcreem   Bryllcreem
    (hair groomer)
14. Toys Я-Us   Toys-Я-Us   Toys "Я" Us   Toys Я Us
    (toy store chain)
15. Cheez•Tos   CheeTos   Chee•tos   Chee•Tos
    (cheese-flavored snack chips)
16. Malox   Maalox   Maaloxe   Malloxe
    (antacid)
17. Tipparillo   Tiparillo   Tiparilo   Tipparilo
    (cigar)

18. U-Needa U-needa Uneeda Uneed-A
  (biscuit)

19. Redi-Whip Redd-i-wip Reddi-Wip RediWip
  (instant whipped cream)

20. Spic-and-Span Spic 'n' Span Spic and Span Spic-N-Span
  (household cleanser)

21. Jel-Lo Jello Jell-O JellO
  (gelatin dessert)

22. Raisonettes Raisinettes Raisonets Raisinets
  (candy)

23. LazeeBoy La-Zee-Boy La-Z-Boy La-Z Boy
  (reclining chair)

24. Wash-n-Dri Wash and Dry Wash'n Dry Wash 'n Dri
  (instant skin-cleansing packet)

25. Gore-Tex Goretex Gore-Texe Gor-Tex
  (sportswear synthetic fabric)

Alternative Words

a. Hoola-Hoop Hula Hoop Hula-Hoop HoolaHoop
  (hoop for hip-swiveling exercise or fun)

b. Piper-Heidsekt Piper-Heidsieck Piper-Hiedsiek
   Piper-Heidseckt
  (champagne)

c. S-O-S S.O.S. S O.S. S.O.S
  (steel wool pads)

d. Teliprompter TelePrompTer TelePrompter
   Tele-Prompter
  (off-camera script magnifier for television performers)

e. Mazzola Mazzolla Mazolla Mazola
  (corn oil)

> *Before consulting the answers on page 299:*
> I think I spelled ＿＿ words correctly on this test.
> (If your estimate is correct, add one point to your score.)

Castles and Fortifications

1. crenel   crenell   crennel   crennelle
   (notchlike space in a battlement)
2. terreplein   terraplein   terraplain   terreplain
   (gun platform on a rampart)
3. machiccolation   mashicolation   machicolation
   machicollation
   (high-up opening through which missiles can be thrown downward)
4. embraceur   embraseur   embrasure   embraisure
   (opening, loophole)
5. portecullis   portcullis   porteculis   portculiss
   (gateway grating that can be lowered)
6. dunjeon   dunjon   donjon   dunngeon
   (interior stronghold, keep, or tower)
7. truneon   trunion   trunnion   trunneon
   (cylinder supporting a cannon barrel)
8. glaicis   glaccis   glaciss   glacis
   (earthen bank or slope before a counterscarp)
9. castilated   castelated   castellated   castillated
   (built like a castle)
10. balistraria   ballestraria   ballistraria   balestraria
    (cross-shaped opening for use of a crossbow)
11. bas-court   base-court   bass-court   bas-corte
    (castle's lower or outer court)
12. palisado   pallisado   palissado   pallissado
    (defensive fence of stakes)
13. chevaut-de-frise   chevaux-de-fries   chevaut-de-fries
    chevaux-de-frise
    (portable spiked or barbed obstacles)
14. reddan   redon   redan   reddon
    (V-shaped fortification)
15. abatus   abatis   abbatus   abbatis
    (defensive barricade of sharpened tree branches)
16. piel   piele   peel   peale
    (small fortified tower)
17. tenail   tenaille   taenail   taenaille
    (ditch outwork between two bastions)

18. bortizon   bortizan   bartizon   bartizan
    (overhanging wall turret)

19. demielune   demilune   demylune   demmilune
    (outwork with a crescent-shaped gorge)

20. barbequan   barbecan   barbican   barbiquan
    (outwork or outpost)

21. circumvellation   circumvelation   circumvalation
    circumvallation
    (surrounding rampart)

22. merlon   merlin   murlon   murlin
    (toothlike projection atop a castle wall)

23. bayley   bailee   baily   bailey
    (wall around a castle's outer court)

24. mot   mautte   motte   matte
    (underlying, often conical and palisaded mound)

25. crosslet   croslet   crosslette   croslette
    (loophole)

Alternative Words

a. parrados   paradose   parados   paridos
   (bank of earth behind a trench)

b. yut   yet   yutte   yett
   (iron-grille gate)

c. gardarobe   gardrobe   garderobe   gardirobe
   (castle latrine)

d. battlement   battelment   batailment   battailment
   (defensive parapet)

e. enceint   enceinte   encente   encent
   (enclosure or its wall)

> *Before consulting the answers on page 299:*
> I think I spelled ＿＿ words correctly on this test.
> (If your estimate is correct, add one point to your score.)

Cats

1. catery   cattery   kattery   chatry
(place for boarding or breeding cats)

2. Abissinian   Abysinian   Abyssinian   Abyssinean
(breed)

3. vibrissi   vibrissae   vibbrisae   vibbrisi
(cat whiskers)

4. cobie   cobbie   cobbi   cobby
(stocky, bulky)

5. caccomistel   cacomistel   cacomistle   caccomistle
(raccoonlike pet that kills rats)

6. Birman   Berman   Birmann   Bermann
(breed)

7. grimalkin   grimmalkin   grimalquin   grimaulkin
(old female cat)

8. Cimryc   Cymric   Cimric   Cymryc
(breed)

9. calico   callicoe   calicoe   callico
(white with black and red patches)

10. Bahst   Bast   Baste   Bhast
(ancient Egyptian goddess with cat's, or lion's, head)

11. Karot   Karrot   Korat   Korrat
(breed)

12. feliform   feleform   felliform   feloform
(resembling a cat)

13. Chartreux   Charteus   Chartreuse   Chartreu
(breed)

14. polidactilism   polydactilism   polydactylism   polidactylism
(having six or more toes)

15. trichobezour   tricobezoar   trichobezoar   trichobezoor
(hairball)

16. aileurophile   ailleurophile   ailurophile   ailorophile
(cat lover)

17. clouder   klowder   clowder   klouder
(group of cats)

18. onchyectomy   onychectomy   onchiectomy   onichectomy
(declawing)

19. marggé   marguay   margay   marguey
    (small tiger cat)

20. nictotating membrane   niccatating membrane
    nictitating membrane   nictating membrane
    ("third eyelid")

21. feline panlukopenia   feline panleukopenia   feline panlucopenia
    feline panleukoponia
    (distemper)

22. chatayant   chattayant   chatoyant   chattoyant
    (changing in luster, like the eye of a cat)

23. nipatalactone   nepetalactone   napetaloctone   nipatalacton
    (attractant in catnip)

24. Chinchilla   Chynchilla   Chinnchilla   Chinchila
    (breed)

25. mattatabi   matatabi   matitabbi   matitobi
    (cat excitant)

Alternative Words

a. torbee   torby   torbie   torbey
   (having a tabby pattern with tortoiseshell coloring)

b. Singapoora   Singipoora   Singapura   Singapurra
   (breed)

c. Tonkenese   Tonkeenese   Tonkinese   Tonquinese
   (breed)

d. Seal-Lynx point   Seal-Linx point   Sealynxe point
   Seallinx point
   (breed)

e. catterwall   caterwall   catarwaul   caterwaul
   (to cry at rutting time)

Before consulting the answers on page 300:
I think I spelled _____ words correctly on this test.
(If your estimate is correct, add one point to your score.)

Chemistry

1. berillium   beryllium   berylium   burillium
   (element: Be, atomic number 4)

2. immissible   immissable   immiscible   immiscable
   (not mixable)

3. sulfanate   sulfinate   sulfonate   sulfunate
   (ester or salt from a particular acid)

4. arilate   arrilate   arylate   arrylate
   (to introduce a certain group into a compound)

5. monosacaride   monosaccaride   monosacharide
   monosaccharide
   (carbohydrate that does not hydrolyze)

6. ellutriate   illutriate   elutriate   ilutriate
   (to purify or separate by washing)

7. sinerisis   syneresis   synaresis   synoresis
   (contracting of a gel while liquid is exuded)

8. tridiated   tritiated   trytiated   trityated
   (containing a certain element)

9. heteromerous   heterommerous   heterammerous
   heteramerous
   (not related in chemical composition)

10. Mischerlich's law   Mitscherlich's law   Mitcherlich's law
    Micherlich's law
    ("isomorphous substances have similar chemical compositions and
    analogous formulas")

11. thyxotropy   thixotropy   thiksotropy   thigzotropy
    (turning of gels to liquid when shaken or stirred)

12. iterbium   yterbium   ytterbium   ytturbium
    (element: Yb, atomic number 70)

13. sol ammoniac   sal amoniac   sal ammoniac   sel ammoniac
    (ammonium chloride)

14. eudiometer   udiometer   udeometer   eudaeometer
    (gas analysis tube)

15. Wolff bottle   Woulff bottle   Wolfe bottle   Wolf bottle
    (multi-necked bottle used in washing or absorbing gases)

16. hydrolisis   hydrollysis   hydrolysis   hidrolysis
    (chemical decomposition through reaction with water)

17. halligen   hallogen   halogen   haligen
(any of five elements molecularly diatomic in the free state)

18. stochiometry   stoachiometry   stoichiometry   stochyometry
(calculation of quantities in chemical reactions)

19. ethanol   ethynol   ethinol   ethenol
(alcohol)

20. pollimer   polimer   polymer   polymur
(type of large-molecule compound)

21. flockulent   flocculant   floculent   flokulent
(chemical that improves the plasticity of clay)

22. olium   ollium   olleum   oleum
(pyrosulfuric acid)

23. phenalpthalein   phenolpthalein   phenalphthalein
phenolphthalein
(white crystalline compound used as a laxative)

24. alefatic   alephatic   alliphatic   aliphatic
(derived from fat)

25. prasiodymium   praseodymium   praseodimium
prasyodymium
(element: Pr, atomic number 59)

Alternative Words

a. valence   valance   vallence   vallance
(quality determining chemical union of atoms or groups)

b. dialysis   diolysis   diallysis   dyalysis
(separating of colloids from crystalloids)

c. gadalineum   gadolinium   gaddolinium   gadilinium
(element: Gd, atomic number 64)

d. Erlinmaier flask   Erlenmeyer flask   Erlinmeyer flask
Erlenmaier flask
(wide-bottomed conical flask)

e. catephoresis   catiphoresis   cataphoresis   catephorisis
(colloidal particle motion from influence of an electric field)

> *Before consulting the answers on page 300:*
> I think I spelled _____ words correctly on this test.
> (If your estimate is correct, add one point to your score.)

Classical Music

1. solefegio   sollfegio   solefeggio   solfeggio
   (syllabic vocal exercise)

2. melosmatic   melismatic   mellosmatic   mellismatic
   (tuneful; using melodic embellishment)

3. accacature   accaccatura   acciaccatura   acchiacatura
   (simultaneous grace note one-half step below)

4. omboucheur   embouchure   emboucheur   ombouchure
   (wind instrument mouthpiece)

5. pascagaglia   passacaglia   passicaglia   passiccaglia
   (piece with variations on a ground bass)

6. carillonor   carrilonor   carolonneur   carillonneur
   (player of orchestral keyboard bell-like instrument)

7. ritennuto   rittenuto   rittenutto   ritenuto
   (slow down abruptly)

8. dodeccaphony   duodecaphony   duadecaphony
   dodecaphony
   (twelve-tone music)

9. synfonieta   sinfonieta   sinfonnietta   sinfonietta
   (short symphony or small symphony orchestra)

10. affettuoso   afetuoso   affituoso   affittuoso
    (with tenderness)

11. raebec   rebbec   reibec   rebec
    (Renaissance fiddle)

12. taccata   toccatta   tocatta   toccata
    (improvisationlike keyboard composition)

13. melodeon   melodion   mellodion   mellodeon
    (small reed organ or type of accordion)

14. apoggiatura   appoggiatura   appogiatura   apogiatura
    (preceding embellishing note)

15. largissimo   larghissimo   larghissimmo   largessimo
    (as slowly as possible)

16. mixolidean   mixolydean   mixolydian   mixylidean
    (church mode: G to G on white keys)

17. Kousevitsky   Kousevitzky   Koussevitzky   Koussevitsky
    (famed conductor)

18. merimba   marimba   merrimba   marrimba
    (horizontal keyboard percussion instrument popular in Central America)
19. fortomente   fortimente   fortamente   fortemente
    (strongly or loudly)
20. borrée   bourée   bourrée   bourré
    (old French or Spanish dance or music for it)
21. Kachatorian   Khachaturian   Khachatorian   Khachiturian
    (Russian-Armenian composer)
22. mistarioso   misterioso   mysterioso   missterioso
    (mysteriously)
23. therrimin   therimin   theremin   therremin
    (electronic instrument played by moving the hands near antennas)
24. arrpeggio   arpegio   arpeggio   arppegio
    (playing of the tones of a chord in quick succession)
25. Messiane   Messien   Messiaen   Messaien
    (French composer)

Alternative Words

a. fermata   fermatta   fermatto   fermato
    (sustaining of a note or chord, or its symbol   )
b. descante   deskant   deskante   descant
    (contrapuntal melody, usually above the tenor)
c. aleatory   alleatory   aliatory   alliatory
    (using randomness or chance in composing or performing)
d. Saint-Sëns   Saint-Säns   Saint-Seäns   Saint-Saëns
    (French composer)
e. riccercare   riccercar   ricerccare   ricercar
    (motetlike symphonic instrumental form)

> *Before consulting the answers on page 300:*
> I think I spelled _____ words correctly on this test.
> (If your estimate is correct, add one point to your score.)

Clothes and Fabrics

1. titivate   tittevate   tittivate   titavate
   (spruce up)
2. bushler   boushler   busheler   buschler
   (garment repairer)
3. ballbriggan   balbrigan   ballbrigen   balbriggan
   (a plain-stitch knitted fabric)
4. redengot   reddingote   redengote   redingote
   (open-front, belted, lightweight coat worn over a dress)
5. fiechu   fichue   fichu   ficheu
   (triangular woman's shawl or kerchief)
6. riverrs   revers   reverce   revier
   (turned back or lapellike part of a garment)
7. dikky   dickey   dickie   dickee
   (collar- or frontlike separate piece)
8. Borsilino   Boursalino   Borsillino   Borsalino
   (man's brimmed hat)
9. bleuson   blouson   blousan   blouseon
   (woman's blouselike outer garment)
10. baze   baiz   baise   baize
    (feltlike, usually green cotton or woolen fabric)
11. serape   sarrape   serrape   serapie
    (blanketlike shawl)
12. mackinaugh   mackinaw   maccinaw   mackanaw
    (short and thick double-breasted coat)
13. gampe   guimp   gimpe   guimpe
    (neck piece of lace or embroidery worn with a low-cut dress)
14. alpaca   allpaca   allpacca   alpacha
    (silky fabric from hoofed South American animal)
15. organsa   organnza   organza   organnsa
    (sheer plain-weave silk, nylon, or rayon fabric)
16. shaloon   schaloon   shalloon   schalloon
    (lightweight twilled fabric used for linings)
17. falle   faille   faielle   faiell
    (soft, ribbed silken or lightweight taffeta fabric)

18. Queana   Quiana   Qiana   Qyana
     (brand of lustrous nylon fiber)
19. toule   tule   tulle   toulle
     (thin, netlike fabric of silk or synthetic material)
20. bedizenment   bedazinment   beddizinement   bedizinement
     (gaudy or vulgar dressing up)
21. galligaskins   galligasquins   galigasquins   galigaskins
     (loose breeches, leggings, or gaiters)
22. vicunña   viccuña   vicuña   vycuña
     (soft woolen fabric from a South American mountain animal)
23. musquitaire gloves   mousquitaire gloves   mousquetaire gloves
        musketaire gloves
     (woman's long gauntlet gloves)
24. paignoir   peignoir   peignoire   pegnoire
     (woman's dressing gown)
25. bissus   bissis   byssis   byssus
     (ancient cloth)

Alternative Words

a. gussit   gussette   gusset   gusette
    (V-shaped fabric insert to make a garment stronger)
b. pantaloons   panteloons   pantalloons   pantelloons
    (old-style wide breeches)
c. crepe de chene   crape de chine   crepe de chine
       crape de chene
    (soft, light fabric with uneven surface)
d. changsam   chongsam   cheongsam   changhsam
    (oriental slit-skirt dress with mandarin collar)
e. sowester   so'wester   souw'ester   sou'wester
    (sailor's long oilskin coat)

> *Before consulting the answers on page 301:*
> I think I spelled ____ words correctly on this test.
> (If your estimate is correct, add one point to your score.)

Countries of the World (U.N. Members)

1. Moritius   Mouitius   Mauritius   Morritius
(republic in the Indian Ocean)

2. Vanoatto   Vannuatu   Vanuattu   Vanuatu
(republic northeast of Australia)

3. Saychelles   Seychelles   Sechelles   Seycheles
(republic in the Indian Ocean)

4. Brunnai   Brunai   Brunei   Brunnei
(sultanate on the northwest coast of Borneo)

5. Comoros   Komoros   Komorros   Comorros
(republic in the Indian Ocean)

6. Guinia-Bisau   Guinia-Bissau   Guinea-Bissau
     Guinnea-Bissau
(republic on west coast of Africa)

7. Gyana   Guyana   Guiana   Guyanna
(republic on northeast coast of South America)

8. Bahraine   Bahrain   Bahurain   Bahreine
(sheikdom in the Persian Gulf)

9. São Toma e Principe   São Tomé e Princippe
     São Toma e Princippe   São Tomé e Principe
(republic in West Africa)

10. Djeboutie   Djeboutis   Djiboutis   Djibouti
(republic in East Africa)

11. Czechaslavakia   Czechoslavakia   Czechoslovakia
     Czechislovakia
(country in central Europe)

12. Katar   Quatar   Qatar   Kaatar
(emirate in the Persian Gulf)

13. Rwanda   Ruwanda   Rowanda   Roowanda
(republic in central Africa)

14. Lezotho   Lesotho   Lesothoe   Lisotho
(monarchy in South Africa)

15. Malawy   Malawe   Malawi   Malaui
(republic in southeastern Africa)

16. Campuchia   Kampuchia   Kampuchea   Campuchea
(official name of Cambodia)

17. Barundi   Borundi   Burundi   Boroundi
    (republic in central Africa)
18. Belorussia   Bylarussia   Bilorussia   Bilourussia
    (republic of the Soviet Union)
19. Sorinam   Surinam   Surrinam   Suranam
    (republic on northeast coast of South America)
20. Antiegua and Barbudda   Antigua and Barbuda
    Antiga and Barbouda   Antigua and Barbouda
    (island state in the West Indies)
21. Sri Lankha   Sri Lanka   Sri Lankuh   Sri Lankka
    (republic, formerly Ceylon)
22. Afganistan   Affghanistan   Afghanistan   Afhghanistan
    (republic in southern Asia)
23. Moritania   Mouritania   Mauretania   Mauritania
    (republic in West Africa)
24. Bangledesh   Banggladesh   Banghladesh   Bangladesh
    (republic in southern Asia)
25. Honduras   Hondooras   Hondoras   Hondoris
    (republic in northeastern Central America)

Alternative Words

a. Buttan   Bhuttan   Bhutan   Butthan
   (kingdom northeast of India)
b. Luxemberg   Luxemborg   Luxembourg   Luxembourge
   (grand duchy in western Europe)
c. Bellese   Belise   Bellize   Belize
   (Central American country, formerly British)
d. Gambia   Ghambia   Ghambea   Gombia
   (republic in West Africa)
e. Zimbobbwe   Zimbobwe   Zimbabwe   Zimbabbwe
   (republic in southern Africa)

> *Before consulting the answers on page 301:*
> I think I spelled _____ words correctly on this test.
> (If your estimate is correct, add one point to your score.)

Dance and Ballet

1. coriphée   corriphée   corryphée   coryphée
   (ballet company small-group member)

2. pirouet   pirouette   piruette   pirrouette
   (a whirling around on one foot)

3. shotische   shottische   schottische   schottiche
   (polkalike round dance)

4. batment   battment   battement   bottement
   (brief fluttering movement by one leg)

5. labinotation   labbinotation   labbanotation   labanotation
   (written system of dance movement)

6. ballonée   ballonné   ballenée   ballennée
   (broad leap with a fluttering of one leg)

7. sisonne   sissonne   sisanne   sissanne
   (jump and landing on one foot with the other extended)

8. habenera   habanera   habinera   habannera
   (a Cuban dance)

9. pachanga   pashanga   paschanga   patchanga
   (Latin ballroom dance)

10. entrichat   entrechat   entrechatte   entrachat
    (jump and crossing of the feet in midair)

11. fuetté   fueté   fuité   fouetté
    (whiplike movement of one leg during a turn)

12. carioca   cariocca   carrioca   carriocca
    (ballroom samba)

13. maxsixe   maxxixe   maxixe   maxix
    (Brazilian ballroom dance)

14. polanais   polonaise   polonais   polanaise
    (slow, triple-time Polish dance)

15. bugalu   bugaloo   boogaloo   boogalu
    (fast Afro-American dance for a couple)

16. porte de bra   port de bras   porte de bras   port de bra
    (arm-movement technique)

17. callipso   calypso   callypso   calipso
    (West Indian dance)

18. balloté   ballotté   ballottée   ballotée
    (of a leap: with a rocking movement, free leg to the side)

19. garguillade   gargouillade   gargeuillade   garguiellade
    (pas de chat with a double rond de jambe)

20. pas de bourée   pas de borré   pas de bouré   pas de bourrée
    (short running step)

21. merengue   maringue   marenge   merengé
    (Dominican-Haitian ballroom dance)

22. begine   beguin   beguinne   beguine
    (bolero dance from Martinique)

23. Nickolai   Nikolais   Nikolai   Nikolei
    (American choreographer)

24. paso double   paso doble   paso dobele   passo doble
    (Latin American march step associated with bullfighting)

25. tarentella   tarrantella   tarrentella   tarantella
    (fast, whirling Italian dance)

Alternative Words

a. eurythmics   eurythmiks   eurhythmix   eurithmics
   (method of body-movement interpretation of music)

b. malaguenia   mallaguenia   malaguena   malleguena
   (fandangolike Spanish dance for a couple)

c. Diaghilev   Diagilov   Diaghillev   Diagghilov
   (Russian ballet producer)

d. pass-pied   passpied   passepied   passe-pied
   (lively triple-meter French dance)

e. Ballenchine   Balanchine   Balenchine   Ballanchine
   (Russian-born American choreographer)

> *Before consulting the answers on page 301:*
> I think I spelled ＿＿ words correctly on this test.
> (If your estimate is correct, add one point to your score.)

Desserts and Sweets

1. joujoubie   jujubie   jujube   jujoubie
   (fruit-flavored candy)

2. strausel   streusel   streusle   strausle
   (crumbly cake filling or topping)

3. petite foure   petit four   petit foure   petite Four
   (small frosted teacake)

4. maccaroon   macarroon   maccarroon   macaroon
   (cookie with ground almonds or coconut)

5. briosch   breosch   brioshe   brioche
   (type of sweet bread)

6. fasnakt   fasnacht   fasnocht   fassnacht
   (deep-fried raised doughnut)

7. rennet   renet   rennit   rennat
   (ingredient in junket)

8. frappe   frape   frappee   frap
   (ice cream milkshake)

9. shtollen   stollen   schtollen   stohlen
   (German bread containing fruit and nuts)

10. Sacker tort   Sacher tort   Sacher torte   Sacher tarte
    (chocolate cake with apricot jam filling)

11. pistaschio   pastashio   pistachio   pistashio
    (ice cream flavor)

12. savarin   savvarin   savarrin   salverin
    (rum-soaked rich cake baked in a ring mold)

13. Häagen-Das   Häagen-Dasz   Häagen-Dazs   Häagen Daz
    (brand of ice cream)

14. croquimbouch   croquembouche   croqembouche
    croquimbouche
    (caramelized pyramid of cream puffs)

15. pandowdy   pandoudy   pandowdie   pandowdee
    (deep-dish dessert with spiced apple)

16. baclava   baklava   bakklava   baklavva
    (nuts-and-honey dessert in a thin pastry)

17. zeballione   zabaglione   zabagglione   zebagglione
    (Italian frothy sauce often served on fruit)

18. charlotte russe   charlette russe   charlot russe
    charlotte ruse
    (layered sponge cake and whipped cream filling)

19. marzapan   marzepan   marzipann   marzipan
    (often shaped confection made of crushed almonds)

20. babbah   babba   boba   baba
    (rum-soaked cake)

21. jelati   gelati   jellati   gelatti
    (rich but low-butterfat Italian ice cream)

22. parfet   parfee   parfait   parfaite
    (dessert of ice cream and syrup layers)

23. blankmange   blanckmange   blancmange   blancmonge
    (vanilla-flavored starchy pudding)

24. tutti-frutti   tutty-frutty   tooty-frooty   tootie-frootie
    (ice cream with candied fruits)

25. prailine   praline   prailene   pralene
    (nut-kernel confection)

Alternative Words

a. compot   kompot   kompote   compote
   (fruit cooked in a syrup)

b. horehound   horhound   horrhound   hoorhound
   (bitter mint used as a flavoring)

c. bon bouche   bonne bouche   bon-bouch   bonne-bouche
   (delicacy or treat)

d. pattisery   pattisserie   patiserie   patisserie
   (shop selling French pastries)

e. pfefernüss   pfeffernüsse   pfeffernüss   feffernüsse
   (small and hard spiced Christmas cookie)

> *Before consulting the answers on page 301:*
> I think I spelled ＿＿ words correctly on this test.
> (If your estimate is correct, add one point to your score.)

Dogs

1. synologist cynologist sinologist psinologist
    (dog trainer)
2. Shnauzer Shnouzer Schnouzer Schnauzer
    (breed)
3. Affghan hound Afghan hound Aphghan hound
    Afghannn hound
    (breed)
4. Rautwiler Rottwyler Rotweiler Rottweiler
    (breed)
5. Selluki Salluka Saluki Salluki
    (breed)
6. Aerdale Airdale Airedail Airedale
    (breed)
7. llasa aphso lhasa apso lasa ahpso lhasah apso
    (breed)
8. Bechon Friese Bichon Frise Bichon Fris Bechon Frise
    (breed)
9. malamute mallamute mallemute malimute
    (breed)
10. Chewawa Chiehwahwa Chihuahua Cheehuahua
    (breed)
11. masstif mastif mastiff massetiffe
    (large and strong short-haired dog)
12. schiperkie schipperke shipperke shiperkie
    (breed)
13. Brettany spaniel Britanny spaniel Brittany spaniel
    Bretanny spaniel
    (breed)
14. whymariner weimariner weimaraner weimarrener
    (breed)
15. afenpinscher affenpinscher affinpinscher afinpinscher
    (breed)
16. Pomoranian Pommeranian Pomeranian Pommeranian
    (breed)
17. whippet whippit whyppet whipett
    (small, slender dog that is very swift)

18. breyarde   breard   briard   briarde
    (breed)
19. dackshund   dachshond   dachshund   dachkshund
    (breed)
20. Dalmatian   Dallmatian   Dalmaition   Dalmayshin
    (breed)
21. Seelyham terrier   Seeliham terrier   Sealyham terrier
    Seallyham terrier
    (breed)
22. Bassette hound   Basset hound   Bassett hound
    Basett hound
    (breed)
23. dingho   dinngo   dingo   dingoe
    (Australian wild dog)
24. Samoyed   Simoyed   Sammoyed   Sammoyede
    (breed)
25. Cyrberos   Cerberos   Cerberus   Cerberrus
    (mythology: three-headed dog guarding infernal regions)

Alternative Words

a. huskie   huskey   husky   huski
   (arctic working dog)
b. Shar-Pay   Char-Pay   Shar-Pei   Zhar-Pei
   (breed)
c. Beddlington terrier   Bedlington terrier   Bedlyngton terrier
   Bed'lington terrier
   (breed)
d. bondog   bann-dog   bandog   band-dog
   (dog kept tied up or chained)
e. Kuvasz   Kuvaaz   Kuvvasz   Kuvasze
   (breed)

Before consulting the answers on page 302:
I think I spelled _____ words correctly on this test.
(If your estimate is correct, add one point to your score.)

Drugs, Antibiotics, and Analgesics

1. barbituate   barbetuate   barbiturate   barbitturate
(sedative or hypnotic drug)

2. Dexidreen   Dexedreen   Dexidrene   Dexedrine
(brand of dextroamphetamine)

3. Melarill   Mellaril   Melaril   Melleril
(brand of thioridazine)

4. Quaalude   Quallude   Qualude   Qualuud
(brand of methaqualone)

5. amphetimine   amphetimin   amphetamin   amphetamine
(mood-elevating or appetite-controlling stimulative drug)

6. methydon   methadone   methidone   methydone
(morphinelike narcotic used to treat heroin addicts)

7. Secconal   Seconal   Seconnal   Seconall
(brand of secobarbital)

8. Delauded   Dilauded   Delaudid   Dilaudid
(brand of hydrochloride salt of dihydromorphinone)

9. strepptomycin   streptomycin   strepptomicin   streptomicin
(antibiotic used chiefly for tuberculosis)

10. Amatol   Amatal   Amytol   Amytal
(brand of amobarbital)

11. atropeen   attropine   atropine   atropene
(antispasmodic and pain reliever; racemic hyoscyamine)

12. Compasine   Campazine   Campasine   Compazine
(brand of prochlorperazine)

13. sodium pentathal   sodium pentothol   sodium pentithol
sodium pentathol
(sodium salt of thiopental)

14. Demerol   Demeral   Demmerol   Demmeral
(brand of meperidine)

15. Nemmbutol   Nembutal   Nemmbutal   Nembeutal
(brand of pentobarbital)

16. codiene   codien   codeine   codein
(opium alkaloid used as a sedative or analgesic)

17. Perckodan   Percodan   Purcodan   Percadan
(brand name for pain reliever containing aspirin and caffeine)

18. psilycibin   psilicybin   psilocybin   psillocybin
(hallucinogenic mushroom substance)

19. meconism   mekonism   mecconism   mekkonism
(opium addiction)

20. pharmacopie   pharmacopea   pharmicopoeia
pharmacopoeia
(technical guidebook to drugs, stock of drugs)

21. pariphenalia   paraphenalia   paraphernalia   pariphernalia
(utensils)

22. Ridolin   Ritolin   Ritalin   Rittalin
(brand of methylphenidate in its hydrochloride form)

23. nargeel   nargheel   narghile   narrghil
(water pipe)

24. Miltowne   Miltown   Milletown   Milltown
(brand of meprobamate)

25. ascetisalicylic acid   acetylsalicylic acid   acetalsalicylic acid
acetysalycylic acid
(aspirin)

Alternative Words

a. Dramamene   Drammamine   Dramamine   Dramimin
(brand of dimenhydrinate)

b. sulfidiazene   sulfadiazine   sulfadyazene   sulfadyazine
(drug used for urinary infections and malaria)

c. tetracycline   tetricycline   tetracyclin   tetrecycline
(antibiotic used to treat many infections)

d. Mercurocrome   Mercurochrome   Mercurichrome
Mercurechrome
(brand of merbromin)

e. cannibism   cannaebism   canibism   cannabism
(marijuana addiction)

> *Before consulting the answers on page 302:*
> I think I spelled _____ words correctly on this test.
> (If your estimate is correct, add one point to your score.)

Economics, Business, and Finance

1. entreprenorial   entrepreneureal   entreprenourial
    entrepreneurial
    (venturesome in business)
2. debinture   debtenture   debenture   debenteur
    (bond backed by issuer's general credit)
3. surityship   suretiship   suretyship   surettyship
    (legal relationship between parties)
4. replevin   replevvin   replaevin   repplevin
    (legal action to recover wrongfully taken goods)
5. hypothecate   hypothicate   hypothacate   hypothocate
    (to pledge or mortgage)
6. thurbligg   therbligg   thurblig   therblig
    (task element analyzed in a time and motion study)
7. tali quale   tali quali   tale quale   tale quali
    (as is)
8. empignerate   impignerate   impignorate   empignourate
    (to pawn)
9. Chancelor of the Excheqer   Chancellor of the Excheqer
    Chancellor of the Exchequer   Chancellor of the Exchequor
    (British finance minister)
10. cetaris paribus   ceteris parribus   cetaris parribus
    ceteris paribus
    (other things being equal)
11. cum dividend   qum dividend   kum dividend
    cumm dividend
    (with the stock price including a previously declared dividend)
12. arbetrage   arbotrage   arbitrage   arbutrage
    (buying and selling in different markets to profit from unequal prices)
13. Kaynsian   Keynsian   Keynesian   Kaynesian
    (pertaining to famed economist, 1883–1946)
14. defulcation   defilcation   defelcation   defalcation
    (misappropriation of money)
15. ussufruct   usufruct   usuefruct   eusofruct
    (rightful use of another's property)
16. Bretonn Woods Conference   Britton Woods Conference
    Breton Woods Conference   Bretton Woods Conference
    (international conference held in New Hampshire in July 1944)

17. fideuciary   fiduciary   fiduceary   fiducciary
    (requiring public trust for value)

18. cavit emptur   caveat emptor   caveate emptor
    caviat emptor
    (let the buyer beware)

19. seigniorage   senhorage   senorage   seigneurage
    (bullion cost difference that is a source of government revenue)

20. laissez-faire   laisez-faire   lessez-faire   lessee-faire
    (belief in minimal governmental economic intervention)

21. tonteen   tontine   tonntine   tontien
    (group financial arrangement with benefits going to survivors over time)

22. sumpteuary   sumptuary   sumptuory   sumptury
    (pertaining to expenditure or regulation of personal habits)

23. oligopalistic   olligopolistic   oligopolistic   olygopolistic
    (pertaining to a few-sellers market situation)

24. Galbrathean   Galbraithean   Galbrathian   Galbraithian
    (pertaining to the famed Canadian-American economist, 1908–   )

25. paeonage   pionage   peonage   peonnage
    (forced labor)

Alternative Words

a. Rickardean   Riccardian   Ricardean   Ricardian
   (pertaining to the English economist, 1772–1823)

b. cartel   kartel   kartell   cartell
   (international syndicate)

c. brassege   brassage   brasage   braussage
   (charge to cover money-coining costs)

d. cameralist   cammeralist   kammeralist   camerilist
   (seventeenth- or eighteenth-century believer in national power through wealth)

e. Ginnie Mae   Ginny Mae   Ginnie May   Ginny May
   (GNMA bond)

> *Before consulting the answers on page 302:*
> I think I spelled _____ words correctly on this test.
> (If your estimate is correct, add one point to your score.)

English and English Literature

1. metynomy   metanomy   metonymy   metonamy
(figure of speech: using the name of one thing for a similar thing)

2. *Ariopagitika*   *Areopagitica*   *Areopogitica*   *Ariopogitika*
(John Milton's famous essay on censorship)

3. Hudibrastic   Huddibrastic   Hudibrasstic   Hudabrastic
(in the burlesque style of Samuel Butler's poem)

4. picqueresque   picuaresque   picaresque   piquaresque
(characterized by earthiness, roguery, and humor)

5. dactyllic   dachtylic   dachtilic   dactylic
(prosody: verse using a long-short-short metrical foot)

6. mythopesis   mythapesis   mythopouesis   mythopoesis
(myth making)

7. *Rubáyát of Omar Khayám*   *Rubáiyát of Omar Khayyám*
Rubeyát of Omar Khayhám   *Rubáyyát of Omar Khayám*
(Persian verses translated by Edward Fitzgerald)

8. parataxis   paratachsis   paritachsis   paritaxis
(sentence style without using connectives)

9. Kaellyard School   Kaelyard School   Kailleyard School
Kailyard School
(late nineteenth-century school of Scottish writers)

10. synecdocce   synecdoche   synekdoche   synecdochie
(figure of speech: use of a part for the whole)

11. flyting   flyteing   fliting   flytting
(cursing match in verse)

12. stichomythia   sticomythia   sticomithia   stychomithia
(fiery dialogue exchange in drama)

13. euphoistic   euphuistic   euphooistic   euphouistic
(in the floridly rhetorical and artificial prose style of John Lyly)

14. kening   kaening   kenning   keanning
(Anglo-Saxon metaphorical epithet)

15. "Mac Fleckno"   "Mc Flecknoe"   "Mac Flekno"
"Mac Flecknoe"
(satirical poem by John Dryden)

16. Pepsian   Pepesian   Pepysian   Pypsian
(of or like the diary or writing of the eighteenth-century diarist)

17. Charles Lutwidge Dodgson   Charles Luttwidge Dodgson
     Charles Lutwidg Dodgeson   Charles Luttwidge Dodgsen
     (Lewis Carroll)

18. *Finegans Wake*   *Finnegans Wake*   *Finegans' Wake*
     Finnegan's Wake
     (work by James Joyce)

19. aposiopeisis   aposeopesis   aposiopesis   aposiopoesis
     (breaking off in midsentence)

20. concetism   conncetism   concettism   concettisme
     (use or love of conceits)

21. belletrist   bel-lettrist   bellettrist   belle-lettrist
     (lightly or refinedly aesthetic writer or poet)

22. Sceltonic   Skeltonic   Scelltonic   Skelltonic
     (in the short-lined, doggerellike verse used by the early Renaissance poet)

23. villanelle   villinelle   villainelle   vilanelle
     (verse form of five tercets followed by a quatrain)

24. esimplastic   escemplastic   essemplastic   esemplastic
     (Coleridge term: imaginatively shaping into a whole)

25. Houhnhym   Houghnhum   Hougghnhnm   Houyhnhm
     (race of superior, reasoning horses in Gulliver's Travels)

Alternative Words

a. tmesis   tmescis   tmoesis   tmiesis
     (sandwiching into a word another word or word element)

b. Hackloyt   Hakloyt   Hakluyt   Hakkloyt
     (chronicler and source used by Shakespeare)

c. *Penndennis*   *Pendenis*   *Pendennis*   *Penndenis*
     (William Thackeray novel)

d. mimisis   memnesis   memnisis   mimesis
     (imitation or aesthetic representation)

e. crestomathy   chrestomathy   chrystomathy   krestomathy
     (selection of literary passages)

> *Before consulting the answers on page 303:*
> I think I spelled ____ words correctly on this test.
> (If your estimate is correct, add one point to your score.)

Furniture and Antiques

1. escritoire   escritoir   eskritoire   escrytoire
   (writing desk)

2. Bedermaier   Bedermeyer   Biedermeyer   Biedermeier
   (nineteenth-century furniture style)

3. gyrendole   girendole   girandole   gyrindole
   (ornate wall bracket for candelabra)

4. bommbé   bombée   bombé   baumbé
   (curving outward)

5. cabriol   cabreole   cabriole   cabbriole
   (curved leg often with a clawlike bottom)

6. Duncan Phyf   Duncan Fife   Duncan Phyfe   Duncan Phife
   (furniture style of Scottish-born U.S. cabinetmaker)

7. vargano   vargenno   varguano   vargueno
   (Spanish fall-front desk)

8. pri-dieux   prie-dieu   pre-dieu   prie-diue
   (prayer desk, for kneeling)

9. Savanerola chair   Savanarolo chair   Savonerola chair
   Savonarola chair
   (Renaissance chair with a somewhat curved-X form)

10. fautauil   fauteuil   fautueil   fauteuille
    (upholstered armchair with open sides)

11. Coromandel work   Coramandel work   Corromandel work
    Corromandell work
    (English lacquer work popular at beginning of the eighteenth century)

12. éttagaire   étagère   étager   étagaire
    (whatnot, open-shelved cabinet)

13. triphid foot   trifid foot   tryphid foot   triffid foot
    (three-lobed pad foot; drake foot)

14. chinnoisery   chinoiserie   chinoisserie   chinoisry
    (eighteenth-century ornamentation using elaborate "Chinese" patterns)

15. boul   buhle   bulle   boulle
    (elaborate wood, ivory, etc., inlay work)

16. encoineur   encoinure   encoignure   encoigneur
    (low corner cabinet)

17. taberet   taboret   taberette   taborette
    (stoollike seat)

18. creedance   credance   credenze   credence
(Renaissance sideboard)

19. setee   settee   settie   settey
(long seat for more than one person)

20. aurmoulu   aurmolu   ormolu   ormollu
(goldlike brass)

21. Emes chair   Eammes chair   Eimes chair   Eames chair
(slender tube-frame chair of plywood)

22. chevail glass   chevel glass   cheval glass   chevalle glass
(tiltable full-length mirror in a frame)

23. gadruning   gadrooning   gaddrooning   gadarooning
(decorative ovallike fluting)

24. parketterie   parqueterie   parquetry   parquettrie
(wood mosaic work)

25. rattan   rattain   rattane   rhatan
(palm stem used to make furniture)

Alternative Words

a. Chippendale   Chippindale   Chipendale   Chippendall
(late-eighteenth-century English furniture style or one similar)

b. trivett table   tryvette table   tryvet table   trivet table
(three-legged table)

c. Circassian walnut   Cercasian walnut   Cercassian walnut
Circassean walnut
(hardwood from the English walnut)

d. damasque   damasc   damask   damaske
(fabric made from satins)

e. scutcheon   scutchion   skutchon   skutchin
(ornamental plate, as on a drawer)

> *Before consulting the answers on page 303:*
> I think I spelled ＿＿ words correctly on this test.
> (If your estimate is correct, add one point to your score.)

Gems and Crystals

1. bijoutery   bijuterie   bijouterie   bijeuxterie
    (jewelry)
2. amythyst   amithyst   amythest   amethyst
    (purple quartz)
3. tormuline   tourmaline   tourmalene   torrmaline
    (transparent black or colored silicate gem)
4. chalcydony   chalcedony   challcydony   challcedony
    (grayish or milky translucent quartz)
5. onyxe   onyx   onyxx   onnyx
    (variety of above gem with parallel bands of alternating color)
6. cabbouchon   cabbuchon   cabochon   cabochin
    (precious oval or hemispherical stone cut convexly, not faceted)
7. smeragyd   smaragyd   smarragd   smaragd
    (emerald)
8. peridot   perridot   perredote   peredot
    (transparent green variety of olivine)
9. jadyt   jadite   jadeite   jadyte
    (form of jade)
10. Mos scale   Moes scale   Mohs' scale   Maux scale
    (hardness scale used in mineralogy, from 1 (talc) to 10 (diamond))
11. lapis lazulli   lappis lazuli   lapis lazule   lapis lazuli
    (deep blue semiprecious stone)
12. adoulorescent   adularescent   adulorescent   addulorescent
    (having a milky bluish luster)
13. sfeen   sfene   spheen   sphene
    (small wedge-shaped crystal; titanite)
14. porfory   porphory   porphyry   porphery
    (hard, purplish red rock containing feldspar crystals)
15. grossularite   grosoulorite   grosularite   grossulorite
    (gray white to pinkish crystal of a garnet)
16. Pahdporadshah   Padparadschah   Padhporadshah
    Padperadshah
    (rare Sri Lankan yellow-orange sapphire)
17. carnealean   carnelean   carnelian   carnellian
    (red variety of number 4 in this test)

18. trikroism   trichroism   trikroizm   tricroism
    (crystallography: showing three colors when viewed differently)
19. asteriated   astoriated   astyriated   astyreated
    (showing a luminous starlike figure)
20. crysoberyll   chrysoberyl   crysoberyl   chrysoberyll
    (green or yellow crystal of beryllium aluminate)
21. girasol   girosole   gyrasol   giresol
    (brightly reflected opal)
22. briolet   breolet   breolette   briolette
    (pear-shaped gem with triangular facets)
23. chevey   chevie   chevee   chevvi
    (gemstone with smooth, slightly depressed surface)
24. meilee   maylee   melee   mellee
    (group of diamonds each of which weighs less than .25 carat)
25. rutile   reutile   routile   ruttile
    (common reddish brown mineral with bright metallic luster found in
       crystals)

Alternative Words

a. cat's eye   cat's-eye   catseye   cattseye
    (gem with a chatoyant luster)
b. nefrite   nephrite   neffrite   nephryt
    (whitish to dark green form of jade)
c. obsydian   obsidian   obsideon   obsydion
    (dark but, when thin, transparent volcanic glass)
d. lewcite   lucyte   lucite   leucite
    (whitish or grayish mineral)
e. malachite   malakite   mallechite   malichite
    (green, copper-ore mineral)

> *Before consulting the answers on page 303:*
> I think I spelled _____ words correctly on this test.
> (If your estimate is correct, add one point to your score.)

Geology

1. micaceous   micacious   miccaceous   micatious
    (containing mica)

2. epirogyny   epirogony   epeirogeny   epierogeny
    (movement of the earth's crust)

3. brechia   breccia   brecia   bretchia
    (rock made up of older rocks melded together)

4. allocthenous   alochthenous   allochthonous   allachthonous
    (formed elsewhere than where discovered)

5. cinebar   cinnebar   cinabar   cinnabar
    (red crystalline mineral and the principal ore of mercury)

6. ferruginous   feruginous   pheruginous   ferrugenous
    (containing iron)

7. cairngorm   carngorme   carngorm   cairnegorm
    (smoky quartz)

8. pahoho   pahoehoe   pohoho   pohoehoe
    (smooth-surfaced basaltic lava)

9. stallactite   stalaktite   stylactite   stalactite
    (iciclelike deposit hanging from the roof of a cave)

10. mispickle   mispickel   myspickel   myspickle
    (arsenopyrite)

11. gypsum   gyppsum   gipsum   jipsum
    (hydrated calcium sulfate, used in plaster of Paris)

12. fleisch   flysch   flysh   flaisch
    (marine sedimentary rocks)

13. terigenous   terriginous   terigynous   terrigenous
    (of sea bottom sediments from nearby land)

14. peniplain   peneplain   penniplane   peneplane
    (erosion-produced flatland)

15. icsostacy   isostasy   issostacy   eisostasy
    (balanced condition of the earth's crust)

16. molibdunite   molybdenite   mollybdenite   molybdunite
    (graphitelike mineral)

17. aphenite   affenite   aphanite   aphinite
    (fine-grained, very compact igneous rock)

18. quockwaversal   quokkuaversal   quaquaversal
    quaquaversile
    (sloping down on all sides from the center)

19. klippe   clippe   klyppe   clyppe
    (erosional outlier of a nappe)

20. congellifraction   conjelifraction   congelifraction
    conjellifraction
    (splitting of a rock or frozen soil because of frost)

21. gabroe   gabbroe   gabbro   gabrow
    (dark granular igneous rock)

22. pergellisol   pergelisol   perjellisol   purgelisol
    (permafrost)

23. arinaceous   arrinacious   arenaceous   arynaceous
    (sandy)

24. cuprious   cupreous   cupryous   cupprious
    (containing copper)

25. phriatic   phreatik   phryatic   phreatic
    (of ground water)

Alternative Words

a. horneblend   horneblende   hornblend   hornblende
   (dark green or black amphibole mineral)

b. eluveum   elluveum   eluvium   elluvium
   (deposit left from decomposed rock)

c. plageoklas   plageoklase   plagioclase   plagioklas
   (a feldspar mineral found in most igneous rocks)

d. dyorite   diorite   dioryte   dierite
   (granular igneous rock)

e. mantel   mantell   mantle   mantile
   (part of earth between the crust and the core)

Before consulting the answers on page 304:
I think I spelled _____ words correctly on this test.
(If your estimate is correct, add one point to your score.)

Gourmet Cook

1. caciatore   cacciatore   cacciattore   cacciottore
   (cooked with tomatoes, herbs, and sometimes wine)

2. radicchio   raddichio   radiccio   radhiccio
   (type of chicory)

3. vinegrette   vinagrette   vinaigret   vinaigrette
   (oil-and-vinegar-based sauce with onions and herbs)

4. gaspocho   gaszpacho   gazpacho   gazpocho
   (spicy cold vegetable soup)

5. piccilil   piccallili   piccalilli   piccillily
   (relish of chopped vegetables and spices)

6. spetzel   spaetzel   spaetzle   schpetzel
   (German starchy batter dish)

7. aeole   aiole   ayole   aioli
   (sauce of egg yolks, garlic, olive oil, and lemon juice)

8. ratatouille   ratitouille   rattatouille   rattattouille
   (stew of eggplant, tomatoes, green peppers, squash, sometimes meat)

9. ptarrmigon   ptarmigon   ptarmigan   ptarrmigan
   (type of grouse)

10. muenière   maunière   meunière   menière
    (rolled in flour and sautéed in butter)

11. bourgignonne   bouguinonne   bourguignonne   bourgignon
    (made with a red Burgundy wine sauce)

12. tetrazini   tetrazzini   tetrazinni   tetrazzinni
    (prepared with pasta and sherry-seasoned white sauce and served au gratin)

13. silantro   cilantro   sillantro   celantro
    (Chinese parsley; coriander)

14. fenochio   finnochio   fennochio   finocchio
    (type of fennel; Florence fennel)

15. timbale   timbalee   tembali   timbali
    (creamy vegetable or meat mixture or pastry shell containing it)

16. racklet   raclette   raqlette   racqlette
    (Swiss dish with cheese and bread or boiled potatoes)

17. scalloppini   scallopine   scalopine   scaloppine
    (sautéed slices of meat flour-coated and fried)

18. coqille St. Jacques   coccilles St. Jacques   coquilles St. Jacques
    coqilles St. Jacques
(appetizer of minced scallops in a wine and cream sauce)

19. fricasseed   friccaseed   fricassied   friccassied
(stewed and served with a white wine sauce)

20. gard-mange   garde-manger   garde-mange   gard-manger
(cook specializing in cold foods)

21. prociutto   proschiutto   prossciutto   prosciutto
(spiced Italian ham)

22. aruegala   arugula   arrugala   areugala
(a mustard plant)

23. strogenov   strogannov   stroganof   stroganoff
(sautéed meat dish)

24. couse-cous   coos-coos   couscouse   couscous
(North African semolina dish)

25. rémoullade   rémoulade   rémeulade   rémollade
(cold sauce of mayonnaise, herbs, and condiments)

Alternative Words

a. rigatoni   riggitoni   riggattoni   rigattoni
(short and curved macaroni)

b. cannelloni   canaloni   canelloni   cannaloni
(stuffed tubes of pasta)

c. cappeletti   capelletti   cappelletti   cappelleti
(filled, hat-shaped pieces of pasta)

d. bärnaise   béarnaise   bernaise   béarnais
(sauce of egg yolks seasoned with wine, vinegar, and shallots)

e. cuisine manceure   cuisine manseur   cuisine minceur
    cuisine minsieur
(low-calorie French cooking)

> *Before consulting the answers on page 304:*
> I think I spelled _____ words correctly on this test.
> (If your estimate is correct, add one point to your score.)

Historical and Cultural Figures

1. Hammersköld   Hammarskjöld   Hammerskjöld
    Hammarsjöld
    (former Swedish U.N. secretary-general)

2. Anderson   Andersen   Andersonn   Andersson
    (Danish fairy tale writer)

3. Tuttankhamin   Tutankamen   Tutankhamin
    Tutankhamen
    (Egyptian king)

4. O'Kiefe   O'Keefe   O'Keef   O'Keeffe
    (American painter)

5. Boccacio   Bocaccio   Boccaccio   Boccoccio
    (Italian author)

6. Solhzenitsin   Solzhenitsyn   Solzhenitsen   Solhzinitsin
    (Russian novelist)

7. Wencislas   Wenceslas   Wencislos   Wenceslos
    (German king and Holy Roman emperor)

8. Anouil   Anouih   Annouilh   Anouilh
    (French dramatist)

9. Stuyvescunt   Stuyvesent   Styvesent   Stuyvesant
    (Dutch administrator in America)

10. Aeskylos   Aeschalus   Aeschylos   Aeschylus
    (Greek dramatist)

11. Audoubon   Audobonn   Audubon   Audabon
    (Haitian-born American ornithologist)

12. Ghandi   Gandi   Gandhi   Ghandhi
    (Indian leader)

13. Khrushchev   Khruchshev   Khruschov   Kruschchev
    (Soviet premier)

14. Verrazano   Verizzano   Verazzano   Verazzanno
    (Italian explorer)

15. Kozćiuszko   Kościuszko   Kośkiuszko   Kościusko
    (Polish patriot who fought in American Revolution)

16. Materlink   Maeterrlinck   Maetarlinck   Maeterlinck
    (Belgian poet and dramatist)

17. Nebuccadnezar   Nebuchadnezzar   Nebuchadnezar
    Nebuchednezzer
    (Chaldean king of Babylon)

18. Casatte   Cassat   Cassatte   Cassatt
    (American painter in France)
19. Saarrinen   Saarenen   Saarennin   Saarinen
    (American architect)
20. Haile Salasse   Haile Selassie   Haile Selassi   Haile Sellassic
    (Ethiopian emperor)
21. Biederbeck   Biederbecke   Beiderbeck   Beiderbecke
    (American jazz musician and composer)
22. Ho Che Mijn   Ho Chi Minh   Ho Chie Min   Ho Che Minh
    (Vietnamese leader)
23. Kemal Atatürk   Kemal Attitürk   Kemal Attatürk
         Kemal Atetürk
    (Turkish political leader)
24. Montesque   Montesqieu   Montesquieu   Montesqueue
    (French political philosopher)
25. Brezinski   Brezhinsky   Brzezinsky   Bryzinski
    (Polish-born American political scholar)

Alternative Words

a. Kuble Khan   Kublah Khan   Kubla Khan   Kublai Khan
   (Mongol leader)
b. Respiggi   Respigi   Respighi   Resphigi
   (Italian composer)
c. Xanthippe   Xanttippe   Xanthipe   Xantipe
   (wife of Socrates)
d. Sidārrtha Gautama   Sidārtha Gautama   Siddārrtha Gautama
        Siddhārtha Gautama
   (founder of Buddhism)
e. Nieztshe   Nietsche   Nietzsche   Nieztsche
   (German philosopher)

> *Before consulting the answers on page 304:*
> I think I spelled _____ words correctly on this test.
> (If your estimate is correct, add one point to your score.)

History

1. Peloppennesian War   Peleponnesian War   Peloponnesian War   Peleponesian War
    (war between Athens and Sparta in fifth century B.C.)

2. Apomatox   Appomatox   Appommatox   Appomattox
    (Virginia site of Lee's surrender to Grant in 1865)

3. Marseillaise   Marsaillaise   Marrseillaise   Marseilaise
    (French national anthem, written in 1792)

4. Treaty of Aix-le-Chappel   Treaty of Aix-la-Chappelle   Treaty of Aix-la-Chapalle   Treaty of Aix-la-Chapelle
    (1748 treaty ending the War of the Austrian Succession)

5. Fanneull Hall   Faneulle Hall   Faneuil Hall   Faneuille Hall
    (Revolutionary War meeting place for patriots, "Cradle of Liberty")

6. Tippicanoe   Tipiccanoe   Tippecanoe   Tippacanoe
    (Indiana battle site and nickname of President William Henry Harrison)

7. Toqueville   Toqu'ville   Tocqueville   Tocquiville
    (French statesman and observer of America)

8. Mazzarin   Mazarin   Mazarrin   Mazzarrin
    (French cardinal and statesman under Louis XIV)

9. Paschandaelle   Paschendaele   Passchendaele   Paschendaelle
    (World War I campaign)

10. Hohanzollern   Hohenzollern   Hohanzolern   Hohennzollern
    (royal family that ruled in Prussia and the German Empire)

11. Dred Scott   Dread Scott   Dred Skott   Dread Scot
    (nineteenth century Supreme Court case involving a slave's rights)

12. Gibheline   Ghibeline   Ghibelline   Gibbheline
    (medieval party opposed to the Guelphs)

13. Battle of Crécie   Battle of Craicy   Battle of Créccy   Battle of Crécy
    (English victory over France in 1346)

14. Antheatam   Antiatam   Antietam   Anthietam
    (Maryland site of Civil War battle)

15. Auffklarüng   Auffclaerung   Aufklaïrung   Aufklärung
    (the Enlightenment, an eighteenth-century philosophical movement)

16. Zvingleyanism   Zwingleyanism   Zwinglianism   Zwinglyanism
    (doctrine of sixteenth-century Swiss Protestant reformer)

17. Anne Boleyn   Ann Bolleyn   Anne Bolleyn   Ann Boleyn
    (second wife of England's Henry VIII)

18. Bertchesgarden   Berchesgaden   Berchtesgaden   Bertchesgaden
(Bavarian site of Hitler's mountain chalet)

19. witenagemot   wittanagamot   witanagamot   wittenagamot
(national council in early English history)

20. *Merimack*   *Merrimac*   *Marrimack*   *Merimac*
(warship used by the Confederacy, and renamed *Virginia,* against
the *Monitor*)

21. Chikamaugga   Chickimauga   Chickamauga   Chicamauga
(Georgia site of an 1863 Civil War battle)

22. Ballfore Declaration   Balfour Declaration   Balfore Declaration
Balfoure Declaration
(1917 British position regarding Palestine)

23. Cannossa   Canassa   Canossa   Kannossa
(castle where Emperor Henry IV did penance before Pope Gregory VII
in 1077)

24. Dreifuss Affair   Dreyfus Affair   Dreyfuss Affair   Dreifus Affair
(French political scandal involving anti-Semitism)

25. Thermopoley   Thermopolae   Thermopylae   Thermopyli
(Greek pass where the Persians defeated Sparta in 480 B.C.)

Alternative Words

a. Burgoigne   Burgoyne   Bergoyne   Burgoyn
(British Revolutionary War general who surrendered at Saratoga)

b. Seepoy Mutiny   Sepoi Mutiny   Seppoy Mutiny   Sepoy Mutiny
(nineteenth century troop revolt in British India)

c. Guarnicca   Guarnica   Guernicca   Guernica
(Basque town bombed in 1937 in the Spanish Civil War)

d. Atchison   Acheson   Achison   Atcheson
(U.S. Secretary of State, 1949–1953)

e. Liebensraume   Lebensraume   Lebensraum   Lebennsraum
(Nazi policy of need for additional "living space" territory)

> *Before consulting the answers on page 305:*
> I think I spelled _____ words correctly on this test.
> (If your estimate is correct, add one point to your score.)

Horses

1. equestrianne equestrien equestrienne equestriane
    (female horse rider)
2. hyppology hippology hypology hipology
    (study of horses)
3. winny whinny whinney whinie
    (to make a horselike sound)
4. croup croop croupe creup
    (top of a horse's rump)
5. Purchuron Percherone Percheron Percherron
    (French gray or black draft horse)
6. lorrimer laurimer lorimer lurimer
    (maker of spurs and bits)
7. pasterne posterne pastern postern
    (part of the foot between the hoof and the fetlock)
8. skuebald skewbald skoobald scewbold
    (with brown and white patches)
9. manege manage mannege mannage
    (movements or paces of trained horses)
10. cantle cantel cantell cantil
    (rear part of a saddle)
11. spaevin spavvin spavan spavin
    (hock joint disease or enlargement)
12. gymkana gymkhana gimkana gimkhana
    (exhibition of horsemanship)
13. Clydsdale Clydesdale Clydesdalle Klydesdale
    (sturdy Scottish draft horse with long wisps along the backs of the legs)
14. sursingle surrsingle surrcingle surcingle
    (belt buckled on the horse's back)
15. pommell pommel pummell pomele
    (top protuberance on a saddle)
16. sorel soral sorrel sorral
    (light reddish-brown horse)
17. rosanante rosinnante rosinante rossinante
    (broken-down horse, nag)

18. gennet   jinnet   jennet   genette
    (small Spanish horse)

19. caracole   carracole   carricole   caricole
    (half turn by a horse and rider)

20. summter   sumpter   sumter   summpter
    (packhorse or mule)

21. cavilleti   cavalleti   cavalletti   cavaletti
    (series of adjustable jumps for horses)

22. farriar   farier   farrier   farrior
    (cavalry noncommissioned officer who has charge of horses)

23. canīn   canon   cannon   canōn
    (shank of the horse's leg)

24. Bucephalus   Boucephalos   Bucephalos   Buccephalus
    (Alexander the Great's horse)

25. Prezhevalski's horse   Przhevalski's horse   Przhevolski's horse
    Przezhevalski's horse
    (endangered breed of wild Mongolian horse)

Alternative Words

a. nummna   numna   numnah   numnuh
   (pad beneath a saddle)

b. hackamoor   hackemoor   hackamore   hockamore
   (horse-breaking or -training bridle)

c. cavilry   cavallry   calvary   cavalry
   (military contingent mounted on horseback)

d. martingale   martengale   martengail   martingail
   (part of a horse's harness, a strap between the forelegs)

e. Pegassus   Peggassos   Pegasus   Pegosus
   (Muses' winged horse)

> *Before consulting the answers on page 305:*
> I think I spelled ____ words correctly on this test.
> (If your estimate is correct, add one point to your score.)

Hypochondriac

1. valatudinarian   valitudinarian   vallitudinarian   valetudinarian
   (sickly person; invalid)

2. impiteigo   impetaigo   impetigo   impetigoe
   (acute skin disease)

3. appoplexy   apoplexy   appoplexie   apoplexie
   (stroke)

4. lumbago   lummbago   lumbagoe   lombago
   (lower back or loin pain)

5. collitis   colitis   colitus   collytis
   (inflammation of the colon)

6. soriasis   psoriasis   psorriasis   psoriassis
   (chronic skin disease)

7. Kayopectate   Kayo-pectate   Kaopectate   Kaopecctate
   (brand of contra-diarrhea medicine)

8. *schadenfreude*   *schattenfreude*   *schatenfreude*   *schadenfreud*
   (pleasure in another's suffering)

9. seditive   sedative   sedditive   seddative
   (tranquilizing medication)

10. vacinator   vacsinator   vaccinater   vaccinator
    (one who inoculates against smallpox)

11. iatrogenic   yatrogenic   iattrigenic   yatrigenic
    (caused by a physician or a physician's treatment)

12. Breosci   Briosci   Brioschi   Brioscci
    (brand of antacid)

13. absesses   abscesses   abbscesses   abbsesses
    (pus-filled inflammations)

14. hemoroid   hemmorhoid   hemorrhoid   hemmorrhoid
    (anal swelling)

15. mygrain   migrain   migraine   meigrain
    (recurrent severe headache)

16. Robbatusin   Robitusin   Robitussin   Robytussin
    (cough syrup)

17. kwetch   kavech   kvech   kvetch
    (*Slang:* complain)

18. cephilalgia   sephilalgia   cephalalgia   cepholalgia
    (headache)

19. halucinate   haluccinate   hallucinate   halluccinate
    (to imagine perceptually or have visions)

20. proritis   pruritis   pruritus   proritus
    (itching)

21. cacheksy   cachecsy   cachexy   chachexy
    (wasting away)

22. rhumatism   rheumitism   rheumatism   rhumitism
    (muscle or joint disorder causing pain)

23. charlie horse   charley horse   charly horse   charleyhorse
    (painful cramp of a leg or arm muscle)

24. tissain   tisain   tisane   tissan
    (herbal tea as a medicinal infusion)

25. psychasommatic   psychosomatic   psychosomactic
    psychosomattic
    (relating to symptoms caused mentally or emotionally)

Alternative Words

a. constupation   constapation   constepation   constipation
   (abnormally infrequent defecation)

b. catar   cattarhe   catarrhe   catarrh
   (respiratory inflammation)

c. tonnsilitis   tonsilitus   tonsillitis   tonsilitis
   (inflammation of two lymphoid masses at the back of the throat)

d. sacroilliac   sacroileac   sacroiliac   sacroilleac
   (pelvic cartilage area)

e. chilblain   chilblaine   chillblaine   chillblane
   (swelling caused by cold)

> *Before consulting the answers on page 305:*
> I think I spelled _____ words correctly on this test.
> (If your estimate is correct, add one point to your score.)

Insects, Spiders, Ants, and Butterflies

1. tarrantula   tarantella   tarantula   tarrantulla
(large hairy spider)

2. proboscis   probosscis   proboskis   probosciss
(protruding mouth part)

3. mantice   mantis   mantace   mantiss
(predatory insect with raised forelegs bent as if kneeling)

4. scarrab   scarab   scarabe   skarab
(beetle once held sacred by the Egyptians)

5. afid   aphid   aphed   affid
(tiny sap-sucking pest of fruit trees and vegetable crops)

6. murmicophile   myrmecophile   murmecophile
myrmicophile
(insect sharing an ant's nest)

7. spineret   spinneret   spinnerette   spinerrette
(spider's or larva's spinning organ)

8. vespid   vaespid   vesped   vespide
(wasp)

9. ceccropia moth   secropia moth   cicropia moth
cecropia moth
(large North American silkworm moth)

10. drasaphila   drasophila   drosophila   drossophila
(genus of fly)

11. cockchaffer   cockchafer   cockchaefer   cockchefer
(type of beetle)

12. ichnumon fly   ichnoumon fly   ichneumon fly
ichnuemon fly
(wasplike parasite of caterpillars)

13. mandibel   mandibal   mandible   mandable
(jawlike mouth part)

14. choleopteron   coleopteron   coleopteran   choleopteran
(beetle)

15. amophila   emophila   ammophila   amaphila
(sand wasp)

16. forresy   phoresy   phorasy   fourresy
(nonparasitic "carrying" relationship between two insects)

17. piralid   pirallid   pyralid   pyralyd
    (slender-bodied moth)

18. cades fly   cadis fly   kadis fly   caddis fly
    (aquatic, mothlike insect)

19. whirligig beetle   whirlygig beetle   whirleygig beetle
     whirigigg beetle
    (aquatic beetle that circles rapidly on the surface)

20. eo moth   io moth   eau moth   iogh moth
    (brilliant yellow moth with pink and bluish spots)

21. fritillary   frytillary   frittilary   frittillary
    (orange-brown butterfly)

22. grylloblattid   grilloblatid   griloblatid   gryloblatid
    (wingless, eyeless mountain insect living under stones)

23. imagos   immagos   immagoes   imagoes
    (adult insects)

24. bottefly   bottfly   botfly   battfly
    (fly with larvae that are skin parasites)

25. curcullio   curculio   curkulio   currcullio
    (fruit-feeding weevil)

Alternative Words

a. dinergate   dinnergate   dynergate   dynorgate
    (soldier ant)

b. sirphid   surphid   serphid   syrphid
    (beelike or wasplike nectar-feeding fly)

c. pismire   pysmire   pissmire   pismyre
    (ant)

d. leppidopter   lepidoptor   leppidoptor   lepidopter
    (butterfly or moth)

e. arrachnid   arachnid   aracnid   arracnid
    (any of a class including spiders, ticks, mites, and scorpions)

> *Before consulting the answers on page 306:*
> I think I spelled ____ words correctly on this test.
> (If your estimate is correct, add one point to your score.)

Law

1. subpenaed   suppenaed   subpoenaed   subpaenaed
    (summoned as evidence or to be a witness)

2. lex taleonis   lex talleonis   lex talionis   lex tallionis
    (eye for an eye)

3. courtasy   curtesy   courtesy   curtesey
    (husband's potential interest in wife's real estate when they have a chid)

4. femme covert   femme couvert   feme covert   femme coverte
    (married woman)

5. allange   allonge   alonge   alange
    (supplementary paper for recording additional endorsements)

6. stari deceasis   stare decisis   stare decysis   stari desesis
    (doctrine affirming principles involved in a previous decision)

7. nolli proseque   nolle prosequi   nolle proseque
    nolli prosequi
    (assertion that prosecutor or plaintiff will proceed no further)

8. emphyteusis   emphitusis   emphiteusis   emphitousis
    (Roman and civil law agricultural contract)

9. dissiezine   dissiezin   disseizine   disseizan
    (depriving of possession of land)

10. megne   mesne   meane   mene
    (intermediate or intervening)

11. champertey   champertie   champorty   champerty
    (sharing in litigation proceeds by a supporter)

12. sciantur   scientur   scienter   sciuntur
    (knowingly, willfully)

13. barratry   baratry   baratrie   barrattry
    (stirring up lawsuits)

14. deforceunt   deforsiant   deforciant   deforseant
    (one who wrongfully withholds land from the owner)

15. noncupitive   noncupative   nuncupative   noncuppitive
    (oral, not written)

16. promisor   promissor   promisser   promisceur
    (one who makes a promise)

17. misprysion   misprizion   misprision   misprizon
    (contempt or scorn)

18. cie pre   cy pres   cie pres   cy pre
    (as near as possible)

19. esstopal   esstoppel   estoppel   estoppell
    (prevention of a claim inconsistent with one previously taken)

20. certiarari   certorari   certiorrari   certiorari
    (record summoning writ from a superior court)

21. supersedeus   supercedeas   supersedeas   supercedeus
    (writ ordering a stoppage or suspension)

22. bailor   bailer   baler   baillor
    (one who delivers personal property in bailment)

23. eschete   escheat   escheate   eschiet
    (reverting of property to the state)

24. appelee   appellee   apellee   appelluy
    (defendant in an appeal proceeding)

25. ducis tecum   ducas tecum   duces tecum   ducis taecum
    (summons to appear with a particular document in court)

Alternative Words

a. remittitur   remittittor   remititor   remititur
    (remission of certain damages ruled to be excessive)

b. amicus curiae   amicas curie   amicas curiae   amicus curii
    (person invited to the court for advice)

c. leguleian   legullian   legulian   legulean
    (pettifogger)

d. nomolographer   nommalographer   nomilographer
      nomalographer
    (writer or maker of laws)

e. shreivalty   shrievvaltie   shrievallty   shrievalty
    (office of a sheriff)

> *Before consulting the answers on page 306:*
> I think I spelled _____ words correctly on this test.
> (If your estimate is correct, add one point to your score.)

Mathematics

1. absissa   abcissa   abscissa   abbscissa
   (x-coordinate of a point)

2. nilpotent   nihilpotent   nillpotent   nilpotant
   (equaling zero when raised to a certain power)

3. parallellapiped   parallelepiped   parallelapiped
   parallellepiped
   (type of prism with six faces)

4. googleplex   googelplex   googalplex   googolplex
   ($10^{10^{100}}$)

5. Fibbonacci numbers   Fibbanacci numbers   Fibonacci numbers
   Fibonaci numbers
   (sequence 1, 1, 2, 3, 5, 8 . . . : each term the sum of the two before)

6. addende   addand   addend   addund
   (one of a set of numbers to be added)

7. assymtote   asymptote   assimptote   asymptot
   (straight line approached by a given curve . . .)

8. steradean   sturadian   sterradian   steradian
   (solid angle at the center of a sphere . . .)

9. Riemanian geometry   Riemannian geometry
   Riemmanian geometry   Riemahnian geometry
   (branch of non-Euclidian geometry)

10. catinary   catennary   catinnary   catenary
    (curve of a chain hanging from two points not in same vertical line)

11. lyttuous   lituous   lytuus   lituus
    (trumpet-shaped plane curve)

12. duadnary   duodenary   duadenary   duadinary
    (duodecimal)

13. Meöbius strip   Mubius strip   Möbius strip   Moöbius strip
    (rectangular strip of paper with ends pasted together after half-twist)

14. escribe   ascribe   exscribe   acscribe
    (draw a circle outside a triangle and tangent to one side . . .)

15. colineation   colliniation   collineation   co-liniation
    (arrangements of points on a straight line)

16. Loboshevsky   Lobashevsky   Lobachevsky   Lobochevsky
    (Russian mathematician)

17. baricentric   barycentric   baracentric   barocentric
    (describing a coordinate system for an *n*-dimensional Euclidian space)

18. frustrum   phrustrum   frustrom   phrustrom
    (solid cone part left after top is cut off horizontally)

19. lochsodromic   loxodromic   loccsodromic   loxedromic
    (pertaining to rhumb lines)

20. nappe   napp   nap   mnap
    (one of two equal sections of a cone)

21. harvorsine   halvorsine   halversine   haversine
    (one half the versed sine of a given angle or arc)

22. sinusoidal   sinisoidal   sinesoidal   synusoidal
    (pertaining to a "$y = a \sin x$" curve)

23. dactilonomy   dactillonomy   dactylonomy   dactyllonomy
    (counting on one's fingers)

24. anulis   anulus   annulis   annulus
    (space between concentric circles on a plane)

25. Diaphanteen equation   Diophantine equation
    Diafantene equation   Diofantine equation
    (equation in which it is required to find all integral solutions)

Alternative Words

a. isagonal   isogonal   isaganal   isoganal
   (equal-angled)

b. allgorism   ahlgorism   algorism   algeurism
   (Arabic system of arithmetic: 1, 2, 3, etc.)

c. circumforential   circumferential   circumferrential
   circumforrential
   (pertaining to the periphery of a circle)

d. quinntic   quintic   quinttic   quinetic
   (polynomial equation of the fifth degree)

e. aliquot   aliquote   alliquot   alliquat
   (forming an exact proper divisor)

> *Before consulting the answers on page 306:*
> I think I spelled _____ words correctly on this test.
> (If your estimate is correct, add one point to your score.)

Medicine

1. Esculapius   Aesculapius   Aesculapeus   Aesculappius
   (Roman god of medicine and healing)

2. dispnea   dyspnea   dispnia   dyspnia
   (labored breathing)

3. kwashiorkor   kwoshiorkor   quashiorkor   kwasheorkor
   (children's malnutrition disease)

4. antiarhythmic   antiarrhythmic   antearrhythmic   antiarithmic
   (inhibiting or alleviating irregular heartbeat)

5. balottement   ballotement   balotement   ballottement
   (manual diagnostic technique to detect tumors)

6. sissarcosis   sysarcosis   syssarcosis   syssarkosis
   (bone attachment by means of muscles)

7. graaffian follicle   graafian follicle   graffian follicle
   graafean follicle
   (small ovarian vesicle with a developing ovum)

8. bilharziasis   billharziasis   bilhartziasis   bilharrziasis
   (schistomiasis)

9. pathogneumonic   pathognumonic   pathogmnemonic
   pathognomonic
   (characterizing a specific disease)

10. iatrigenicity   iatragenicity   iatrogenicity   iatrogynicity
    (phenomenon of imagined or doctor-induced illness)

11. cannula   kanula   canulla   cannulla
    (surgical metal tube)

12. ankleosis   ankelosis   ankylosis   ankkylosis
    (union of two or more bones)

13. cholycystectomy   cholicystectomy   cholecystectomy
    cholacystectomy
    (gallbladder removal)

14. mammilary   mammalary   mamimilary   mammillary
    (pertaining to a nipple or nipples)

15. eresypelas   erysipilas   erisypelas   erysipelas
    (infectious febrile streptococcal disease)

16. sphigmomannometer   sphygmomanometer   sphygmimanometer
    spigmimanometer
    (cufflike blood pressure measuring instrument)

17. pollagra   pelagra   polagra   pellagra
(niacin-deficiency disease)

18. tsuzugamushi fever   tsutsugamushi fever   tsuzougamushi fever
tsutsugumushi fever
(scrub typhus)

19. Freedman test   Friedman test   Friedmann test   Freedmann test
("rabbit test")

20. vulcelum   vulselum   vullsellum   vulsellum
(type of surgical forceps)

21. cachechsia   caccexia   cacchexia   cachexia
(emaciation)

22. bystory   bistory   bistoury   bystorry
(surgical knife)

23. ryovirus   riovirus   reohvirus   reovirus
(large virus family, including infantile gastroenteritis)

24. semmiologist   semeologist   semeiologist   semiologist
(practitioner in symptomatology)

25. calenture   calanture   callanture   callenture
(severe tropical fever)

Alternative Words

a. granuloma inguinal   granuloma inguinale   granulloma inguinal
granulloma inguinale
(venereal disease)

b. bisinosis   bysinosis   byssenosis   byssinosis
(brown lung)

c. iskemia   iscemia   ischemia   iscemea
(localized tissue anemia due to arterial obstruction)

d. affibrogenemia   afibrogenemia   afibroganemia   affibroganemia
(blood-clotting abnormality)

e. perulis   parullice   parulis   perullis
(gumboil)

> *Before consulting the answers on page 307:*
> I think I spelled _____ words correctly on this test.
> (If your estimate is correct, add one point to your score.)

Modern Authors

1. John Ashberry John Ashbury John Ashbery
   John Aschbury
   (poet, *Self-Portrait in a Convex Mirror*)

2. A. E. Houssman A. E. Housmann A. E. Housman
   A. E. Houseman
   (poet, "To an Athlete Dying Young")

3. Friedrich Dürrenmatt Friedrich Dürenmatt
   Friedrich Dürrenmat Friedrich Dürrennmat
   (dramatist, *The Visit*)

4. Seán O'Faeláin Seán O'Faoláin Seán O'Fáolin
   Seán O'Failáin
   (writer, *The Vanishing Hero*)

5. Muriel Roukeiser Muriel Rukeysor Muriel Rukeyser
   Muriel Rokeyser
   (poet, "Ajanta")

6. James Gould Cozzens James Gould Cousins
   James Gould Cozzins James Gould Cuzzens
   (novelist, *By Love Possessed*)

7. Nikos Kazenzakis Nikos Kazentzakis Nikos Kazantzakis
   Nikos Kazanzakis
   (novelist, *Zorba the Greek*)

8. Knut Hamson Knute Hamsun Knut Hamsun
   Knut Hammsen
   (novelist, Nobelist, *Growth of the Soil*)

9. Lawrence Ferlingeti Laurance Ferrlinghetti
   Lawrence Ferlinghetti Laurence Ferlinghetti
   (poet, "A Coney Island of the Mind")

10. Archibald Macleish Archibald McLeish Archibald McLiesh
    Archibald MacLeish
    (poet and dramatist, *J.B.*)

11. Dashiell Hammet Dashiel Hammett Dashiell Hammett
    Dashiell Hamett
    (novelist, *The Maltese Falcon*)

12. Pär F. Lagerkwist Pär F. Lagerkvist Pär F. Laggerkvist
    Pär F. Løgerkvist
    (novelist, Nobelist, *Barrabas*)

13. John Betgeman   John Betdgman   John Betjeman
    John Bettjeman
    (poet, *First and Last Loves*)

14. Eugene Ianesco   Eugene Eunesco   Eugene Ionesco
    Eugene Iannesco
    (dramatist, *The Bald Soprano*)

15. Jerzi Kosinsky   Jerzy Kosinski   Jerzy Kosinsky
    Jerzi Kosinski
    (novelist, *The Painted Bird*)

16. Isak Dinnisin   Isaak Dinesen   Isak Dinisin   Isak Dinesen
    (story writer, *Seven Gothic Tales*)

17. Theodore Reuthke   Theodore Rothke   Theodore Roethke
    Theodor Roethke
    (poet, *Words for the Wind*)

18. McKinley Kantor   Mackinlay Kantor   MacKinley Kanter
    MacKinlay Kantor
    (dramatist,*The Andersonville Trial*)

19. Salomon Rushdie   Salmon Rushdy   Salman Rushdie
    Saloman Rushdie
    (novelist, *The Satanic Verses*)

20. Donald Bartehlme   Donald Bartelme   Donald Barthelme
    Donald Barthellme
    (novelist, *Snow White*)

21. Mordecai Richtler   Mordecai Richler   Mordecai Richter
    Mordecai Richlor
    (novelist, *The Apprenticeship of Duddy Kravitz*)

22. Allan Drury   Alan Drury   Allen Drury   Alan Drurry
    (novelist, *Advise and Consent*)

23. Bernard Mallemud   Bernard Malamud   Bernard Malemud
    Bernard Mallamud
    (novelist, *The Natural*)

24. Luigi Pirandello   Luigi Pirendello   Luigi Pirendelo
    Luigi Pirrandello
    (dramatist, Nobelist, *Six Characters in Search of an Author*)

25. Gerhardt Hauptman   Gerhart Hauptmann   Gerhard Hauptman
    Gerhard Hauptmann
    (dramatist, Nobelist, *The Weavers*)

Alternative Words

a. Lawrence Durrel   Laurence Durrell   Laurence Durell
   Lawrence Durrell
   (novelist, *The Alexandria Quartet*)

b. Mark Connolly   Marc Connelly   Mark Connelly
   Marc Connolly
   (dramatist, *The Green Pastures*)

c. Max Bierbom   Max Beerbohm   Max Beerbomb
   Max Beerbom
   (novelist, *Zuleika Dobson*)

d. Gabriel García Marquese   Gabriel García Márquez
   Gabriel García Márques   Gabriel García Marcques
   (novelist, *One Hundred Years of Solitude*)

e. Kurt Vonnagutt   Kurt Vonegut   Kurt Vonnegut
   Kurt Vonnegutt
   (novelist, *Slaughterhouse Five*)

Before consulting the answers on page 307:
I think I spelled _____ words correctly on this test.
(If your estimate is correct, add one point to your score.)

Money and Currencies

1. noumismatics   nummismatics   numismatics   noomismatics
   (study of coins, paper money, etc.)

2. zlotie   czloty   czlotie   zloty
   (currency of Poland)

3. specie   speccie   specey   spiecie
   (money in the form of coins)

4. do-ray-mee   do-re-me   doe-ray-mi   do-re-mi
   (slang for money)

5. ducat   duccat   duckat   duket
   (old European gold coin)

6. markka   markah   marka   marcka
   (currency of Finland)

7. fourint   forint   forrint   forinnt
   (currency of Hungary)

8. bimettallism   bimetalism   bymetalism   bimetallism
   (two-metal monetary standard)

9. cruzzero   cruzero   cruzeiro   cruzairo
   (currency of Brazil)

10. koruna   coruna   korunna   corunna
    (currency of Czechoslovakia)

11. ringgit   ringit   rinngit   ringat
    (currency of Malaysia)

12. poseta   paseta   peseta   pesetta
    (currency of Spain)

13. eirire   eirir   eyrir   irir
    (currency of Iceland)

14. port-monai   porte-monnaie   port-monnaie   porte-monaie
    (small purse)

15. dirham   durhum   durham   dirhum
    (currency of Morocco)

16. florrin   florine   florin   florinn
    (currency of the Netherlands; gulden; guilder)

17. ryhal   rial   ryale   riall
    (currency of Iran)

18. numery   numory   nummory   nummary
    (pertaining to money or coins)

19. Croesus   Croisus   Croissus   Croessus
    (extremely rich man)

20. cambestry   kambistry   cambistry   kambestry
    (science of monetary exchange)

21. gerdon   gurdon   guerdon   gurrdon
    (recompense or reward)

22. Onassis   Onnassus   Onnasis   Onassos
    (Greek shipping-magnate millionaire)

23. dynar   denare   dinarr   dinar
    (currency of Yugoslavia)

24. grochen   groshen   groschen   grosschen
    (currency of Austria)
25. annuit captus   annuit coptus   annuit coeptus
    annuit coeptis
    (words on dollar bill)

Alternative Words

a. ruppee   rupee   rupey   rupi
   (currency of India)
b. annutocism   annatocism   anatocism   anoticism
   (compound interest)
c. burser   bursar   bursor   burseur
   (financial officer or treasurer)
d. impecunious   impeccuneous   impicunious   impeccunious
   (penniless)
e. solacium   solatium   sollacium   sollatium
   (financial compensation for suffering)

Before consulting the answers on page 307:
I think I spelled _____ words correctly on this test.
(If your estimate is correct, add one point to your score.)

Mountains and Mountaineering

1. bergshrunde   bergschrund   berggschrund   burgschrunde
   (crevasse)
2. insulberg   insilberg   inselberg   insalberg
   (solitary hill or mountain on a plain; monadnock)
3. Kilimanjaro   Killimanjaro   Killimunjaro   Kilimonjaro
   (Africa's highest mountain)
4. verglace   verglass   verglas   verglaice
   (thin ice coating; glaze ice)

5. absyle   absile   abseil   absiel
   (descent method by means of a rope looped or fastened above)

6. carabiner   carrabinor   carabinner   carabinnor
   (ring for fastening ropes)

7. arrêt   arêtte   arêtt   arête
   (rugged glacial mountain ridge)

8. névée   névé   nivée   nivé
   (high-altitude snow that becomes glacial ice)

9. aigille   aiguille   aigeul   aigeulle
   (needlelike rock or peak)

10. glisade   glysade   glisaad   glissade
    (gliding descent)

11. crammpon   cramponn   crampon   crammponn
    (spiked boot plate)

12. massiffe   massif   masif   masiff
    (part of a mountain range)

13. rapell   rappel   rappell   rapel
    (gradual steep descent by means of a rope wrapped around body)

14. cordillera   cordalerra   cordilerra   cordallera
    (system of parallel mountain chains)

15. hypsography   hyppsography   hipsography   hipssography
    (measurement of heights on earth)

16. chockstone   chokkstone   chokstone   chakstone
    (wedged rock mass in a mountain chimney)

17. prussick knot   prusick knot   prusik knot   prussik knot
    (type of knot used in rescues)

18. screy   scree   skree   skrey
    (mountainside detritus)

19. Arrarat   Araratt   Arrarrat   Ararat
    (Turkey's highest mountain)

20. Pyronees   Pyrronees   Pyrenees   Pyrrenees
    (mountains between France and Spain)

21. Kanchinjunga   Kangchenjunga   Kangchinjunga
    Kanjchenjunga
    (in Nepal, third highest mountain in the world)

22. Aconcagua   Aconncagua   Aconcogua   Acconcagua
    (in Argentina, highest peak in the Western Hemisphere)
23. accrophobia   agrophobia   akrophobia   acrophobia
    (dread of heights)
24. Lohtse   Lohtsi   Lhotsi   Lhotse
    (in the Himalayas, fourth highest peak in the world)
25. Mount Rainer   Mount Rainier   Mount Raineer
    Mount Rainire
    (peak in Washington)

Alternative Words

a. sarac   serac   sarrac   serrac
    (jagged mass of glacial ice)
b. Ruwenzori   Roowenzoori   Ruwennzori   Rowenzori
    (group of African mountains)
c. Nunga Purbat   Nanga Parbat   Nunga Parbat   Nanga Purbat
    (in the Himalayas, sixth highest peak in the world)
d. morane   morrain   moraine   muraine
    (deposit of glacial material)
e. kletterschuh   clettershoe   kletorschuh   klettershoe
    (lightweight boot)

> *Before consulting the answers on page 307:*
> I think I spelled ____ words correctly on this test.
> (If your estimate is correct, add one point to your score.)

Movie People

1. Darryl Hanna   Daryl Hannah   Darryle Hannah
    Daryl Hanna
    (actress)
2. Martin Scorsese   Martin Scorcese   Martin Scorscese
    Martin Scorrcese
    (director)

3. Anne Margaret   Ann-Margret   Anne-Margrit
   Ann Margret
   (actress)

4. Isabela Rosellini   Isabella Rossellini   Isabela Rosselini
   Isabella Rosellini
   (actress)

5. Kris Kristoforsen   Kris Kristoferrsen   Kris Kristofforsen
   Kris Kristofferson
   (actor)

6. Everett Sloane   Everet Sloane   Everett Sloan   Everet Sloan
   (actor)

7. J. Carole Naish   J. Carroll Naish   J. Caroll Naish
   J. Carrol Naish
   (actor)

8. Dmitri Tiomkin   Dimitri Tiomkin   Dmitri Tiomken
   Dimitri Tiomken
   (composer)

9. Malcolm McDowell   Malcom McDowell   Malcolm MacDowell
   Malcolm McDowel
   (actor)

10. Steven Speilberg   Stephen Spielberg   Steven Spielberg
    Steven Spielburg
    (director)

11. Bernard Herrmann   Bernard Herman   Bernard Hermann
    Bernard Herrman
    (composer)

12. Dom De Louise   Dom DeLouis   Dom De Luise
    Dom DeLuise
    (actor)

13. Dino Di Laurentis   Dino DeLaurentiis   Dino De Laurentiis
    Dino DiLaurentis
    (producer)

14. Claude La Louch   Claude Le Louche   Claude Lalouch
    Claude Lelouch
    (director)

15. Nicholas Roege   Nicolas Roge   Nicholas Roeg
    Nicolas Roeg
    (director)

16. Donald Pleasanse   Donald Pleasance   Donald Pleasence
    Donald Pleasense
    (actor)

17. Ronald Coleman   Ronald Colman   Ronald Colmann
    Ronald Colemann
    (actor)

18. Franco Zefirelli   Franco Zefferelli   Franco Zeferelli
    Franco Zeffirelli
    (director)

19. Heddi LeMar   Heddy LeMar   Hedy Lamarr
    Hedy La Marr
    (actress)

20. Rossanna Arquet   Rosanna Arquette   Rosannah Arquette
    Rossana Arquette
    (actress)

21. Vitorio De Sica   Vittorio De Sica   Vittorio Di Sica
    Vitorio Da Sica
    (director and actor)

22. Brian Dennehy   Brian Denehy   Brian Denehey
    Brian Denahey
    (actor)

23. Hattie MacDaniel   Hatti McDaniel   Hattie McDaniel
    Hatty McDaniel
    (actress)

24. Jeanni Craine   Jeanne Crain   Jeanny Crain   Jeane Crane
    (actress)

25. Rick Schroeder   Rick Schroder   Rick Shroder
    Rick Shroeder
    (actor)

Alternative Words

a. Freddie Bartholemew   Freddie Bartholomew
   Freddie Bartholemue   Freddie Bartholamew
   (actor)

b. John Voigt   John Voight   Jon Voigt   Jon Voight
   (actor)

c. Simone Signoret   Simone Signorette   Simon Sinoret
    Simone Signorete
    (actress)

d. Gina Lollabriggida   Gina Lollobrigida   Gina Lollabrigida
    Gina Lollibrigida
    (actress)

e. Deanna Durban   Diana Durbin   Deana Durbin
    Deanna Durbin
    (actress)

Before consulting the answers on page 308:
I think I spelled _____ words correctly on this test.
(If your estimate is correct, add one point to your score.)

Mythology

1. Charybdiss   Charybdis   Charybbdis   Charibdis
    (mythological whirlpool)

2. Actaian   Actaeon   Actaean   Acteian
    (hunter changed by Diana into a stag)

3. Hygia   Hygea   Hygeia   Hygaia
    (Greek goddess of health)

4. Nausika   Nausica   Nausicca   Nausicaa
    (maiden who befriends Odysseus)

5. Cimmarion   Cimmerian   Cimmereon   Cimmerion
    (pertaining to a people living in perpetual darkness)

6. Rhadimanthis   Rhadymanthis   Rhadamanthus
    Rhadamanthis
    (Underworld judge)

7. Dionisus   Dinyssus   Dionysis   Dionysus
    (Bacchus)

8. Deucalion   Deucallion   Deucallian   Ducalion
    (son of Prometheus who survived the Deluge)

9. Danëae   Danai   Danaë   Danae
    (mother of Perseus)

10. Tiresias   Teresius   Tiresius   Theresius
    (blind Theban seer changed for a while into a woman)

11. Hephestos   Haephestus   Hephaistos   Hephaestus
(Greek god of fire and metalworking)

12. Bellerofon   Bellerophon   Belerophon   Bellarophon
(Corinthian slayer of the Chimera)

13. Agamemnon   Agammemnon   Aggamemnon   Agomemnon
(Greek leader at Troy later murdered by Clytemnestra)

14. Laaocoön   Laocouön   Laocöon   Laoccöon
(priest at Troy killed with his two sons by two serpents)

15. Phaëton   Phaëtton   Phaiton   Phaëthon
(son of Helios who drove chariot of the sun too close to earth)

16. Chorybantes   Coribants   Corybantes   Chorybbantes
(minor divinities of revelry)

17. Sarpadon   Sarpidon   Sarpedon   Sarpodon
(prince killed by Patroclus at Troy)

18. Aries   Arys   Ares   Arries
(Greek god of war)

19. Cybill   Cybile   Cybele   Cybille
(Greek goddess of nature)

20. Minotaur   Minnotaur   Minotaure   Minotor
(Labyrinth monster with a bull's head)

21. Anchyses   Anchises   Ancheises   Ankises
(Aeneas's father)

22. Menalaus   Menaleas   Meneleas   Meneleus
(husband of Helen)

23. Euridice   Eurydice   Euridyce   Eurydyce
(wife of Orpheus)

24. cockatris   cockatrice   cockatryx   cockatrix
(monster with a deadly glance)

25. Iphiginia   Iphigenia   Iphigeneia   Iphigenaia
(sister of Orestes and Elektra rescued as a sacrificial victim)

Alternative Words

a. Atlantaa   Atalanta   Attalanta   Atallanta
(swift huntress who ran in a footrace against suitors)

b. Mommis   Momas   Momus   Momis
(god of ridicule)

c. Galatea   Galaatia   Gallatea   Galaetia
   (Pygmalion's statue brought to life by Aphrodite)

d. Euterpe   Euturpe   Euterpy   Euturpy
   (muse of music and lyric poetry)

e. Dioscurai   Diascuri   Dioscurri   Dioscuri
   (Castor and Pollux, twin sons of Zeus and Leda)

Before consulting the answers on page 308:
I think I spelled _____ words correctly on this test.
(If your estimate is correct, add one point to your score.)

Native Americans (Indians)

1. Chipowa   Chipewa   Chippua   Chippewa
   (Great Lakes-and-west tribe; Ojibwa)

2. wickyup   wickiup   wicciup   wikiup
   (hut of mats or brushwood)

3. Mescalero   Meskilero   Mesquilero   Mesqualero
   (Apache group)

4. Sacajawia   Sachajawea   Sachajawia   Sacajawea
   (Shoshone female guide on Lewis and Clark expedition)

5. Tllingit   Tlinggit   Tlingit   Tlinngit
   (Alaskan people)

6. Tuscarora   Tuskarora   Tuskiroora   Tuscarura
   (people of North Carolina, later of New York and Ontario)

7. hogan   hoegan   hogun   howgan
   (Navajo mud-covered log or stick dwelling)

8. Lenni Lennape   Leni Lenape   Lenni Lenape
   Leni Lennape
   (Delaware group)

9. Pohatan   Pohattan   Powhattan   Powhatan
   (Algonquian people of Virginia)

10. Nez Persé   Nes Percé   Nez Percé   Nez Percée
    (Sahaptin people)

11. Tacumsah   Tecumsah   Tecumseh   Tecummseh
    (Shawnee chief)

12. Penabscott   Penabscot   Penobscot   Penobscott
    (Maine people)
13. katchine   kachina   kochina   kacheena
    (Hopi doll)
14. Kwakiutl   Kwokiutl   Kwokkiutl   Kwakkiutl
    (British Columbian people)
15. travoi   travois   travoise   travvois
    (A-shaped sledge drawn by an animal)
16. Muskhogean   Muskhogian   Muskogian   Musquogian
    (Indian language family of southeastern United States)
17. Onneida   Onaeda   Oniaida   Oneida
    (Iroquois people)
18. Passamaquotte   Passamaquoddy   Passamaquotty
       Passamaquodde
    (people of Maine and New Brunswick)
19. berdash   burdash   berdache   berdach
    (in some tribes, man who adopts women's dress and role)
20. Keowa   Kieowa   Kiowa   Keeowa
    (Plains people of the southwestern United States)
21. Fort Belknap Reservation   Fort Bellnap Reservation
       Fort Belnappe Reservation   Fort Bellknapp Reservation
    (reservation in Montana)
22. kivvah   kiva   kivva   kieva
    (Pueblo partly underground structure for men's activities)
23. Shoshanian   Shoshanean   Shoshonian   Shoshonean
    (language group including Hopi)
24. Peute   Peaute   Piute   Paiute
    (Uto-Aztecan family of the Far West)
25. Zunni   Zune   Zuni   Zunne
    (western New Mexico group)

Alternative Words

a. Aruwak   Arawak   Ariwak   Aruwaak
   (people of northeastern South America)
b. Kimosabi   Kemoesabe   Kemo Sabe   Kimo Sabi
   ("Faithful Friend": the Lone Ranger to Tonto)

c. Kikapoo   Kickapoo   Kikkapoo   Kickapou
(people of Wisconsin)

d. Cochese   Chochis   Cochees   Cochise
(chief of the Chiricahua Apaches)

e. Iraqoian   Iroquoian   Iroquyan   Iroquian
(language family including Cherokee and Mohawk)

Before consulting the answers on page 308:
I think I spelled _____ words correctly on this test.
(If your estimate is correct, add one point to your score.)

Opera

1. reggisseur   regissor   reggiseur   regisseur
(staging director)

2. Sparrafucille   Sparafuccile   Sparafucile   Sparaffucille
(character in *Rigoletto*)

3. *Così Fan Tuti*   *Cosè Fan Tutte*   *Così van Tutti*   *Così Fan Tutte*
(opera by Mozart)

4. fioretura   fioratura   fioritura   fiorratura
(melodic ornamentation)

5. sprecc'stimme   sprechstima   sprechstimme   strechstimma
(vocalizing in a way halfway between speaking and singing)

6. Bepe   Beppi   Beppe   Beppei
(character in *Pagliacci*)

7. portamento   portimento   porte-mento   portomento
(smooth transition from one pitch or tone to another)

8. Schaunard   Shaunerd   Shaunard   Schaunord
(character in *La Bohème*)

9. *Hérodiad*   *Hérodiode*   *Hérodiade*   *Hérodead*
(opera by Massenet)

10. compromario   comprimario   kompremario   komprimario
(company singer of secondary roles)

11. janizary music   janisary music   janissary music
     jannissary music
(imitative percussive and bell-like "Turkish" music)

12. brydnese   brindese   brindisi   brinndese
    (drinking or toasting song)

13. tesatura   tessittura   tessatura   tessitura
    (average vocal range of a piece)

14. cabaletta   cabbaleta   cabaleta   cabballetta
    (short, simple aria).

15. *Cavalleria Rusticana*   *Cavaleria Rusticanna*   *Cavelleria Rusticana*
    Cavallerria Rusticana
    (opera by Mascagni)

16. commedia dl'arte   comedia dell'arte   commedia dell'arte
    comedia del'arte
    (traditional Italian comedy with stock characters)

17. ritornelo   rittornelo   ritornello   retornello
    (instrumental aria-closing passage)

18. Challiapen   Challiapin   Chaliapin   Chaliapine
    (Russian bass)

19. coloraturra   colorotura   coloritura   coloratura
    (soprano specializing in dazzling virtuoso passages)

20. verismo   verizmo   verrismo   veresmo
    (use of everyday realism in opera)

21. gibus   gibbus   gibus   jibus
    (opera hat)

22. Michaëla   Michaëlla   Micaëla   Miccaëla
    (character in *Carmen*)

23. rataplan   rattiplan   rattaplan   rateplan
    (describing the use of drumming, as in a martial scene)

24. Galicurci   Gallicurci   Galli-Curci   Galli-Curcci
    (Italian soprano)

25. Papogueno   Papageno   Pappogueno   Papogeno
    (character in *Die Zauberflöte*)

Alternative Words

a. cavatina   cavotina   cavattina   cavatinna
   (simple operatic solo)

b. soubret   soubrette   subrette   soubrett
   (lady's maid character, often a flirt)

c. *Peléas et Mélisande*   *Pelléas et Mélisand*   *Pelléas et Méllisande*
   Pelléas et Mélisande
   (opera by Debussy)

d. Jacquenno   Jacqueno   Jacquino   Jacquinno
   (character in *Fidelio*)

e. solfège   solfègge   sollfège   sollfègge
   (vocal syllabic exercise)

> *Before consulting the answers on page 309:*
> I think I spelled _____ words correctly on this test.
> (If your estimate is correct, add one point to your score.)

Philosophy and Logic

1. escatology   eschatology   eskatology   aeschatology
   (philosophy of the final matters of life or afterlife)

2. synchretism   syncrotism   syncretism   synchrytism
   (attempt to reconcile differing beliefs or philosophies)

3. Cyrrenaeic   Cyrennaic   Cyrenaeic   Cyrenaic
   (pertaining to Aristippus's philosophy that pleasure is life's aim)

4. ignoratio elenchi   ignoratio ellenchi   ignoratio ilenchae
   ignoratio ilenchi
   (fallacy of proving what is irrelevant)

5. heceity   hecciety   haecceity   hechceity
   (thisness, individuality)

6. Boithius   Boitheus   Boetheus   Boethius
   (Roman philosopher)

7. hylamorphism   hylimorphism   hylomorphism
   hylemorphism
   (theory that physical objects are governed by two principles)

8. Carniadus   Carniadis   Carneadis   Carneades
   (Greek philosopher)

9. dystileological   disteleological   dysteleological
   dysteliological
   (presuming no final cause or purpose in life)

10. casouistry   cassuistry   casuistry   casuistery
    (inquiry into right and wrong, sometimes sophistically)

11. ergetism   ergitism   ergotism   ergottism
(logical or sophistical reasoning)

12. theodecy   theodisy   theodesy   theodicy
(vindication of God's justice in allowing existence of evil)

13. Nietschean   Nietzschean   Nietzschian   Nietschian
(pertaining to the German philosopher)

14. asceity   asseity   aseity   acceity
(self-originating existence)

15. numenon   nummenon   noumenon   nouminon
(object as a nonexperiential reality, opposed to a phenomenon)

16. Ockham's razor   Ockam's razor   Ocham's razor
Okham's razor
(principle that explanations should not be unduly complicated)

17. a posteriari   a postoriari   a posteriori   a posterriari
(deriving a principle from the particular or actual)

18. Maimonides   Maimonnides   Meimonides   Maimanides
(Jewish scholastic philosopher)

19. syncategarematic   syncatigorematic   syncategorematic
syncategorimatic
(pertaining to a word that is not an independent term, such as *all*)

20. enthememe   enthymeme   enthymneme   enthymime
(syllogism with a premise or conclusion implicit, not expressed)

21. Eliatic   Elliatic   Eleatic   Elleatic
(pertaining to Parmenides' phenomenalistic philosophy)

22. Pyrrhenism   Pyrenism   Pyrenism   Pyrrhonism
(extreme skepticism)

23. Fichtean   Fichttian   Fichtian   Fichktian
(pertaining to the German philosopher)

24. zatetic   zitetic   zetetic   zytetic
(proceeding by inquiry)

25. Kierkagard   Kierkegard   Kierkegaard   Kierkegarrd
(Danish philosopher)

Alternative Words

a. Berkleyan   Barkeleyan   Berkelyan   Berkeleian
(pertaining to the English philosopher)

b. Plotinnus   Plotinus   Plautinus   Plauthinus
(Roman Egyptian-born philosopher)

c. apodyctic   apodichtic   apodeictic   appodictic
(demonstrably or provenly true)

d. eristic   erristic   aeristic   errhistic
(pertaining to disputation or controversy)

e. Comptism   Compteism   Comtism   Comteism
(positivism)

Before consulting the answers on page 309:
I think I spelled _____ words correctly on this test.
(If your estimate is correct, add one point to your score.)

Physics and Electricity

1. entholpy   enthelpy   enthalpy   enthallpy
(quantity in a thermodynamic system)

2. manometer   minnometer   minometer   menometer
(instrument to detect stray radiation)

3. barretter   barretor   barettor   barrettor
(early type of radio detector)

4. adiabatic   addiabatic   adyabatic   adiabattic
(without gaining or losing heat)

5. cryogeny   criogeny   cryogony   cryogyny
(extremely low temperature physics)

6. pwos   pwoz   pois   poise
(centimeter-gram-second unit of viscosity)

7. orsted   oersted   errsted   orrsted
(centimeter-gram-second unit of magnetic intensity)

8. abhmo   abmoe   abmho   abmoh
(centimeter-gram-second unit of conductance)

9. sollenoid   solinoid   sollinoid   solenoid
(electrical conductor wound as a helix with small pitch)

10. sher modulus   scher modulus   shear modulus
     schir modulus
     (coefficient of elasticity)

11. debbe   dibye   debye   debie
     (measurement unit for electric dipole moment)

12. Avagadro's law   Avvagadro's law   Avoggadro's law
     Avogadro's law
     (gas volumes at the same temperature and pressure have the same number
       of molecules)

13. Kleistron   Klystron   Klistron   Klysstron
     (brand name for a type of vacuum tube)

14. capillarity   capellarity   capilarity   cappillarity
     (effect on a liquid's surface by contact with a solid)

15. brehmstrahlung   bremmstrahlung   bremsstrahlung
     bremmstrallung
     (radiation emitted by a charged particle during acceleration)

16. ferronickel   feronickel   ferrinickel   ferinickel
     (iron alloy)

17. skweging   squegging   skwegging   squeging
     (producing an oscillating output as an electronic circuit or component)

18. actonism   achtinism   aktinism   actinism
     (chemical-change property of radiant energy)

19. shleeren   schleeren   schlieren   schlearen
     (streaks in a turbulent, transparent fluid)

20. Dewar vessel   Dewer vessel   Deworr vessel   Dieuwar vessel
     (thermos-type, temperature-maintaining flask)

21. Hevyside layer   Heaviside layer   Heavyside layer
     Hevvyside layer
     (E layer, ionospheric layer sixty to seventy-five miles up)

22. stellarater   stellarator   stellorator   stelerator
     (plasma-physics device using magnetic fields)

23. rhentgenopaque   renntgenopaque   roentgenopaque
     reontgenopaque
     (not susceptible to X rays)

24. collimator   columator   colimator   colimater
     (device producing a parallel-path particle beam)

25. K-on   kaon   kaeon   kayon
     (meson with strangeness -1 and positive or zero electric charge)

Alternative Words

a. Plank's constant   Planckk's constant   Planck's constant
   Plannck's constant
   (fundamental constant of quantum mechanics)

b. degause   digaus   degauss   degausse
   (to demagnetize)

c. piccofarod   picofarrad   picoferad   picofarad
   (one trillionth of a unit of capacitance)

d. Leiden jar   Lyden jar   Leidan jar   Leyden jar
   (electric-charge storage device)

e. histerisis   hysterisis   histeresis   hysteresis
   (response lag by a body reacting to magnetic forces)

> *Before consulting the answers on page 309:*
> I think I spelled _____ words correctly on this test.
> (If your estimate is correct, add one point to your score.)

Political Science

1. autarchy   autarrky   autarky   autarche
   (economic self-sufficiency)

2. Stakhonnovite   Stakhonovite   Stakhanovite   Stachanovite
   (exemplary Soviet worker)

3. Kumingtang   Khumintang   Koumintang   Kuomintang
   (Chinese party founded chiefly by Sun Yat-sen)

4. resorgimento   resurgimento   risorgimento   resorggimento
   (political resurgence or rebirth)

5. Kulturkamf   Kultorkampf   Kulturkampfe   Kulturkampf
   (conflict between the state and religious authority)

6. dictat   diktat   diktate   diktatte
   (harsh settlement imposed on a defeated country)

7. apparatchik   apparachik   apparachic   apparatchic
   (member of a Communist power structure)

8. suffragettism   suffragetism   sufragetism   suffragetteism
   (militant belief in women's voting rights)

9. entante cordiale   entente cordiale   entent cordial
     entent cordiale
     (friendly understanding between countries)

10. Tamanyism   Tammanyism   Tammanism   Tamannyism
     (municipal political corruption)

11. suserainty   suzerainty   suzorainty   suzeranty
     (sovereignty)

12. plebiscite   plebbiscite   plaebiscite   plebecite
     (direct public vote on a pertinent issue)

13. plenapotentiary   plenipotentiary   plenopotentiary
     plenepotentiary
     (having full authority or power)

14. ad baculum   ad bacalum   ad bacculum   ad bacallum
     (describing an argument using threat or intimidation)

15. Knaeset   Kneset   Knesset   Knessett
     (Israel's parliament)

16. Falangist   Phalangist   Falangeist   Phalangeist
     (member of a Spanish fascist party disbanded in 1977)

17. attantat   attentat   atentat   attentate
     (attempted act of political violence)

18. mari clausam   mare clausam   mare clausum   mara clausum
     (body of water under a country's jurisdiction)

19. sanscullotteism   sanscullotism   sansculottism   sans-culottism
     (revolutionary beliefs)

20. ultra viris   ultra viras   ultra vires   ultra virus
     (beyond legal authority or power)

21. Blankism   Blannkism   Blanquism   Blancquism
     (socialist belief that the workers must seize power immediately)

22. satiagraha   satyagraha   sateyagraha   sathyagraha
     (Gandhi's policy of passive resistance)

23. posse commitatus   possi commitatus   posse comitatus
     posse cometatus
     (body of citizenry called upon to help keep the peace)

24. revančist   revanshist   revanchiste   revanchist
     (advocate of regaining territory once held but now lost)

25. obblast   oblast   obelast   obolast
     (Soviet administrative division)

Alternative Words

a. hejemony   hegemony   hegimony   hedgimony
    (predominance)

b. Machiavellism   Machiavelism   Macchiavellism
    Macchiavelism
    (belief in or practice of amoral political guile)

c. bycammeral   bicammeral   bicameral   bicammoral
    (having two parliamentary houses)

d. annschlus   anshluss   anschlusse   anschluss
    (1938 union of Germany and Austria)

e. jerrymander   gerymander   jerrimander   gerrymander
    (election-district division for partisan or party purposes)

> *Before consulting the answers on page 310:*
> I think I spelled _____ words correctly on this test.
> (If your estimate is correct, add one point to your score.)

Psychology

1. idetic   eidetic   idettic   eidettic
    (pertaining to vividly recalled visual images)

2. somatotonic   somitatonic   sometatonic   sommatatonic
    (extroverted and mesomorphic)

3. amygdala   amigdula   amygdula   ammygdula
    (brain part involved in emotions of fear and aggression)

4. Kraft-Ebing   Krafft-Ebing   Kraft-Ebbing   Krafft-Ebbing
    (German researcher in sexual pathology)

5. ologophrenia   olligophrenia   oligophrenia   auligophrenia
    (feeblemindedness)

6. encephylon   encepholon   encephelan   encephalon
    (the brain)

7. annankastic   anankastic   anoncastic   anaincastic
    (having a meticulously obsessive or compulsive personality)

8. hyperemnesia   hyperamnesia   hypermnesia   hypernesia
    (acutely good memory)

9. noreponephrine   noreppinephrine   norephinephrine
    norepinephrine
    (neurotransmitter; noradrenaline)

10. disthymic   dysthimic   dystheimic   dysthymic
    (despondent or depressed)

11. pyknik   pyknyk   picnyk   piknik
    (having a rotund body build)

12. Wexler-Belvue   Wechsler-Belview   Wexlor-Bellevue
    Wechsler-Bellevue
    (intelligence scale)

13. glucagen   glucagon   gluccagon   glucogon
    (hormone with effect opposite to that of insulin)

14. Zygarnic effect   Zygarnik effect   Zeigarnik effect
    Ziegarnik effect
    (interrupted tasks are better remembered)

15. telekinesis   telakinesis   telikinesis   tellokinesis
    (purported ability to move objects through mental powers)

16. Eysenck   Eysenkk   Eysenk   Eysennck
    (inventor of neuroticism-extroversion personality inventory)

17. acetylcholin   acetylcolene   acetylcholene   acetylcholine
    (ester involved in neural impulse transmission)

18. zenoglossy   zennoglossy   xenoglossy   xeniglossy
    (trancelike use of a foreign language)

19. haebaphrenia   hebiphrenia   hebephrenia   hebaphrenia
    (type of schizophrenic reaction)

20. dysperunia   dyspareunia   dysporeunia   dyspereunia
    (painful sexual intercourse)

21. Ebinghouse law   Ebinghaus law   Ebbinghaus law
    Ebbinghouse law
    (increased material to be learned demands disproportionately more time)

22. allgolania   algolania   algolannia   algolagnia
    (sexual pleasure from inflicting or suffering pain)

23. psychogoguey   psychogogey   psychagogy   psychegogy
    (therapeutic guidance toward worthy life goals)

24. ionism   eonism   eyonism   iannism
    (adoption of feminine dress and mannerisms by a male)

25. cattamnesis   catamnisis   catymnesis   catamnesis
    (patient's follow-up medical history)

Alternative Words

a. erethism   erythism   erothism   erithism
   (inordinate physical irritability or responsiveness)

b. Bobbinski reflex   Babinski reflex   Babinnski reflex
   Bobinski reflex
   (toe reflex indicative of possible central nervous system damage)

c. hipnogogic   hypnogogique   hypnagogic   hypnigogic
   (denoting the period between wakefulness and sleep)

d. abeyance   abbyence   abience   abbiance
   (tendency to withdraw from a stimulus object)

e. ephasia   apphasia   aphasia   epphasia
   (impairment in power to use words)

Before consulting the answers on page 310:
I think I spelled _____ words correctly on this test.
(If your estimate is correct, add one point to your score.)

Religion

1. sotyriology   souteriology   sauteriology   soteriology
   (doctrine of salvation through Christ)

2. hagiology   hagyology   haggiology   haggyology
   (literature dealing with lives of saints)

3. Karaite   Karyte   Kariate   Karayte
   (adherent of Jewish sect rejecting the Talmud in favor of Bible)

4. theophany   theophony   theopheny   theophani
   (physical manifestation of God)

5. prosalyte   proselyte   prosalite   proselite
   (convert)

6. Upanishad   Upannishad   Uppanishad   Uphanishad
   (Hindu treatise)

7. chrisom   chrism   chrisum   krism
   (consecrated oil)

8. Eucaryst   Eucarist   Euchorist   Eucharist
   (Christian Holy Communion)

9. sabatarian   sabbitarian   sabbatarian   sabbotarian
    (strict observer of the sabbath)

10. abbacey   abbasy   abbosy   abbacy
    (rank or jurisdiction of a monastery superior)

11. simoney   simony   symony   seimony
    (profit made from dealing in sacred things)

12. theopnuste   theophnost   theopneust   theophneust
    (divinely inspired)

13. souty   sootie   suttee   suti
    (self-immolation by a Hindu widow)

14. opheolater   opheolator   ophiolator   ophiolater
    (snake worshiper)

15. Wycliffite   Wyklifite   Wicliffite   Wychlifite
    (follower of English religious reformer)

16. Homoyoosian   Homoioosian   Homoiousian   Homoioosean
    (member of early Christian party maintaining that essence of the Father
    and Son is similar but not the same)

17. Homoousian   Homoeousian   Homousian   Homooesian
    (member of early Christian party maintaining that essence of the Father
    and Son is the same)

18. appostacy   apostacy   apostasy   appostasy
    (desertion of one's religion)

19. Sosinean   Sosinnean   Socinean   Socinian
    (follower of an anti-Trinitarian Christianity)

20. Mishnuh   Mishnah   Mischna   Mischnuh
    (traditional Jewish doctrine or a rabbinical tenet)

21. antinomianism   antenomianism   antignomianism
    antegnomeanism
    (Christian belief that God's gift of grace through the gospels frees one
    from older Mosaic laws)

22. Mahaiana   Mahyanha   Mahayana   Mahayhana
    (sect of Buddhism)

23. keristic   kerystic   cheristic   chyristic
    (pertaining to preaching; homiletic)

24. Mennanite   Menonite   Mennonite   Meninite
    (Protestant sect noted for simple living and dress)

25. nulifidian   nolifidian   nollifidian   nullifidian
    (one lacking faith; skeptic)

Alternative Words

a. eskitology   escatology   eschatology   eskatology
(branch of theology dealing with final events in human history)

b. Sihkism   Sikkism   Sikhism   Sikkhism
(religion of a Hindu sect opposed to the caste system)

c. Cistursion   Cisturcian   Cistercian   Cisstercian
(member of a monastic order founded near Dijon, France)

d. infrilapsarianism   infrolapsarianism   infralapsarianism
infralappsarianism
(doctrine that after the Fall God decreed the election of some)

e. apotheosis   apothyosis   apathiosis   apothiocys
(person's becoming a god)

Before consulting the answers on page 310:
I think I spelled _____ words correctly on this test.
(If your estimate is correct, add one point to your score.)

Sociology

1. misscegination   mysegenation   miscegenation
missegenation
(marriage between people of different races)

2. anthropophegy   anthropophygy   anthropophagy
anthropophogy
(cannibalism)

3. residivism   rescidivism   recidivism   residdivism
(relapsing into criminal activity)

4. levorate   levvirate   leverate   levirate
(marriage of a man to his brother's widow)

5. telesis   telusis   telosis   tellosis
(deliberate use of natural and social processes to achieve goals)

6. bracerro   bracero   braccero   brasairo
(seasonal Mexican agricultural laborer in the United States)

7. fratery   fratry   phratre   phratry
(grouping of subtribes or clans)

8. uvunculocal   avvunculocal   avunculocal   uvunkulocal
    (centered on the husband's maternal uncle)

9. bina marriage   bena marriage   biena marriage
       beena marriage
    (marriage in which husband lives with wife's family)

10. aphenal   affenal   aphinal   affinal
    (related by marriage)

11. xenophobia   zenophobia   xeniphobia   zeniphobia
    (fear or dislike of foreigners)

12. anamy   annomy   anomie   annomie
    (societal breakdown)

13. Kalikak   Kalikkak   Kallikak   Kallikakk
    (fictitious name, with Jukes, in actual sociological study of heredity and
       intelligence)

14. potlache   pottlatch   potlach   potlatch
    (Kwakiutl festival of lavish gift giving and destruction by the host of his
       own property)

15. saternalia   satyrnalia   saturnalia   satirnalia
    (unrestrained celebration or orgy)

16. architype   archotype   arkatype   archetype
    (original model or prime example)

17. moyeties   moyetes   moieties   moities
    (complementary tribal subdivisions)

18. ajelicism   agelicism   aggelicism   ajellicism
    (belief that society determines individuals' thoughts and actions)

19. poligeny   polygeny   polygyny   poligyny
    (having two or more wives simultaneously)

20. gerontology   gerentology   geruntology   geriuntology
    (science of aging and the problems of old people)

21. Geminschaft   Gemeinschafft   Gemienschafft   Gemeinschaft
    (ideal society of kinship and friendship ties)

22. bracycephaly   brachycephaly   braccicephaly   bracacephaly
    (short-headedness)

23. Appallachia   Apalachea   Appalachia   Apallachia
    (southeastern region of the United States)

24. gynococrasy   gynecocracy   gynicocrasy   gynococracy
    (government by women; gynarchy)

25. lumpinproletariat   loomp'nproletariat   lumpenproletariat
   lumponproletariat
   (lowest level of the common people)

Alternative Words

a. Weltenshauung   Weltanshauung   Weltanschauung
   Weltunschauung
   (world view or philosophy of life)

b. chatel   chattel   chatell   chattell
   (slave)

c. amatate   amitate   ammitate   ammatate
   (special niece-aunt relationship in a society)

d. petit bourgoisy   petite bourgeoisie   petite bourboise
   petit burgoisy
   (lower middle class)

e. matrapotestal   matripautestal   matripothestal   matropotestal
   (pertaining to authority of a mother or her blood relatives)

> *Before consulting the answers on page 311:*
> I think I spelled _____ words correctly on this test.
> (If your estimate is correct, add one point to your score.)

Sports

1. annebolic   annibolic   anabolic   annabolic
   (type of steroid)

2. ephus pitch   eephus pitch   ephis pitch   eephis pitch
   (baseball: ridiculously lobbed, high-arc pitch)

3. Yamashita   Yommoshito   Yomashita   Yamishita
   (gymnastics: type of woman's vault)

4. mashy niblick   mashie niblick   mashy niblik   mashie niblik
   (gold: number six iron)

5. pyste   piste   piest   pistte
   (fencing strip on which bouts are held)

6.   pfartleck   fartlek   pfartlek   farrtlek
     (running: speed training)

7.   knokking point   knocking point   nocking point
         nokking point
     (archery: bowstring part for placement of arrow)

8.   spherestika   sphairistika   sphairistike   spharisticha
     (ancient name for tennis)

9.   cesstuh   chestuh   cesta   cestta
     (jai alai: player's curved basket for hurling and catching)

10. Worcester   Worchester   Wooster   wusstor
     (bowling: split leaving all but the 1 and 5 pins)

11. tellamark   telamark   telemark   telamarkk
     (skiing: type of ski turn)

12. Marquess of Queensberry rules   Marquis of Queensbury rules
         Marquis of Queensberry rules   Marquess of Queensbury rules
     (fair-play code governing boxing matches)

13. Naismith   Nasmyth   Nasmith   Nasmythe
     (inventor of basketball)

14. Heismann trophy   Heisman trophy   Hiesmann trophy
         Heissman trophy
     (award to college football's player of the year)

15. chukker   chukha   chukkor   chuckah
     (period of a polo match)

16. tarpolin   tarpulin   tarpalin   tarpaulin
     (field-protective rain sheet used in baseball games)

17. deek   deke   deeke   deeque
     (ice hockey: deceptive move or feint)

18. repeschage   reppishage   repechage   repichage
     (rowing: second-chance trial heat)

19. totalizator   totallisator   totalisateur   totalizateur
     (horse racing: pari-mutuel machine)

20. pellota   pelata   pellata   pelota
     (jai alai ball)

21. trugeon stroke   trugin stroke   trudgen stroke
         trudgin stroke
     (swimming: double overarm stroke with a scissors kick)

22. Wimbelton   Wimbledon   Wimbleton   Wimbeldon
     (tennis: site of the British Open)

23. leuge   louge   luge   lujj
(type of toboggan and Olympic event)
24. ally-oop   alley-oop   allie-oop   alley-oup
(basketball: soaring pass to teammate close to the basket)
25. ochser   oxer   oksor   okksor
(obstacle in equestrian show jumping)

Alternative Words

a. bonnespeel   bonspeel   bonspiel   bonespiel
(curling tournament)
b. flèsch   flèshe   flèche   flàische
(fencing: running attack)
c. forcaddy   forecaddy   forcaddie   forecaddie
(golf: advance assistant who indicates where the ball is)
d. clyster   klyster   klister   klistor
(ski wax for use on wet snow)
e. cauliflour ear   calliflower ear   cauliflower ear
   caullyflour ear
(misshapen ear of a boxer)

> *Before consulting the answers on page 311:*
> I think I spelled ＿＿ words correctly on this test.
> (If your estimate is correct, add one point to your score.)

Wines

1. somelié   sommelié   somelier   sommelier
(wine steward)
2. Lafite-Rothschild   La Fit-Rothschild   Lafitte-Rothschild
   La Fitte-Rothschild
(claret)
3. Médok   Médoc   Mèdoc   Méddoc
(red Bordeaux wine)
4. allage   ullage   ulage   eulage
(remaining wine in a container)

5. Gewertztraminer   Gewörtztraminer   Gewürztraminer
     Gewürztramminer
(dry white table wine)

6. Châteaunuf-de-Pape   Châteauneuf-du-Papp
     Châteauneuff-du-Pape   Châteaunneuf-de-Pape
(dry Rhone red or white wine)

7. Schpätlese   Spätlase   Schpätlase   Spätlese
(late-harvested and sweeter than a Kabinett wine)

8. bottritized   bottrytised   botrytized   botritized
(affected in flavor by "noble rot" mold or yeast)

9. Valpolicella   Vallpollicella   Valpollicella   Vallpolicella
(Italian dry red table wine)

10. grapa   gropa   groppa   grappa
(Italian brandy)

11. méthode champainoise   méthode champanoise
     méthode champenoise   méthode champannoise
(Champagne process)

12. Bernkastlor   Berncasteler   Bernkasteler   Bernkast'ler
(German Mosel vintage)

13. ampulography   ampillography   amplography
     ampelography
(study of vines or cultivation of grapes)

14. Sémmilon   Sémillon   Sémmillon   Sémilon
(French variety of white grape)

15. *tastevin*   *tostevin*   *tasttevin*   *testevin*
(silver cup for wine tasting)

16. patilant   petilant   petillant   patillant
(slightly sparkling)

17. Asti spumanti   Aste spumante   Aste spumanti
     Asti spumante
(Italian sweet sparkling wine)

18. Chenine Blanc   Chennin Blanc   Chennin Blanc
     Chenin Blanc
(white wine grape of the Loire Valley and California)

19. Trockenbarenauslese   Trockenbeerenauslese
     Trokenbarenauslese   Trokenbeerenauslese
(rare, very sweet German wine; T.B.A.)

20. skupernong   scuppernong   scupernong   skuppernong
    (amber green muscadine grape)
21. Manichevitz   Manischevitz   Manischewitz   Manischewitze
    (kosher wine from Concord grapes)
22. Pouilé-Fuissé   Pouille-Fuissé   Pouilly-Fuissé   Pouilly-Fuissée
    (dry white Burgundy wine)
23. zymurgy   symergy   zymergy   symurgy
    (chemical science of fermentation)
24. Verdicchio   Verrdiccio   Verrdicchio   Verdichio
    (Italian Adriatic white wine)
25. amontallado   amontillado   ammontillado   amontilado
    (pale dry Spanish sherry)

Alternative Words

a. chianti   cheanti   chiante   chiantti
   (Italian dry red table wine)
b. punchon   punchen   puncheon   punchin
   (large eighty-gallon cask)
c. Rheoboame   Rehoboam   Rehaboame   Rohaboam
   (five-quart champagne bottle)
d. rettsina   rezina   retsina   retsinna
   (Greek red or white resin-flavored wine)
e. Rioja   Riojja   Rioha   Reoja
   (Spanish dry red table wine)

> *Before consulting the answers on page 311:*
> I think I spelled _____ words correctly on this test.
> (If your estimate is correct, add one point to your score.)

World Geography

1. Timbucktoo   Timbuktoo   Timbuktu   Timbucto
   (West African town near the Niger River)
2. Lichtinstein   Liechtenstein   Leichtenstein   Liechtonstein
   (principality between Switzerland and Austria)

3. Koala Lampur   Kuala Lompur   Kuala Lumpur
       Koala Lumpur
   (Malaysian city)

4. Adelaide   Adelaid   Adelade   Addelaide
   (Australian city)

5. Machue Pichu   Maccu Picchu   Machu Pichu   Machu Picchu
   (ancient Inca ruins site near Cuzco, Peru)

6. Quom   Qum   Qom   Quam
   (Iranian city)

7. Abu Dabbi   Abhu Dhabi   Abu Dhabi   Abbu Dhabi
   (United Arab Emirates sheikhdom)

8. Reyahd   Riyadh   Riadh   Riyahd
   (Saudi Arabian city)

9. Saskachuan   Saskatchuan   Saskachewan   Saskatchewan
   (Canadian province)

10. Upsalla   Upssala   Upsala   Uppsala
    (Swedish city)

11. Pnom Pen   Pnom Phen   Phnom Penh   Phnom Phen
    (Cambodian city)

12. Schyllkill River   Schuyllkill River   Schuylkill River
        Schuyllkil River
    (Pennsylvania river)

13. Djebooti   Djibouti   Djibbouti   Djibboute
    (East African country)

14. Rekyjavík   Reykjavík   Rekjavík   Reykhjavík
    (Icelandic city)

15. Lake Winnepesaukee   Lake Winnipesauke   Lake Winnipesaukee
        Lake Winnepesauke
    (New Hampshire lake)

16. Mikonas   Miknos   Mykonos   Mykonnos
    (Greek island)

17. Würtemburg   Würtemberg   Würrtemberg   Württemberg
    (German region, formerly a duchy, kingdom, and state)

18. Edinborgh   Edinborough   Edinburgh   Edinbrough
    (Scottish city)

19. Tallahatchie River   Tallahachee River   Tallahatchee River
        Tallahachie River
    (Mississippi river)

20. Novosubersk   Novosibirsk   Novosobersk   Novosobirsk
(U.S.S.R. city)

21. Allagheny Mountains   Allegany Mountains
Allegheny Mountains   Alleghany Mountains
(mountains of eastern United States)

22. Montovideo   Montivideo   Montevideo   Montevidio
(Uruguayan city)

23. Guadalajara   Guadhalajara   Guadalajhara   Guadelajarha
(Mexican city)

24. Dneipper River   Dniepper River   Dnieper River
Dneiper River
(U.S.S.R. river)

25. Bophutatswana   Bophuthatswana   Bophothatswana
Bophutathswana
(region of enclaves in South Africa)

Alternative Words

a. Marrekech   Marrakecch   Marakecch   Marrakech
(Moroccan city)

b. Portabello   Portobello   Portabelo   Portobelo
(Panamanian town)

c. Balearic Islands   Balaric Islands   Ballearic Islands
Balairic Islands
(Spanish islands in the Mediterranean)

d. Saulte Saint Marie   Sault Sainte Marie   Soulte Sainte Marie
Soulte Saint Marie
(Canadian city)

e. Lake Titikaka   Lake Titticaca   Lake Titicaca   Lake Tittikaka
(lake at boundary of Peru and Bolivia)

Before consulting the answers on page 311:
I think I spelled ____ words correctly on this test.
(If your estimate is correct, add one point to your score.)

... viewed as a science, spelling is probably somewhat less rigid than nuclear physics, and, as an art, slightly more arcane than astrology. Even those magicians of the computer age, electronic spelling checkers, are capable of pulling a goose out of the hat that should have held a rabbit. Knowledge of spelling rules can save valuable time, but so far there is no magic, no substitute for a well-worn dictionary.

Jeanne Hecker

Spelling Rules

As primarily a festival of tests, this book is an unmitigated celebration of the ornery difficulties of English spelling—not a guide to spelling self-improvement.

Spelling rules, abounding in exceptions, do nonetheless exist, and for what they are worth we provide a number of them here.

Because of the chaotic orthography of English, knowing spelling rules is a little like a soldier's possessing an old map of a onetime friendly village that in fact is swarming with enemy agents and whose exact perimeters are now unknown and continually shifting. As Patricia Fergus says in *Spelling Improvement*, it's wiser to consider spelling rules as "spelling generalizations."

There are numerous exception-words to many of the rules, or else the particular rule has one or two complicating qualifying clauses—ifs, and, and buts. Sometimes it's as if the basic rules are reframed and reworded to accommodate the exceptions. Many seem suspiciously ex post facto, contrived to seem rules when they aren't; or Procrustean—stretched to try to sum up what isn't so easily or reliably summed up. They're also sometimes formulated according to how a word is pronounced (rather than pure orthography), to some a dubiously backward approach.

Is it worth the trouble to learn them? For some people, definitely. It is also worth it to become more of a reader, and better yet, a careful reader.

Nobody likes memorizing rules. The thing to do is to keep referring to them and "applying" or testing them in your reading and writing. Slowly but surely, you can acquire a sixth sense of the principles in the rules. You'll absorb them, begin to know them almost unconsciously.

Besides rules, there are also mnemonics, or verbal or conceptual memory aids, to help with particular spelling problems. For example, if you can never remember whether it's *inoculate* or *innoculate,* you can store in the back of your mind the sentence or thought "I no see you late"; or be sure of the spelling of *harass* by associating the word with "Ha! Razz!" If you don't find ready-made mnemonics in improve-your-spelling books, you can have fun making up your own. The only trouble with mnemonics, besides their often being strained or sophomoric, is that they're a kind of mental baggage. Not everybody's brain will want to offer unlimited occupancy to such mental Post-it notes.

Another way to learn problem spelling words is to break them into pronounceable syllables and try to memorize them in pieces, possibly exaggerating the pronunciation of the troublesome syllables (e.g., *cal-en-DAR*).

If you've done poorly on tests in this book, you might take in a few of the following rules. When you know them fairly well, let some time pass (to forget the test answers) and take the tests a second time.

If you don't take to rules as a route to better spelling, read, read, and read, and that includes dictionaries.

DOUBLING CONSONANTS

Broadly speaking, double a consonant when the preceding vowel sound is short rather than long (*plan: planned* but *plane: planed*).

A word ending in a single consonant after a single vowel (or vowel *y*), when the word is accented on the final syllable, doubles the consonant before a vowel-beginning suffix provided that the accented syllable remains accented (*deter: deterred, deterring, deterrence;* but *resist: resisted, resisting, resistance,* and similarly *profited, preference, benefited, appeared*). Exceptions include *transference* and *chagrined.*

One-syllable words ending in a single consonant after a single vowel (or vowel *y*) double the consonant in inflections (*swim: swimmer; sob: sobbed; glom: glommed; map: mapped; quiz: quizzed;* also, *buggy, gladden*).

Etymology—knowing the derivation of a word—can also be invaluable in deducing whether certain words have a single or double letter (*inoculate, in-*

terregnum, calligraphy, bellicose, desiccated, dilettante, guttural, battalion).

Note that in some cases variant spellings violating the just-given doubling rule are found in dictionaries (both *kidnaped* and *kidnapped, canceled* and *cancelled*). And the British (and *The New Yorker* magazine) double final consonants even when the accent is on the first syllable of the word *(travelled, carolled, worshipping, marvellous)*.

PLURALS

The plural is *-es,* not *-s,* when the word ends in *s, ch, sh, x,* or *z (stresses, belches, sashes, roaches, squelches, sexes, wishes, taxes, fezzes).*

Words ending in *-ey, -ay,* or *-oy* do not have *-ies* plurals *(ploys, trays, clays, valleys, abbeys, jitneys).*

IE OR EI

Most long-*e*-sound words are spelled *-ie (bier, yield, relieve, piece).* But there are many exceptions *(weird, seize, protein, either, leisure, codeine).*

Long-*e*-sound words after a *c* that is pronounced like an *s* use *-ei (perceive, conceit, receipt).* An exception is *financier.*

After a *c* pronounced like *sh,* the spelling is *-ie (coefficient, conscientious, prescience, ancient).*

Rule of thumb:

> Put *i* before *e,*
> Except after *c,*
> Or when sounded like *a,*
> As in *neighbor* or *weigh.*

Exceptions to this include *glacier, neither,* and *counterfeit.*

Words using *i* and *e* pronounced with a long *a* sound are always spelled *-ei,* never *-ie (neigh, sleigh, vein, eight, peignoir, feign).*

With long-*i*-sounding words the spelling is usually *-ei,* not *-ie (height, leitmotif, feisty, gemütlichkeit, stein, seismic).* Exceptions (followed by *r*) are *hierarchy, fiery, hieroglyphic, hieratic.*

With short-sound words, it's usually *-ie,* not *-ei (mischief, handkerchief, transient, friend, sieve, patient).* Exceptions include *nonpareil, heifer,* and *Seidlitz* and the *-eign* and *-feit* words *(foreign, sovereign, counterfeit, surfeit).*

-ANCE OR -ENCE

For the troublesome question of *-ance/-ant* or *-ence/-ent,* there is unfortunately no spelling rule to go by.

In general (with fingers crossed), *-ence* words are more common than *-ance* words except after the letters *t* and *v (reluctance, pittance, assistance, observance, relevance).*

After a *c* or *g* pronounced soft, it's *-ence (munificence, phosphorescence, intel-*

ligence, diligence); if the c or g is pronounced hard, it's -ance (significance, extravagance).

-ABLE OR -IBLE

There are more -able words than -ible words.

After a complete word, it's usually -able (bendable, findable, breakable, workable, predictable). Exceptions include resistible, flexible, discernible, gullible, dismissible.

A word ending in e preceded by a single consonant usually drops the e and takes -able (except when the word ends in -ce or -ge). Thus writable, measurable, blamable, desirable, usable, lovable, comparable. But in many instances dictionaries permit either of two spellings (sizable or sizeable).

Words ending in -ce or -ge, when the c or g has a "soft" sound, keep the e before -able endings (to retain the soft pronunciation: peaceable, changeable).

It's implacable, practicable, despicable, and navigable because c and g are hard, not soft, before the vowel a.

After the letter i, it's always -able (reliable, appreciable, amiable, enviable, sociable, insatiable, classifiable, justifiable).

For a word like irritable—where there is no word irrit—if the related verb ends in -ate, it's -able (demonstrable, tolerable, estimable, inimitable, impenetrable).

Otherwise, it follows that after noncomplete words and after soft-sound-ing g's, it's usually -ible (negligible, intelligible, eligible, tangible).

When the word ending is -miss, it's always -ible (permissible, dismissible, admissible, transmissible). Likewise with -ns word endings (ostensible, comprehensible, expansible, defensible). Exceptions include dispensable and indispensable.

Like the earlier rule pertaining to -ate-related words, many roots having a related -ion form end in -ible (digestible, expansible, collectible, exhaustible, suppressible, contractible, accessible, repressible). Exceptions include predictable, detectable, correctable.

Similarly, with roots having an -sion form, it's -ible (suppressible, pervertible, erodible, corrodible, convertible).

DROPPING FINAL E

When a suffix begins with a consonant, a word ending in e retains the e (sorely, disparagement, blueness, profusely, management, barely, trueness). Exceptions include awful, only, wholly, truly, duly, ninth and the -dge words (acknowledgment, abridgment, judgment, lodgment—but these have variant spellings).

Drop all final e's, no matter what the preceding consonant, before any vowel-beginning suffix (puling, illustrative, enclosure, desiring, arguing, aching, hoping). This also applies to y suffixes (mangy, wiry, spongy, stony). Exceptions include cagey, homey, mileage, and advantageous.

-IFY OR -EFY

It's usually an *-ify* ending, not *-efy*. Exceptions inlcude *putrefy, rarefy, liquefy, stupefy.*

WORDS ENDING IN Y OR IE

A word ending in *-y* (with a vowel sound), when preceded by a consonant, changes the *y* to *i* before a suffix not beginning with *i (ponies, queries, bellies, compliance, daintiness, mopiness)*. Exceptions include *spryness, miscellaneous,* and *implying.*

Words ending in *-ly* retain the *y* in the plural *(doilys, bialys)*. Exceptions include *dollies* and *lilies.*

A word ending in *y* changes the *y* to *i* before *-ness* or *-ly (happiness, loopiness, tastiness, heaviness, yeastiness, iciness, coziness, clumsily, airily, busily)*.

A word ending in *-ie* changes the *ie* to *y* before *-ing (dying, vying, lying)*.

-C OR -CK

A word ending in a hard *c* adds a *k* before a vowel-beginning suffix *(picnicker, shellacker, frolicking, panicky, mimicking)*.

-ISE OR -IZE

After the letter *v*, it's *-ise*, never *-ize (advise, supervise, revise)*.

-FUL OR -FULL

The suffix is *-ful*, never *-full (vengeful, wakeful, handful, mouthful, cupful)*.

When the suffix is *-ful* plus *-ly*, there are two *l*'s *(restfully, balefully, thankfully, mirthfully, artfully, zestfully)*.

-SEDE, -CEED, OR -CEDE

The only word ending in *-sede* is *supersede.*

The only words ending in *-ceed* are *exceed, succeed,* and *proceed.*

The ending for other words is *-cede (recede, intercede, precede)*.

-ERY OR -ARY

Only six common words end in *-ery*, as opposed to *-ary: stationery* (writing paper), *monastery, cemetery, millinery, distillery,* and *confectionery.*

For further reading on spelling improvement, books you may find in your local library or bookstore include Patricia Fergus's *Spelling Improvement,* Edna Furness's *Spelling for the Millions,* Norman Lewis's *Correct Spelling Made Easy* and *Dictionary of Correct Spelling,* Joseph Mersand and Francis Griffith's *Spelling Your Way to Success,* Stephen Ross's *Spelling Made Simple,* Charles Ryan's *Spelling for Adults,* Harry Shefter's *6 Minutes a Day to Perfect Spelling,* John Stratton and Michael Montgomery's *The Fast-Track Program for Perfect Spelling,* and Veronica Towers's *Spelling and Vocabulary Simplified and Self-Taught.*

Diachronic [i.e., historical or developed over time] spelling rules are forever subdividing and bifurcating; rules keep begetting rules.

Louis Jay Herman

Ultimate Death by Spelling

(A Final Round of Tests)

Some of the following fifteen tests focus on particular, classic types of spelling problems. Others are general tests gathering together some of the tougher words you've encountered earlier in the book—review tests, but not easy ones. (Ultimate Death test answers begin on page 313.)

Spelling became not merely the shibboleth that distinguished one as a gent, or even a lady. A century later bad spelling could ruin one's career as well as one's social standing. Dr. Morell, a famous Inspector of Schools in England, was quoted in 1877 as remarking that: "out of 1,972 failures in the Civil Service examinations, 1,866 candidates were *plucked for spelling*. That is, eighteen out of every nineteen who failed, failed in Spelling."

Philip Howard

THE ESQUIRE TEST

Way back in the turbulent, spelling-destroying 1960s, a spelling test of sixty difficult words was given to some eight hundred college graduates, many of whom were editors, teachers, journalists, proofreaders, and advertising people. Needless to say, not a single person got a perfect score.

From this sixty-word test, a test of the twenty most frequently misspelled words was derived, and this was given to a sampling of average Americans, college graduates and nongraduates alike.

The test was brought to public attention in *Esquire* in April 1967 by T. K. Brown III and soon thereafter was reprinted in *Reader's Digest*. More than fifteen years later, it showed up embedded in a droll piece on the op-ed page of the *New York Times*. Which is to say it's been handed down: It's a classic. It's also the test that, back in the early 1970s, got me interested in spelling tests.

Interested?

If you get six right, you're at the median level. If you get twelve right, you're one person in ten. If you get eighteen words correct, you're at the college professor level.

The test is reprinted here, phonetically, just as it was originally given. Variant spellings for some of the words will be found in dictionaries, but only one answer was allowed on this test—and shall be here.

The Esquire Test

Write in the correct spelling.

1. ass'-uh-9 _____
2. brag-uh-doe'-C-O _____
3. rare'-uff-I _____
4. lick'-wuff-I _____
5. puh-vill'-yun _____
6. ver-mill'-yun _____
7. im-pah'-stir _____
8. mock'-uh-sun _____
9. uh-kahm'-uh-date _____
10. kon-sen'-sus _____
11. roe-ko'-ko _____
12. tit'-tle-8 _____
13. sack-ruh-li'-jus _____
14. may-uh-naz' _____

15. im-pray-sor'-ry-O   _____
16. in-ock'-U-late   _____
17. soo-per-seed'   _____
18. ob-ly-gah'-to   _____
19. des'-suh-Kate   _____
20. re-sus'-suh-tate   _____

> *Before consulting the answers on page 313:*
> I think I spelled _____ words correctly on this test.
> (If your estimate is correct, add one point to your score.)

ULTIMATE DEATH WORDS OF ONE SYLLABLE

For the articulately monosyllabic, a se-
lection of short spelling words that
have appeared earlier in the book.

Ultimate Death Words of One Syllable Test

Write in the correct spelling.

1. zist   _____   (ancient covered portico or promenade)
2. nef   _____   (table ornament or holder shaped like a ship)
3. dou   _____   (Arab sailing boat)
4. piks   _____   (Holy Communion bread container)
5. ko͞om   _____   (steep bowllike basin on a mountain)
6. mō   _____   (unit of electrical conductance)
7. les   _____   (yellowish brown loamy deposit)
8. fī'(ə)l   _____   (close-woven fabric with slight ribs in the weft)
9. ouf   _____   (elf)
10. dalz   _____   (river rapids in a gorge)

Pronunciation key on page 10.

> *Before consulting the answers on page 313:*
> I think I spelled _____ words correctly on this test.
> (If your estimate is correct, add one point to your score.)

-IE OR -EI

Let's see, it's "I before E, except after . . ." or was it "E before I, except . . ." You wondered why the tests in the book haven't had more "ie" and "ei" words? Why, we've been saving them to give them to you all at once.

-Ie or -Ei Test

Complete the correct spelling by filling in the space.

1. w___rd
2. sh___kh
3. f___nd
4. sk___n
5. fr___ze
6. dec___ve
7. s___ze
8. forf___t
9. g___sha
10. w___r

11. h___fer
12. Sh___la
13. nonpar___l
14. cod___ne
15. Pl___ades
16. caff___ne
17. pleb___an
18. s___ve
19. s___ge
20. c___ling

21. f___fdom
22. w___ld
23. conc___ve
24. rec___pt
25. retr___ve
    a. n___ce
    b. S___gfr___d line
    c. k___lbasa
    d. l___der
    e. h___nous

Before consulting the answers on page 313:
I think I spelled _____ words correctly on this test.
(If your estimate is correct, add one point to your score.)

-ANCE (-ANT) OR -ENCE (-ENT)

In case you have ance in your pance,
or are enxious about your endings.

-Ance (-Ant) or -Ence (-Ent) Test

Complete the correct spelling by filling in the
space.

1. aberr__nce	11. anteced__nt	21. decad__nt
2. suffer__nce	12. relev__nt	22. deced__nt
3. resplend__nt	13. appet__nce	23. defend__nt
4. imped__nce	14. opul__nce	24. quitt__nce
5. cogniz__nt	15. dalli__nce	25. pench__nt
6. despond__nt	16. admitt__nce	a. preponder__nt
7. abid__nce	17. lieuten__nt	b. retard__nt
8. petul__nce	18. trucul__nt	c. disput__nt
9. reflect__nce	19. intermitt__nt	d. mord__nt (biting)
10. nurtur__nt	20. attract__nt	e. adher__nt

> *Before consulting the answers on page 313:*
> I think I spelled _____ words correctly on this test.
> (If your estimate is correct, add one point to your score.)

-OS OR -OES

Yet another vile vowel dilemma. But at
least you can spell your mistakes *pecca-
dilloes* or *peccadillos* and be correct.

-Os or -Oes Test

Complete the correct spelling by filling in the space with an o or oe.

1. ech_____s
2. kimon_____s
3. fung_____s
4. bagni_____s
5. gring_____s
6. fandang_____s
7. ling_____s
8. jing_____s
9. her_____s
10. farrag_____s

11. caballer_____s
12. fats_____s
13. dild_____s
14. majordom_____s
15. boler_____s
16. curi_____s
17. boz_____s
18. albin_____s
19. gess_____s
20. sopran_____s

21. vet_____s
22. pistachi_____s
23. potat_____s
24. tomat_____s
25. embry_____s
  a. seragli_____s
  b. Merin_____s
  c. fiasc_____s
  d. bass_____s
  e. hidalg_____s

Before consulting the answers on page 314:
I think I spelled _____ words correctly on this test.
(If your estimate is correct, add one point to your score.)

A glaring example of the inadequacies of English spelling appeared in a test given to sixty-four graduate students of journalism at Columbia University. The average was twenty-five misspellings out of seventy-eight words. Typical words used in the test were *analogous, dissension, harassed, siege, canoeist, ecstasy, restaurateur, vilification, dietitian, guerrilla, supersede,* and appropriately, *misspell.* Foreign students did better than the native-born, pointing up the advantages of bilingualism. Another series of spellings so ghastly as to be almost unbelievable is submitted by Professor Arnold Hartoch of the Chicago Navy Pier branch of the University of Illinois: *dumnb, middnite, lieutendent, wisch, rifel, cowtch, natly* (naturally), *tyered, youniform, sodiers, speach, aliet* (alight), *theirfour, theorhea* (theory).

Mario Pei

-ER OR -OR TESTS

Here are two tests of words sometimes called agent nouns. You and only you can be the perpetrat__r.

-Er or -Or Test No. 1

Complete the correct spelling by filling in the space.

1. estimat____
2. facilitat____
3. hallucinat____
4. mutilat____
5. repudiat____
6. infect____
7. separat____
8. discriminat____
9. rebutt____
10. forfeit____

11. seced____
12. extirpat____
13. depredat____
14. placat____
15. constrict____
16. inculcat____
17. insinuat____
18. predict____
19. perpetuat____
20. enumerat____

21. cultivat____
22. requit____
23. accumulat____
24. pollinat____
25. educat____
   a. consummat____
   b. proselytiz____
   c. improvisat____
   d. arbit____
   e. acquitt____

> *Before consulting the answers on page 314:*
> I think I spelled ____ words correctly on this test.
> (If your estimate is correct, add one point to your score.)

-Er or -Or Test No. 2

Complete the correct spelling by filling in the space.

1. massacr____
2. abbreviat____
3. confiscat____
4. sojourn____
5. formulat____
6. masticat____
7. emboss____
8. subjugat____
9. obliterat____
10. dissertat____

11. abscond____
12. punctuat____
13. initiat____
14. contest____
15. tergiversat____
16. execrat____
17. perpetrat____
18. inveigh____
19. advocat____
20. disburs____

21. illuminat____
22. extrapolat____
23. attract____
24. pontificat____
25. alienat____
   a. denigrat____
   b. underli____
   c. dissimulat____
   d. irrigat____
   e. chastis____

> *Before consulting the answers on page 314:*
> I think I spelled ____ words correctly on this test.
> (If your estimate is correct, add one point to your score.)

-ABLE OR -IBLE

There are two tests here, and you're dared to take them one after the other, but not if you're mentally unstible.

The root word is given. Merely provide each with the appropriate ending, ably or ibly—and remember the *e* or doubled letter that may or may not precede the endings.

-Able or -Ible Test No. 1

Write the root's correct -able *or* -ible *form.*

1. analyze   _____
2. assess   _____
3. bid   _____
4. censure   _____
5. code   _____
6. compass   _____
7. compat___   _____
8. comprehend   _____
9. condemn   _____
10. confuse   _____
11. corrode   _____
12. cut   _____
13. dim   _____
14. dip   _____
15. distract   _____
16. enforce   _____
17. erect   _____
18. excerpt   _____
19. exhaust   _____
20. expand   _____
21. expans___   _____
22. fuse   _____
23. gauge   _____
24. gel   _____
25. illimit___   _____

a. illumin____ _____
b. impass _____
c. indestruct____ _____
d. induce _____
e. inelud____ _____

Before consulting the answers on page 315:
I think I spelled ____ words correctly on this test.
(If your estimate is correct, add one point to your score.)

-Able or -Ible Test No. 2

Write the root word's correct -able or -ible form.

1. infect _____
2. invert _____
3. irrefrag____ _____
4. lease _____
5. misc____ _____
6. part _____
7. postpone _____
8. produce _____
9. prove _____
10. putresc____ _____
11. resist _____
12. salvage _____
13. scale _____
14. scrut____ _____

15. spare　　　　　　　＿＿＿＿＿＿＿＿＿＿
16. sue　　　　　　　　＿＿＿＿＿＿＿＿＿＿
17. submerge　　　　　＿＿＿＿＿＿＿＿＿＿
18. subsume　　　　　 ＿＿＿＿＿＿＿＿＿＿
19. suppress　　　　　＿＿＿＿＿＿＿＿＿＿
20. tithe　　　　　　　＿＿＿＿＿＿＿＿＿＿
21. tract___　　　　　 ＿＿＿＿＿＿＿＿＿＿
22. traverse　　　　　 ＿＿＿＿＿＿＿＿＿＿
23. destruct___　　　　＿＿＿＿＿＿＿＿＿＿
24. unbudg___　　　　＿＿＿＿＿＿＿＿＿＿
25. unreproduc___　　 ＿＿＿＿＿＿＿＿＿＿
　a. vanquish
　b. win　　　　　　　＿＿＿＿＿＿＿＿＿＿
　c. ingest
　d. interrupt　　　　 ＿＿＿＿＿＿＿＿＿＿
　e. locate　　　　　　＿＿＿＿＿＿＿＿＿＿

Before consulting the answers on page 315:
I think I spelled ＿＿ words correctly on this test.
(If your estimate is correct, add one point to your score.)

SPELL THE PLURAL

For most plurals of nouns in English, a good old *s* or *es* usually suffices. But then there are those odd words, the ones with the nightmare plurals. They're back . . .

Spell the Plural Test

Singular	*Plural*
1. auto-da-fé (burning of a heretic)	＿＿＿＿＿＿＿
2. ignis fatuus (deceptive goal)	＿＿＿＿＿＿＿
3. court-martial (military trial)	＿＿＿＿＿＿＿

4. heir apparent (presumed inheritor) _____
5. kielbasa (Polish smoked sausage) _____
6. torii (Japanese ∏-shaped
   shrine gateway) _____
7. billet-doux (love-letter) _____
8. coccyx (end of spinal column) _____
9. annus mirabilis (wondrous year) _____
10. kohlrabi (thick-stemmed cabbage) _____
11. marchesa (Italian marquis) _____
12. croquis (sketch) _____
13. starets (Eastern Orthodox leader) _____
14. pince-nez (nose-clip eyeglasses) _____
15. metastasis (secondary malignant growth) _____
16. mot juste (the perfectly apt word) _____
17. goosefoot (herb with greenish flowers) _____
18. kuvasz (Hungarian dog breed) _____
19. oyez ("Hear!" cry use in courtrooms) _____
20. chassis (automobile body frame) _____
   a. beau geste (noble gesture) _____
   b. nouveau riche (newly rich person) _____
   c. entremets (side dish) _____
   d. plaice (European flounder) _____
   e. nexus (connection or interconnection) _____

> *Before consulting the answers on page 315:*
> I think I spelled _____ words correctly on this test.
> (If your estimate is correct, add one point to your score.)

ACCENT MARK OR NONE

Here, to give you a break, your words are prespelled. But you're invited to determine where those darn foreign squiggly marks (acutes, graves, circumflexes, umlauts, and tildes) go. Or don't they?

Accent Mark or None Test

Where appropriate, place accent marks over letters of the words.

1. manana — tomorrow (Spanish)
2. melee — confused fight (French)
3. pieta — representation of Virgin Mary cradling the dead body of Christ (Italian)
4. boite — nightclub (French)
5. panache — dash and flair (French)
6. arrividerci — good-bye for now (Italian)
7. porte cochere — passageway to a courtyard (French)
8. Gotterdammerung — catastrophic disorder (German)
9. dolce vita — the sweet, lazy life (Italian)
10. mano a mano — head-on, competing directly (Spanish)
11. crepes suzette — rolled, liqueur-sprinkled pancakes *flambé* (French)
12. aloha oe — hello or farewell (Hawaiian)
13. virtu, vertu — love for artistic curios (French)
14. zabaglione — Italian dessert sauce (Italian)
15. deja vu — sensation of having experienced something before (French)
16. emigre — person departing a country for political reasons (French)
17. creche — Nativity scene representation (French)
18. lese majeste — affront to those higher up (French)
19. objet d'art — valuable article of art (French)
20. fuhrer — fascist dictator (German)
21. ciao — hello or good-bye (Italian)
22. gemutlichkeit — friendliness or coziness (German)
23. forte — strong point (French)
24. kielbasa — Polish sausage (Polish)
25. tete-a-tete — private conversation (French)
   a. Chicano — Mexican-American (Spanish)
   b. dacha — Russian country cottage (Russian)

c. detente   relaxation of tension between two countries
(French)
d. machismo   masculine preening or posturing (Spanish)
e. hasta la vista   till we meet again (Spanish)

> *Before consulting the answers on page 315:*
> I think I spelled _____ words correctly on this test.
> (If your estimate is correct, add one point to your score.)

> One research study is that of Thomas Pollock, of New York University, conducted between 1950 and 1964. In this study, English teachers in high schools and colleges throughout the country reported 90,000 instances of misspellings. But a large percentage of the 90,000 misspellings involved only nine words: *their (there), too (to), receive, believe (belief), all right, separate, coming, until,* and *character.*
>
> Edna L. Furness

WEBSTER'S SECOND (ONE SPELLING ONLY) TESTS

For those of you—terrific spellers—who deplore Webster's Third New International Dictionary and its permissiveness (or unreadable small print), and who long for the days when a word had *one* correct spelling, here is a retro opportunity. Answers here are all according to Webster's (Second) New International, with variant or deviant spellings absolutely not allowed. Nostalgia shouldn't be short-lived, so there are two tests here.

Webster's Second (One Spelling Only) Test No. 1

Write in the correct spelling.

1. ə fish yun ä′dō   _____ devotee
2. chan′səl rē   _____ court office
3. kī′rə man sē   _____ palm reading

4.	kol'ən dər	_____	kitchen draining utensil
5.	gə lumf'	_____	tread clumsily
6.	man'ə kin	_____	little man
7.	rum'bə	_____	Cuban ballroom dance
8.	yōō kə lā'lē	_____	small guitar
9.	gē'gô	_____	trinket
10.	pleb'ə sīt	_____	popular vote
11.	plə bē'ən	_____	common person
12.	sə rōō'lē ən	_____	sky blue
13.	fə nēsh'ən	_____	ancient Mediterranean resident
14.	kos moj'ə nē	_____	universe creation theory
15.	rig'(ə) mə rōl	_____	complicated procedure
16.	vāl'əns	_____	drapery hung along an edge
17.	sal mə gun'dāe	_____	salad plate; mixture
18.	brok'ə lē	_____	green vegetable
19.	kwes chə nâr'	_____	set of things asked
20.	bar'bə kyōō	_____	to cook over coals
a.	bab'i trē	_____	middle-class conformity
b.	kar'ə van ər	_____	traveler in remote regions
c.	eks hā'lənt	_____	emitting
d.	kak'ē	_____	light yellowish brown
e.	rach'it	_____	toothed mechanism

Pronunciation key on page 10.

Before consulting the answers on page 316:
I think I spelled _____ words correctly on this test.
(If your estimate is correct, add one point to your score.)

Webster's Second (One Spelling Only) Test No. 2

Write in the correct spelling.

1.	ā ri<u>th</u>'mē ə	_____	heartbeat irregularity
2.	bas ə net'	_____	baby's bed
3.	chik'ə dē	_____	crestless titmouse

4.	dā zhä voo′	_____	sense of the familiar
5.	kā′tē did	_____	shrill-sounding grasshopper
6.	âr′ē ən	_____	Indo-European; Nordic
7.	kroo′it	_____	condiment bottle
8.	but in′skē	_____	meddler
9.	shap ə ral′	_____	thicket of dwarf trees
10.	pal i sād′	_____	line of cliffs
11.	sä′kē	_____	Japanese alcoholic drink
12.	chär′däsh	_____	Hungarian dance
13.	ä kə pel′ə	_____	sung without accompaniment
14.	shän ti klâr′, shan ti klēr′	_____	rooster
15.	kan′ə stər	_____	can or container
16.	chan′sē	_____	uncertain or risky
17.	kē′loid	_____	fibrous tissue scar
18.	də krep′it	_____	worn-out or run-down
19.	rō′pē	_____	stringy; like rope
20.	duf′əl	_____	cylindrical belongings bag
a.	bē′zhoo	_____	jewels
b.	sel ə ret′	_____	wine case or sideboard
c.	rə doo′si bəl	_____	capable of being lessened
d.	loo′kə sīt	_____	white blood cell
e.	hom′ə log	_____	something of similar origin or form

Pronunciation key on page 10.

Before consulting the answers on page 316:
I think I spelled _____ words correctly on this test.
(If your estimate is correct, add one point to your score.)

ULTIMATE DEATH BIG FIFTY REVIEW

A grand reprise of words already encountered in previous tests in *Death by Spelling*, this review test is drawn from both the multiple-choice and the phonetically presented twenty- and twenty-five-word tests.

Ultimate Death Big Fifty Review Test

Write in the correct spelling.

1. kōm′pōs men′tis   _____   sound of mind
2. pə ral′ə jiz′əm   _____   logically false argument
3. ver′ə kōs   _____   warty
4. nik′ə lik   _____   containing nickel
5. shmēr′kā zə   _____   cottage cheese
6. non ə jə nār′ē ən   _____   ninety-year-old person
7. ab sīz′   _____   to cut off
8. kroch′i tē   _____   irritable
9. par ə kwät   _____   type of weed killer
10. nô′gə hīd′   _____   vinyl-coated fabric
11. klə mid′ē ə   _____   venereal disease
12. sə läm′   _____   Eastern bow with hand to forehead
13. af ri käns′   _____   language of South Africa
14. milk′tōst   _____   meek person
15. si kwē′lē   _____   disease or injury aftereffect
16. flī′tī′ər   _____   maker of fishing flies
17. fef′ē, fē fē′   _____   recipient of a fee
18. kə pēsh′   _____   *Italian:* Understand?
19. kar′ə fôr   _____   crossroads or square
20. sin′sə mil′ə   _____   type of marijuana
21. ə mûrs′ing   _____   punishing by fining
22. bom′bə sēn   _____   pertaining to silkworms
23. mä jông′   _____   board game
24. tsoo nä′mē   _____   great seismic sea wave
25. lä′mə ser′ē   _____   Buddhist monastery
26. div′ēd   _____   divided
27. sə rôr′əl   _____   sisterly
28. pop ə rä′tsē   _____   celebrity-pursuing photographers
29. sin′jər   _____   one who singes
30. riv′yoo let   _____   small stream
31. pol′ē klin ik   _____   outpatient department

32.	vī ə lən chel′ō	_____	large stringed instrument
33.	stā tol′ə trē	_____	belief in powerful central government
34.	bûr′dē ing	_____	achieving one under par in golf
35.	pal′ing	_____	becoming comrades
36.	krō shā′ər	_____	needlework [looped stitches] practitioner
37.	thon′ik	_____	infernal
38.	mar ē ä′chē	_____	Mexican folk musical group
39.	shif′ə rōb	_____	wardrobe chest of drawers
40.	glâr′ē	_____	brightly reflective or dazzling
41.	i kis′tiks	_____	science of human settlements and building
42.	zhə lā′	_____	cosmetic gel
43.	kon sen tā′nē əs	_____	in agreement, unanimous
44.	zom′bē iz əm	_____	cult of the living dead
45.	ō′lē ō	_____	hodgepodge
46.	də sēd′ənt	_____	dead person
47.	ə man yōō en′sēs	_____	copyists or dictation takers
48.	mə rid′ē ə nəl	_____	southern
49.	sib′ə līn	_____	oracular
50.	kyōō′bə chər	_____	cubic content

Pronunciation key on page 10.

Before consulting the answers on page 316:
I think I spelled _____ words correctly on this test.
(If your estimate is correct, add one point to your score.)

LAST RITES: DEATH BY SPELLING'S TOP TWENTY TEST

As most of the general tests in the book consist of twenty words (with five alternatives to choose from), it's appropriate to make the coup de grace an Author's Favorite Toughest Twenty. These are only my picks; one man's poison is another man's meat, and that goes for women, too.

Again, there are five alternative words to choose from should they look like better bets to you. All but one of these words have one correct answer, and each has appeared in an earlier test in the book.

If you're an ace speller and have turned right to this test after buying the book, that's okay. It proves you're a supercompetitor with hopefully awesome hubris, as a modern professional athlete might put it. You probably sneak peeks at the ends of mystery novels, too.

Last Rites

Write in the correct spelling.

1.	tal′kē	_____	containing a soft silicate used in powder
2.	shə lā′lē	_____	Irish cudgel
3.	grā′nə rē	_____	grain storage place
4.	bē ä′lē	_____	flat roll with central indentation
5.	ap ə loo′sə	_____	Western blotched saddle horse
6.	də sen′ə rē	_____	period of ten years
7.	fī′ə rē ər	_____	more in flame, more passionate
8.	tī′kwon dō′	_____	Korean martial art
9.	yoo′lə lāt, ul′yə lāt	_____	to wail or howl
10.	vish ē swäz′	_____	cold pureed soup
11.	pom′ə gra nət	_____	large fruitlike berry
12.	par ə myoo′t(y)oo əl	_____	betting pool with shared proceeds
13.	kak ə nā′shən	_____	loud laughing
14.	bī sex′til	_____	pertaining to leap year
15.	flib′ûr tee jib′ə tē		silly and flighty
16.	whip′ər wil	_____	nocturnal bird, goatsucker
17.	kap ə chē′no	_____	espresso coffee with hot milk
18.	kyoo′pē	_____	doll with a topknot
19.	pik′ ə dôr	_____	bullfight horseman
20.	shrap′nəl	_____	deadly bomb or mine fragments
a.	ploo′mē	_____	downy, feathery

b. kō′lē   _____   containing or like coal
c. bī mil′ə nûr ē   _____   two thousandth anniversary
d. shē′shē   _____   fashionable or la-di-da
e. sen yŏor′   _____   Portuguese gentleman or title for
                                         him

Pronunciation key on page 10.

> *Before consulting the answers on page 317:*
> I think I spelled ____ words correctly on this test.
> (If your estimate is correct, add one point to your score.)

ANSWERS

"Scoring Yourself on the Tests," Death by Spelling's *grading system, appears on page 8.*

Death by Spelling Admissions Test

1. macaroni
2. vinegar
3. gumption
4. gallivant
5. pineapple
6. mischievous
7. introvert
8. homage
9. aching
10. vassal
11. laryngitis
12. excerpt
13. ordnance
14. gizzard
15. scintillating
16. absorption
17. exhilaration
18. alumnae
19. vacuum
20. superintendent
  a. separate
  b. tariff
  c. privilege
  d. corroborate
  e. bachelor

Count the Misspellings Test

Answers follow the test. See page 7.

SAT-Level Test

1. heterogeneity
2. ancillary
3. casuistry
4. malaise
5. undescried
6. beatific
7. satiety
8. chicanery
9. frangible
10. dysphoria
11. cutaneous
12. desuetude
13. millipede
14. paucity
15. bucolic
16. sari
17. ubiquitous
18. apogee
19. seismometer
20. onerous

GRE-Level Test

1. accoutre
2. beleaguer
3. agglomeration
4. panacea
5. cataclysm
6. talisman
7. vellum
8. apothecary
9. paranoiac
10. tocsin
11. codicil
12. aberration
13. cynosure
14. denizen
15. lagniappe
16. apiary
17. connivance
18. viand
19. acquiescent
20. malediction

Words of One Syllable Test No. 1

1. adz, adze
2. queue
3. weir
4. maize
5. khan
6. schist, shist
7. quire
8. crwth, cruth, crouth
9. xyst
10. flue
11. scrip
12. bight
13. shirr
14. retch
15. spilth
16. brougham
17. ankh
18. gloze
19. stirps
20. ouph, ouphe
a. whorl, wharl
b. brume
c. kine
d. bleb
e. mousse

Multiple Choice Test No. 1

1. deliquesce
2. hoi polloi
3. diphthongal
4. parasol
5. litterateur
6. latchet
7. hominy
8. bombycine
9. lanolin, lanoline
10. rheostat
11. farina
12. paparazzi
13. otiose
14. inchoate
15. cuneiform
16. myrmidon
17. kaleidoscopic
18. megillah
19. Mah-Jongg
20. bêtise
a. bacillus
b. okra, okro
c. chasuble
d. schmierkase
e. kepi

Say It and Spell It Test No. 1

1. Mardi Gras
2. outlier
3. sapphire
4. willfully
5. willfulness
6. Uruguay
7. transmissible
8. gelée
9. treacly
10. turtlet
11. formatter
12. abysmal

13. perspicacious
14. anneal
15. paraph
16. braised, braized
17. macadam
18. discomfiter
19. carrel, carrell
20. anodyne
a. pronounceable
b. Ferris wheel
c. redactor
d. friable
e. Jacuzzi

Words of One Syllable Test No. 2

1. Lapp
2. stile
3. shiv
4. nous
5. nef
6. auk
7. oomph
8. bisque, bisk
9. pyx
10. crèche
11. boîte
12. sieve
13. gorse
14. wen
15. shroff
16. sough
17. taupe
18. coign
19. mulct
20. trough
a. phlox
b. fiend
c. seiche
d. frieze
e. bourse

Multiple Choice Test No. 2

1. sinsemilla
2. amercing
3. formaldehyde
4. chrysanthemum
5. ukase
6. farinaceous
7. palomino, palamino
8. cicada
9. temerarious
10. piscicide
11. Pocahontas
12. melanoma
13. cacophony
14. filament
15. kowtow
16. tambourine
17. proselyte
18. bourgeoise
19. meringue
20. tsetse fly
a. batik
b. wampum
c. nougat
d. tattersall
e. yarmulke, yarmelke

Two Words or One Test

1. snowball
2. taillight
3. backseat
4. redbrick
5. wastewater
6. salesclerk
7. filmmaker
8. pot holder
9. birdbath
10. hair shirt
11. passionflower
12. locker room
13. tollbooth
14. stepladder
15. nightclub
16. bow tie
17. barbell
18. hammerlock
19. lawsuit
20. windowsill
21. peephole
22. artwork
23. paper clip
24. barroom
25. lamppost
a. landowner
b. mouthpart
c. gallbladder
d. seabird
e. cream puff

Say It and Spell It Test No. 2

1. distal
2. amanuenses
3. Baedeker
4. glary
5. dialysis
6. toboggan
7. patroon
8. caitiff
9. assessable
10. ideate
11. paraboloid
12. imprest
13. potash
14. oxidization
15. ekistics
16. demesne

17. ceorl
18. kibitzer
19. proselytize

20. cocoon
a. ack-ack

b. boracic
c. catheter

d. pyorrhea
e. nonagenarian

Words of One Syllable Test No. 3

1. gel
2. plaid
3. hoe
4. flense
5. phlegm
6. teal
7. whey

8. ketch
9. mouth
10. banns
11. shawm, shalm
12. crosse
13. dhow
14. sonde

15. dyne
16. fleche
17. thrips
18. quash
19. stoup
20. drupe
a. sconce

b. toile
c. guimpe
d. thew
e. fosse, foss

Multiple Choice Test No. 3

1. flytier
2. ensorcellment
3. carrefour
4. jalapeño
5. Rorschach
6. strychnine
7. bimillenary

8. aquarellist
9. feoffee
10. cocotte
11. skedaddle
12. bizarrerie
13. naiad
14. tae kwon do

15. aeolian
16. palliasse
17. banquette
18. koine
19. anopheles
20. *capisce*
a. lachrymose

b. bedizen
c. Quonset
d. croupier
e. obloquy

Minute Minute Waltz Test

1. bonhomie
2. segue
3. shelfful

4. épéeist
5. comeuppance
6. mopiness

7. abbutal
8. transference

9. vilify
10. consommé

Say It and Spell It Test No. 3

1. devoirs
2. conferee
3. mucilage
4. serried
5. chamois
6. tutelage
7. couturiere

8. soigné, soignée
9. chifforobe
10. pretzel
11. decedent
12. lovey-dovey
13. peripatetic
14. Judaism

15. flotilla
16. shallot
17. excursus
18. terrazzo
19. gallimaufry
20. psephology
a. braggadocio

b. virescence
c. fidgetiness
d. mariachi
e. tassel

Pairs or Pears Test

1. True
2. True

3. False
4. True

5. False
6. False

7. False
8. True

9. True	15. False	21. False	a. False
10. False	16. False	22. True	b. True
11. True	17. True	23. True	c. True
12. False	18. True	24. False	d. True
13. False	19. True	25. False	e. False
14. False	20. False		

Multiple Choice Test No. 4

1. moiety	8. tinnitus	14. senhor	20. Huguenot
2. solfeggio	9. fracases	15. tourniquet,	a. chintziness
3. parallelism	10. phooey	tourniquet	b. fuchsia
4. manacle	11. scurrilous	16. falafel, felafel	c. picayune
5. platelet	12. dysmenorrhea,	17. bissextile	d. aggiornamento
6. flibbertigibbety	dysmenorrhoea	18. truncheon	e. easel
7. stiletto, stilletto	13. acidophilus	19. guyot	

Say It and Spell It Test No. 4

1. intercalate	8. episcopacy	15. phthalein	b. mnemonic
2. cauliflower	9. gondolier	16. dahlia	c. ctenoid
3. jonquil	10. scuttlebutt	17. ignis fatuus	d. marchioness
4. zwieback	11. caparison	18. shibboleth	e. chthonic
5. hibachi	12. tamale	19. bellwether	
6. caisson	13. shaman	20. thurifer	
7. rapprochement	14. olio	a. mbira	

Words of One Syllable Test No. 4

1. ghat, ghaut	8. spore	15. squeg	b. spitz
2. cwm	9. gneiss	16. baht, bat	c. claque
3. giaour	10. slype	17. rhumb	d. luff
4. thyrse	11. bloc	18. pelf	e. doge
5. gaff	12. gnat	19. gigue	
6. winze	13. sluice	20. tsine	
7. mho	14. putsch	a. sylph	

Multiple Choice Test No. 5

1. catechumen	5. fierier	9. measly	13. centenary
2. menorah	6. trichinosis	10. quisling	14. boutonniere
3. conniption	7. malapropos	11. braille	15. sequelae
4. scintilla	8. Milquetoast	12. debouch	16. baccalaureate

17. poultice
18. glazier
19. aniline

20. meerschaum
a. rebutter

b. bacchanal
c. antediluvian

d. isosceles
e. philippic

Double Letter or Not Test

1. misspelling
2. pastime
3. nighttime
4. poetaster
5. drunkenness
6. coattail
7. sonneteer
8. occurrence
9. withhold
10. dumbbell
11. newsstand
12. duress
13. misshapen
14. threshold
15. bookkeeper
16. roommate
17. headdress
18. musketeer
19. teammate
20. suddenness
a. accommodate
b. commemorate
c. necessity
d. pusillanimous
e. commitment

Say It and Spell It Test No. 5

1. chicanery
2. simpatico
3. palling
4. culotte
5. depilate
6. cul-de-sac
7. Pollyanna
8. accrual
9. hookah, hooka
10. vying
11. patrilineal
12. bibliolater
13. hairbreadth, hairsbreadth
14. effervesces
15. curvature
16. crocheter
17. teleology
18. pantywaist
19. venereology, venerology
20. teetotum
a. paraffin, paraffine
b. surplice
c. maillot
d. abhorrent
e. rowel

Multiple Choice Test No. 6

1. palazzo
2. mulatto
3. espadrille
4. narcissist
5. paraquat
6. Naugahyde
7. encryption
8. chlamydia
9. Szechuan, Szechwan, Sichuan
10. abscise
11. salaam
12. habeas corpus
13. commissary
14. Methuselah
15. Afrikaans
16. paramountcy
17. generalissimo
18. balustrade
19. passel
20. herculean
a. cicatrix
b. discombobulate
c. oleander
d. divagation
e. hebdomadal

Say It and Spell It Test No. 6

1. birdieing
2. canniness
3. styptic
4. caravel
5. evanescing
6. Parsons table
7. bivouacking
8. ululate
9. granite
10. billet
11. conquistador
12. dumdum
13. dum-dum
14. topaz
15. olio
16. tinniness

17. auld lang syne
18. terra-cotta
19. lapful
20. duress
a. annulling
b. covey
c. sisal
d. dowsing rod
e. solder

Multiple Choice Test No. 7

1. cicerone
2. inamorata
3. sebaceous
4. cranny
5. colossal
6. veterinarian
7. gutta-percha
8. titillate
9. silhouette
10. glutenous
11. brummagem
12. penicillin
13. hors d'oeuvres
14. skivvies, scivvies
15. galoshes
16. piccolo
17. icicle
18. tam-o'-shanter
19. trivet
20. succotash
a. eucalyptus
b. chichi
c. battalion
d. dromedary
e. astrakhan, astrachan

Words of One Syllable Test No. 5

1. Mach
2. scree
3. conte
4. leach
5. yurt
6. skoal
7. brooch
8. yacht
9. veld, veldt
10. moue
11. loess
12. swatch
13. yegg
14. wraith
15. mien
16. vane
17. scourge
18. breve
19. mete
20. gar
a. cloche
b. deign
c. baal
d. grebe
e. joule

Multiple Choice Test No. 8

1. kohlrabi
2. phylogeny
3. rickety
4. semaphore
5. participatory
6. habiliments
7. Dramamine
8. doily
9. calamine
10. tergiversate
11. talcky
12. ipecac
13. bludgeon
14. poinsettia
15. crotchety
16. affidavit
17. hemorrhage
18. cappuccino
19. Capuchin
20. obelisk
a. inveigle
b. molasses
c. complaisant
d. pasteurize
e. tupelo

Say It and Spell It Test No. 7

1. isthmus
2. policlinic
3. hymeneal
4. phthisic
5. violoncello
6. bated
7. caffeine
8. accruement
9. statolatry
10. zombiism
11. shoofly
12. abutment
13. acned
14. disc harrow
15. galoot
16. nonsked

17. Wedgwood
18. missilery, missilry
19. décolletage

20. hawser
a. cravat

b. handsel, hansel
c. currieries

d. eunuch
e. pomade

Words of One Syllable Test No. 6

1. faille
2. nil
3. cirque
4. dight
5. coif, coiffe
6. sphex
7. wrasse

8. gyle
9. daube
10. cyst
11. strep
12. conch
13. toque
14. nosh

15. gault, galt
16. dalles
17. swathe
18. sclaff
19. plaice
20. dun
a. seine

b. wort
c. Sekt
d. frass
e. wreathe

Multiple Choice Test No. 9

1. cinnamon
2. tintinnabulation
3. placket
4. daguerreotype
5. rutabaga
6. dinghies
7. aqueous

8. genealogically
9. panegyric
10. solstitial
11. bicentenary
12. mallet
13. abacuses
14. rimy

15. naphtha
16. Antaean
17. littoral
18. acetylene
19. catenary
20. fedora
a. maraschino

b. geodesy
c. phantasmagoria
d. Tagalog
e. gigolo

Say It and Spell It Test No. 8

1. seminal
2. harass
3. commemorate
4. playwright
5. anoint
6. deferment
7. stupefy

8. foreordain
9. sulky
10. consentaneous
11. vitriol
12. conferral
13. rivulet
14. lintel

15. oppugn
16. wall-less
17. guttural
18. owlet
19. armature
20. freshet
a. extirpate

b. casteism
c. rarities
d. pabulum
e. genteelly

Multiple Choice Test No. 10

1. de rigueur
2. adenoidal
3. chameleon,
   cameleon

4. philately
5. bougainvillea,
   bougainvillaea
6. prestidigitator

7. spinet
8. octoroon
9. brisket
10. demurral

11. minaret
12. homburg
13. caballero
14. passementerie

15. chautauqua
16. dilatation
17. garret
18. colophon
19. ptomaine
20. trekker
a. antimacassar
b. betel
c. revetment, revêtement
d. chrysalis
e. anise

Say It and Spell It Test No. 9

1. deserts
2. meridional
3. grippe
4. obstreperous
5. consensual
6. intendance
7. pittance
8. plumy
9. shooed
10. avalanche
11. pro tem
12. divvied
13. infinitesimal
14. sororal
15. phaeton
16. lensless
17. funereal
18. parricide
19. harebrained
20. singer
a. satchel
b. liaison
c. enchilada
d. saltcellar
e. embarrass

Multiple Choice Test No. 11

1. pomegranate
2. nimiety
3. decennary
4. brusquerie
5. bituminous
6. aneroid
7. roentgen, röntgen
8. Armageddon
9. paralogism
10. velleity
11. caoutchouc
12. monadnock
13. vermeil
14. pharaoh
15. verrucose
16. papilionaceous
17. fluorescent
18. rhadamanthine
19. niccolic
20. shekel
a. beelzebub
b. mistletoe
c. gouache
d. propaedeutic
e. myrrh

British Spellings Test

1. aeon
2. haemorrhage
3. kerb
4. carburettor, carburetter
5. speciality
6. waggon
7. artefact
8. connexion
9. homoeopathy
10. apologise
11. enrol
12. cyder
13. to-morrow
14. gaol
15. enthralment
16. dulness
17. syphon
18. pyjamas
19. faecal
20. nought
21. vice
22. pretence
23. manoeuvre
24. anaemic
25. harbour
a. biassed
b. worshipper
c. behove
d. diarrhoea
e. mediaeval

Multiple Choice Test No. 12

1. hasenpfeffer, hassenpfeffer
2. loupe
3. kiosk, kiosque
4. palette
5. coquetry
6. innards
7. opalescent
8. sarsaparilla
9. buccaneer
10. napery
11. paregoric

12. aperitif
13. compos mentis
14. reveille
15. schnapps, schnaps
16. psychedelic

17. eleemosynary
18. Demerol
19. hermeneutics
20. piranha, piraña

a. chicle
b. shrapnel
c. syphilis

d. adscititious,
   ascititious
e. plankton

Multiple Choice Test No. 13

1. liniment
2. ophthalmology
3. bouillabaisse
4. caduceus
5. Sheol
6. camellia, camelia
7. sibilant

8. smorgasbord
9. camaraderie
10. jitney
11. censer
12. maggoty
13. chukka
14. peccadillo

15. chapleted
16. zeppelin
17. muumuu
18. nickelodeon
19. cirrhosis
20. macaroon
 a. cemeteries

b. quinquennium
c. empyrean
d. picador
e. gypper

Multiple Choice Test No. 14

1. gelignite
2. vaqueros
3. daiquiri
4. balalaika
5. topsy-turviness
6. topsy-turvydom
7. luau

8. spinnaker
9. dirndl
10. finagle, fenagle
11. trellis
12. lamasery
13. kindergartner,
    kindergartener

14. jodhpurs
15. barrette
16. manicotti
17. paean, pean
18. slaveys
19. fricassee
20. marquee

a. Sisyphean,
   Sisyphian
b. nigritude
c. carousel,
   carrousel
d. kitsch
e. stevedore

Multiple Choice Test No. 15

1. odysseys
2. shillelagh,
   shillalah
3. whippoorwill
4. vichyssoise
5. pari-mutuel
6. sassafras
7. Appaloosa

8. castanets
9. diocesan
10. Filipinos
11. granary
12. hullabaloo,
    hullaballoo
13. Kewpie
14. millennium

15. bialys
16. obeisance
17. Weimaraner
18. tinselry
19. simoleon
20. babushka
 a. spermaceti
 b. winnable

c. diphtheria
d. antihistamine
e. spittoon

Two Spellings Allowed Test No. 1

1. aneurysm, aneurism
2. bourn, bourne
3. caravansary, caravanserai

4. inexpungible, inexpungeable
5. keister, keester
6. shtetl, shtetel

7. tumbrel, tumbril
8. wainscoting, wainscotting
9. mavourneen, mavournin
10. persnickety, persnickity
11. esophagus, oesophagus
12. chiaroscuro, chiaro-oscuro
13. wisenheimer, weisenheimer
14. genuflection, genuflexion
15. hoopla, houp-la
16. counselor, counsellor

17. Legionnaires' disease,
    Legionnaire's disease
18. teetotaler, teetotaller
19. cockamamy, cockamamie
20. kaput, kaputt
    a. bark, barque
    b. wadable, wadeable
    c. epaulet, epaulette
    d. moniker, monicker
    e. parallelly, paralelly

Two Spellings Allowed Test No. 2

1. gauntlet, gantlet
2. chocolaty, chocolatey
3. calamari, calamary
4. linguine, linguini
5. whodunit, whodunnit
6. syllabub, sillabub
7. caliper, calliper
8. loofah, luffa
9. Manichaean, Manichean
10. bonhomie, bonhommie
11. lanyard, laniard
12. omelet, omelette
13. quay, quai

14. grommet, grummet
15. slew, slue
16. absinthe, absinth
17. brier, briar
18. sty, stye
19. clarinetist, clarinettist
20. barcarole, barcarolle
    a. extrovert, extravert
    b. caulk, calk
    c. tricorne, tricorn
    d. dreadnought, dreadnaught
    e. janissary, janizary

Two Spellings Allowed Test No. 3

1. nitroglycerin, nitroglycerine
2. cornetist, cornettist
3. envoi, envoy
4. beldam, beldame
5. mortise, mortice
6. grandam, grandame
7. grotesquerie, grotesquery
8. enjambment, enjambement
9. bluing, blueing
10. appanage, apanage
11. Ghanaian, Ghanian
12. letch, lech
13. chlorophyll, chlorophyl

14. omicron, omikron
15. sateen, satine
16. myna, mynah
17. briquette, briquet
18. bandanna, bandana
19. willful, wilful
20. casino, cassino
    a. aerogram, aerogramme
    b. christie, christy
    c. Christmasy, Christmassy
    d. crime passionel, crime passionnel
    e. autogiro, autogyro

Death by Spelling College
(50 special-subject tests)

American Cities

1. Tallahassee
2. Albuquerque
3. Ypsilanti
4. Wahpeton
5. Corvallis
6. Oskaloosa
7. Chattanooga
8. Schenectady
9. Wilkes-Barre
10. Chillicothe
11. Amarillo
12. Champaign
13. Bogalusa
14. Casper
15. Manasquan
16. Elkhart
17. Meriden
18. Fredericksburg
19. Montpelier
20. Savannah
21. Sheboygan
22. Missoula
23. Paragould
24. Phenix City
25. Brainerd
26. Atchison
27. McAlester
28. Tooele
29. Petaluma
30. Pocatello
31. Spartanburg
32. Paducah
33. Vermillion
34. Woonsocket
35. Buckhannon
36. Chicopee
37. Wenatchee
38. Ketchikan
39. Wailuku
40. Hattiesburg
41. Walsenburg
42. Plaistow
43. Millinocket
44. Sedalia
45. Winnemucca
46. Dundalk
47. Smyrna
48. Kannapolis
49. Holdrege
50. Bisbee

Anatomy

1. malleolus
2. gracilis
3. periosteum
4. gastrocnemius
5. apophysis
6. triquetrum
7. ischium
8. masseter
9. supraspinatus
10. xiphoid
11. gemellus
12. teres
13. serratus
14. sternocleido-mastoid
15. phalanges
16. obturator
17. bregma
18. hypothenar
19. coracobrachialis
20. sesamoid
21. iliopsoas
22. pterygoideus
23. interosseus
24. trochanter
25. piriformis
    a. psoas major
    b. epicondyle
    c. platysma
    d. calcaneus
    e. humerus

Animals and Dinosaurs

1. peccary
2. dormouse
3. pterodactyl
4. ocelot
5. hartebeest
6. hippopotamus
7. wallaby
8. llama
9. macaque
10. megathere
11. gemsbok
12. triceratops

13. oryx
14. capybara, capibara, capivara
15. platypus
16. terrapin
17. okapi
18. agouti, agouty
19. coatimundi, coatimondi
20. manatee
21. dimetrodon
22. Komodo dragon
23. caiman, cayman
24. Gila monster
25. archaeopteryx
a. tyrannosaur, tyrannosaurus
b. kinkajou
c. marmot
d. quokka
e. nutria

Anthropology

1. shamanism
2. cromlech
3. Australopithecus
4. ethnogeny
5. Nilotic
6. mythopoeia
7. adelphic
8. dolichocephalic
9. labret
10. Melanesian
11. teknonymy
12. polygyny
13. quadrumanous
14. Kulturkreis
15. totemism
16. Olduvai Gorge
17. cymotrichous
18. infibulation
19. euhemerism
20. Cycladic
21. Boskopoid
22. xylomancy
23. catarrhine, catarhine
24. Choukoutien, Choukoutienian, Zhoukoudian
25. corroboree
a. baalism
b. Caucasoid
c. Eleusinian mysteries
d. henotheism
e. apotropaism

Archeology

1. skeuomorph
2. calumet
3. midden
4. Acheulean, Acheulian
5. varve dating
6. sgraffito, scraffiato
7. burin
8. Mycenaean, Mycenian
9. oculus
10. souterrain
11. Pleistocene
12. aryballos, aryballus
13. Nineveh
14. crannog
15. fibula
16. Schliemann
17. homotaxis
18. syllabary
19. cist, kist
20. Chichén Itzá
21. paleolimnology
22. canopic jar
23. palaetiology, paletiology
24. terramara
25. Tiahuanaco
a. Solutrean, Solutrian
b. fluviatile
c. mattock
d. cenotaph
e. carination

Architecture History

1. clerestory, clearstory
2. finial
3. tympanum
4. grimthorpe
5. voussoir
6. cartouche, cartouch
7. stylobate
8. muntin, munting
9. galilee
10. intrados
11. eurythmy, eurhythmy
12. cinquefoil
13. aqueduct
14. Brunelleschi, Brunellesco
15. guilloche

16. Colosseum, Coliseum
17. metope
18. volute
19. tierceron
20. plateresque, plateresco

21. lancet
22. reliquary
23. campanile
24. baldachin
25. pilaster

a. loggia
b. Palladian
c. Bauhaus
d. acanthus
e. coffered

Art History

1. Phidias
2. glyptic
3. de Stijl
4. craquelure
5. Botticelli
6. sfumato
7. caryatid
8. Rouault
9. putto
10. trompe l'oeil
11. Brueghel, Breughel, Bruegel

12. tesselated
13. marmoreal
14. Beaux-Arts
15. quattrocento
16. triptych, triptich
17. Kokoschka
18. churrigueresque
19. tenebrism
20. Valázquez, Velásquez
21. contrapposto
22. Pissarro
23. Ghirlandajo, Ghirlandaio

24. pleinairism
25. Canaletto
a. Buonarroti
b. grisaille
c. limner
d. synthetism
e. nabi

Astronomy

1. gibbous
2. Pleiades
3. aphelion
4. selenodesy
5. deferent
6. Cassegrain
7. interferometry
8. areocentric
9. parallax
10. Deimos
11. gegenschein

12. collimator
13. Betelgeuse
14. facula
15. astrolabe
16. almucantar, almacantar
17. Cepheid variable
18. Magellanic cloud
19. epact
20. coelostat
21. cislunar
22. aurora borealis

23. kiloparsec
24. telluric
25. syzygy
a. Foucault pendulum
b. Boötes
c. sidereal
d. Chandrasekhar limit
e. Cassiopeia

Automobiles

1. magneto
2. landau
3. Pininfarina
4. ohmmeter
5. Peugeot

6. coolant
7. solenoid unit
8. cowl
9. Indianapolis 500

10. flivver
11. Lamborghini
12. chicane
13. tachometer
14. macadam

15. tappet
16. ethylene glycol
17. Aston Martin
18. tonneau
19. ammeter

20. taillight
21. Reo
22. Graham-Paige

23. Cardan joint
24. catalytic
      converter

25. pinion
  a. shims
  b. Darracq

  c. synchromesh
  d. gasket
  e. camber

Barfly

1. bacchanalianism
2. julep
3. amaretto
4. Campari
5. mai-tai
6. Kahlúa
7. ouzo
8. Mickey Finn

9. Galliano
10. pousse-café
11. aquavit
12. Tsingtao
13. margarita
14. curaçao,
      curaçoa
15. seidel

16. glögg
17. kirsch
18. crème de cacao
19. Drambuie
20. Calvados
21. anisette
22. kümmel
23. cassis

24. sambuca
25. Dubonnet
  a. Rob Roy
  b. shandygaff
  c. piña colada
  d. pilsner, pilsener
  e. Dos Equis

Bible

1. Douay Bible
2. Pentateuch
3. Colossians
4. Balaam
5. Gilead
6. Nicodemus
7. Ananias
8. diatessaron

9. Gomorrah
10. Elohist
11. Capernaum
12. Philippians
13. Galilean, Galilaean
14. Septuagint
15. Jehoshaphat
16. Golgotha

17. Zadok
18. canonical
19. Gadite
20. Johannine
21. Paralipomenon
22. Ecclesiastes
23. Judas
      Maccabaeus

24. Nahum
25. Gnostic
  a. exegetics
  b. Sadducean,
      Sadducaean
  c. Torah, Tora
  d. Qumran
  e. Galatians

Biology

1. Linnaean, Linnean
2. ecesis
3. prokaryote
4. transferase
5. mitochondrion
6. annelid
7. deoxyribonucleic acid
8. phylogeny
9. gnotobiotic
10. Coelenterata

11. ocellus
12. cytolysis
13. auxesis
14. nephridium
15. allele
16. organelle
17. Lysenkoism
18. crustacean
19. mesentery
20. testaceous

21. allantois
22. phytoplankton
23. scolex
24. meiosis
25. therology
  a. nucleolus
  b. vacuole
  c. cladistics
  d. gametophyte
  e. centriole

Birds

1. toucan
2. grosbeak
3. curlew
4. gyrfalcon
5. bobolink
6. tanager
7. kookaburra
8. nidifugous
9. barbet
10. phalarope
11. ratite
12. egret
13. chaffinch
14. lammergeier, lammergeyer
15. pileated
16. whydah
17. neossology
18. dickcissel
19. psittacosis
20. altricial
21. pipit
22. guillemot
23. cygnet
24. merganser
25. avocet
a. jaeger
b. passerine
c. cormorant
d. petrel
e. vireo

Botany

1. xylem
2. dicotyledon
3. saprophytic
4. bracteole
5. batology
6. lenticel
7. anther
8. connivent
9. phloem
10. braky
11. rhizome
12. caespitose, cespitose
13. abscisic acid
14. peduncle
15. involucre
16. pomology
17. ligule
18. efflorescence
19. calyx
20. deciduous
21. corymb
22. Cycadofilicales
23. Gnetum
24. bryophyte
25. calamite
a. lichen
b. thallus
c. mycology
d. phytology
e. Ginkgoales

Brand Name Shopper

1. Jacuzzi
2. Sweet 'n Low
3. Dr Pepper
4. ChapStick
5. Procter & Gamble
6. Handi Wipes
7. Tinkertoy
8. K mart
9. NutraSweet
10. Ty-D-bol
11. Jujyfruits
12. Levi's
13. Brylcreem
14. Toys "Я" Us
15. Chee•tos
16. Maalox
17. Tiparillo
18. Uneeda
19. Reddi-Wip
20. Spic and Span
21. Jell-O
22. Raisinets
23. La-Z-Boy
24. Wash 'n Dri
25. Gore-Tex
a. Hula-Hoop
b. Piper-Heidsieck
c. S.O.S
d. TelePrompTer
e. Mazola

Castles and Fortifications

1. crenel, crenelle
2. terreplein
3. machicolation
4. embrasure
5. portcullis
6. donjon
7. trunnion
8. glacis
9. castellated
10. balistraria
11. base-court
12. palisado
13. chevaux-de-frise
14. redan
15. abatis, abattis
16. peel
17. tenaille
18. bartizan
19. demilune
20. barbican
21. circumvallation
22. merlon
23. bailey
24. motte
25. crosslet
a. parados
b. yett
c. garderobe
d. battlement
e. enceinte

Cats

1. cattery
2. Abyssinian
3. vibrissae
4. cobby
5. cacomistle
6. Birman
7. grimalkin
8. Cymric
9. calico
10. Bast
11. Korat
12. feliform
13. Chartreux
14. polydactylism
15. trichobezoar
16. ailurophile, aelurophile
17. clowder
18. onychectomy
19. margay
20. nictitating membrane
21. feline panleukopenia, feline panleucopenia
22. chatoyant
23. nepatalactone
24. Chinchilla
25. matatabi
a. torbie
b. Singapura
c. Tonkinese
d. Seal-Lynx point
e. caterwaul

Chemistry

1. beryllium
2. immiscible
3. sulfonate, sulphonate
4. arylate
5. monosaccharide
6. elutriate
7. syneresis, synaeresis
8. tritiated
9. heteromerous
10. Mitscherlich's law
11. thixotropy
12. ytterbium
13. sal ammoniac
14. eudiometer
15. Woulff bottle
16. hydrolysis
17. halogen
18. stoichiometry
19. ethanol
20. polymer
21. flocculant
22. oleum
23. phenolphthalein
24. aliphatic
25. praseodymium
a. valence
b. dialysis
c. gadolinium
d. Erlenmeyer flask
e. cataphoresis

Classical Music

1. solfeggio
2. melismatic
3. acciaccatura
4. embouchure
5. passacaglia
6. carillonneur, carilloneur
7. ritenuto
8. dodecaphony
9. sinfonietta
10. affettuoso
11. rebec, rebeck
12. toccata
13. melodeon
14. appoggiatura
15. larghissimo
16. mixolydian
17. Koussevitzky
18. marimba
19. fortemente
20. bourrée
21. Khachaturian
22. misterioso
23. theremin
24. arpeggio
25. Messiaen
a. fermata
b. descant
c. aleatory
d. Saint-Saëns
e. ricercar, ricercare

Clothes and Fabrics

1. titivate
2. busheler
3. balbriggan, ballbrigan
4. redingote
5. fichu
6. revers
7. dickey, dicky
8. Borsalino
9. blouson
10. baize
11. serape, sarape
12. mackinaw
13. guimpe
14. alpaca
15. organza
16. shalloon
17. faille
18. Qiana
19. tulle
20. bedizenment
21. galligaskins
22. vicuña, vicuna, vicugna
23. mousquetaire gloves
24. peignoir
25. byssus
a. gusset
b. pantaloons
c. crepe de chine
d. cheongsam
e. sou'wester

Countries of the World

1. Mauritius
2. Vanuatu
3. Seychelles
4. Brunei
5. Comoros
6. Guinea-Bissau
7. Guyana
8. Bahrain, Bahrein
9. São Tomé e Principe
10. Djibouti
11. Czechoslovakia
12. Qatar
13. Rwanda
14. Lesotho
15. Malawi
16. Kampuchea
17. Burundi
18. Belorussia, Byelorussia
19. Surinam, Suriname
20. Antigua and Barbuda
21. Sri Lanka
22. Afghanistan
23. Mauritania
24. Bangladesh
25. Honduras
a. Bhutan
b. Luxembourg, Luxemburg
c. Belize
d. Gambia
e. Zimbabwe

Dance and Ballet

1. coryphée
2. pirouette
3. schottische
4. battement
5. labanotation
6. ballonné
7. sissonne, sissone
8. habanera
9. pachanga
10. entrechat
11. fouetté
12. carioca
13. maxixe
14. polonaise
15. bugaloo
16. port de bras
17. calypso
18. ballotté
19. gargouillade
20. pas de bourrée
21. merengue, méringue
22. beguine
23. Nikolais
24. paso doble
25. tarantella, tarentelle
a. eurythmics, eurhythmics
b. malaguena
c. Diaghilev
d. passepied, passpy
e. Balanchine

Desserts and Sweets

1. jujube
2. streusel
3. petit four
4. macaroon
5. brioche
6. fasnacht, fastnacht
7. rennet
8. frappe, frappé
9. stollen

10. Sacher torte
11. pistachio
12. savarin
13. Häagen-Dazs
14. croquembouche
15. pandowdy
16. baklava
17. zabaglione
18. charlotte russe
19. marzipan
20. baba
21. gelati, gelato
22. parfait
23. blancmange
24. tutti-frutti
25. praline
a. compote
b. horehound, hoarhound
c. bonne bouche
d. patisserie
e. pfeffernüss

Dogs

1. cynologist
2. Schnauzer
3. Afghan hound
4. Rottweiler
5. Saluki
6. Airedale
7. lhasa apso
8. Bichon Frise
9. malamute, malemute
10. Chihuahua
11. mastiff
12. schipperke
13. Brittany spaniel
14. weimaraner
15. affenpinscher
16. Pomeranian
17. whippet
18. briard
19. dachshund
20. Dalmatian
21. Sealyham terrier
22. Basset hound
23. dingo
24. Samoyed
25. Cerberus
a. husky
b. Shar-Pei
c. Bedlington terrier
d. bandog
e. Kuvasz

Drugs, Antibiotics, Etc.

1. barbiturate
2. Dexedrine
3. Mellaril
4. Quaalude
5. amphetamine
6. methadone, methadon
7. Seconal
8. Dilaudid
9. streptomycin
10. Amytal
11. atropine
12. Compazine
13. sodium pentothol
14. Demerol
15. Nembutal
16. codeine
17. Percodan
18. psilocybin
19. meconism
20. pharmacopoeia, pharmacopeia
21. paraphernalia
22. Ritalin
23. narghile, nargileh
24. Miltown
25. acetylsalicylic acid
a. Dramamine
b. sulfadiazine
c. tetracycline
d. Mercurochrome
e. cannabism

Economics, Business, and Finance

1. entrepreneurial
2. debenture
3. suretyship
4. replevin
5. hypothecate
6. therblig
7. tale quale
8. impignorate
9. Chancellor of the Exchequer
10. ceteris paribus
11. cum dividend
12. arbitrage
13. Keynesian
14. defalcation

15. usufruct
16. Bretton Woods Conference
17. fiduciary
18. caveat emptor
19. seigniorage, seignorage
20. laissez-faire
21. tontine
22. sumptuary
23. oligopolistic
24. Galbraithean
25. peonage
a. Ricardian
b. cartel
c. brassage
d. cameralist
e. Ginnie Mae

English and English Literature

1. metonymy
2. *Areopagitica*
3. Hudibrastic
4. picaresque
5. dactylic
6. mythopoesis
7. *Rubáiyát of Omar Khayyám*
8. parataxis
9. Kailyard School, Kaleyard School
10. synecdoche
11. flyting
12. stichomythia, stichomythy
13. euphuistic
14. kenning
15. "Mac Flecknoe"
16. Pepysian
17. Charles Lutwidge Dodgson
18. *Finnegans Wake*
19. aposiopesis
20. concettism
21. belletrist
22. Skeltonic
23. villanelle
24. esemplastic
25. Houyhnhnm
a. tmesis
b. Hakluyt
c. *Pendennis*
d. mimesis
e. chrestomathy

Furniture and Antiques

1. escritoire
2. Biedermeier
3. girandole
4. bombé
5. cabriole
6. Duncan Phyfe
7. vargueno
8. prie-dieu
9. Savonarola chair
10. fauteuil
11. Coromandel work
12. étagère, etagere
13. trifid foot
14. chinoiserie
15. boulle, buhl, boule
16. encoignure
17. taboret, tabouret
18. credence
19. settee
20. ormolu
21. Eames chair
22. cheval glass
23. gadrooning
24. parquetry
25. rattan, ratan
a. Chippendale
b. trivet table
c. Circassian walnut
d. damask
e. scutcheon

Gems and Crystals

1. bijouterie
2. amethyst
3. tourmaline, turmaline
4. chalcedony, calcedony
5. onyx
6. cabochon
7. smaragd
8. peridot, peridote
9. jadeite
10. Mohs' scale
11. lapis lazuli
12. adularescent
13. sphene
14. porphyry
15. grossularite
16. Padparadschah
17. carnelian, cornelian
18. trichroism

19. asteriated
20. chrysoberyl
21. girasol, girasole
22. briolette, brilliolette, brillolette

23. chevee
24. melee
25. rutile
a. cat's-eye

b. nephrite
c. obsidian
d. leucite
e. malachite

Geology

1. micaceous
2. epeirogeny, epirogeny
3. breccia
4. allochthonous, allocthonous
5. cinnabar
6. ferruginous
7. cairngorm
8. pahoehoe
9. stalactite
10. mispickel

11. gypsum
12. flysch
13. terrigenous
14. peneplain, peniplane
15. isostasy, isostacy
16. molybdenite
17. aphanite
18. quaquaversal
19. klippe, klip
20. congelifraction
21. gabbro

22. pergelisol
23. arenaceous
24. cupreous
25. phreatic
a. hornblende
b. eluvium
c. plagioclase
d. diorite
e. mantle

Gourmet Cook

1. cacciatore
2. radicchio, radichio
3. vinaigrette
4. gazpacho
5. piccalilli
6. spaetzle, spätzle
7. aioli
8. ratatouille
9. ptarmigan
10. meunière
11. bourguignonne, bourguignon

12. tetrazzini
13. cilantro
14. finocchio, finochio
15. timbale
16. raclette
17. scaloppine, scallopini
18. coquilles St. Jacques
19. fricasseed
20. garde-manger
21. prosciutto
22. arugula
23. stroganoff

24. couscous, cuscousou, cuscusu
25. rémoulade, remoulade, remolade
a. rigatoni
b. cannelloni
c. cappelletti
d. béarnaise
e. cuisine minceur

Historical and Cultural Figures

1. Hammarskjöld
2. Andersen
3. Tutankhamen
4. O'Keeffe
5. Boccaccio

6. Solzhenitsyn
7. Wenceslas
8. Anouilh
9. Stuyvesant
10. Aeschylus

11. Audubon
12. Gandhi
13. Khrushchev
14. Verrazano, Verrazzano
15. Kościuszko

16. Maeterlinck
17. Nebuchadnezzar, Nebuchadrezzar
18. Cassatt
19. Saarinen
20. Haile Selassie
21. Beiderbecke
22. Ho Chi Minh
23. Kemal Atatürk
24. Montesquieu
25. Brzezinsky
    a. Kublai Khan
b. Respighi
c. Xanthippe
d. Siddhārtha Gautama
e. Nietzsche

History

1. Peloponnesian War
2. Appomattox
3. Marseillaise
4. Treaty of Aix-la-Chapelle
5. Faneuil Hall
6. Tippecanoe
7. Tocqueville
8. Mazarin
9. Passchendaele
10. Hohenzollern
11. Dred Scott
12. Ghibelline
13. Battle of Crécy
14. Antietam
15. Aufklärung
16. Zwinglianism
17. Anne Boleyn
18. Berchtesgaden
19. witenagemot, witenagemote
20. *Merrimac, Merrimack*
21. Chickamauga
22. Balfour Declaration
23. Canossa
24. Dreyfus Affair
25. Thermopylae
    a. Burgoyne
    b. Sepoy Mutiny
    c. Guernica
    d. Acheson
    e. Lebensraum

Horses

1. equestrienne
2. hippology
3. whinny
4. croup
5. Percheron
6. lorimer, loriner
7. pastern
8. skewbald
9. manege, manège
10. cantle
11. spavin, spavine
12. gymkhana
13. Clydesdale
14. surcingle, circingle
15. pommel, pummel
16. sorrel
17. rosinante
18. jennet, genet
19. caracole
20. sumpter
21. cavalletti
22. farrier
23. cannon
24. Bucephalus
25. Przhevalski's horse, Przewalski's horse, Prjevalski's horse
    a. numnah
    b. hackamore
    c. cavalry
    d. martingale
    e. Pegasus

Hypochondriac

1. valetudinarian
2. impetigo
3. apoplexy
4. lumbago
5. colitis
6. psoriasis
7. Kaopectate
8. *schadenfreude*
9. sedative
10. vaccinator
11. iatrogenic
12. Brioschi
13. abscesses
14. hemorrhoid
15. migraine
16. Robitussin
17. kvetch
18. cephalalgia
19. hallucinate
20. pruritus

21. cachexy,
    cachexia
22. rheumatism

23. charley horse
24. tisane, ptisan
25. psychosomatic

a. constipation
b. catarrh
c. tonsillitis

d. sacroiliac
e. chilblain

Insects, Spiders, Ants, and Butterflies

1. tarantula
2. proboscis
3. mantis
4. scarab
5. aphid
6. myrmecophile
7. spinneret
8. vespid

9. cecropia moth
10. drosophila
11. cockchafer
12. ichneumon fly
13. mandible
14. coleopteran
15. ammophila
16. phoresy

17. pyralid
18. caddis fly,
    caddice fly
19. whirligig beetle
20. io moth
21. fritillary
22. grylloblattid
23. imagoes

24. botfly
25. curculio
a. dinergate
b. syrphid
c. pismire
d. lepidopter
e. arachnid

Law

1. subpoenaed
2. lex talionis
3. curtesy
4. feme covert
5. allonge
6. stare decisis
7. nolle prosequi
8. emphyteusis
9. disseizin, disseisin
10. mesne

11. champerty, champarty
12. scienter
13. barratry
14. deforciant
15. nuncupative
16. promisor
17. misprision
18. cy pres
19. estoppel
20. certiorari

21. supersedeas
22. bailor
23. escheat
24. appellee
25. duces tecum
a. remittitur
b. amicus curiae
c. leguleian
d. nomolographer
e. shrievalty

Mathematics

1. abscissa
2. nilpotent
3. parallelepiped,
   parallelepipedon,
   parallelopiped,
   parallelopipedon
4. googolplex
5. Fibonacci numbers
6. addend
7. asymptote
8. steradian

9. Riemannian geometry
10. catenary
11. lituus
12. duodenary
13. Möbius strip
14. escribe
15. collineation
16. Lobachevsky
17. barycentric
18. frustrum, frustum
19. loxodromic

20. nappe
21. haversine
22. sinusoidal
23. dactylonomy
24. annulus
25. Diophantine equation
a. isogonal
b. algorism
c. circumferential
d. quintic
e. aliquot

Medicine

1. Aesculapius
2. dyspnea, dispnoea
3. kwashiorkor
4. antiarrhythmic
5. ballottement
6. syssarcosis
7. graafian follicle
8. bilharziasis
9. pathognomonic
10. iatrogenicity
11. cannula, canula
12. ankylosis, anchylosis, ancylosis
13. cholecystectomy
14. mammillary
15. erysipelas
16. sphygmomanometer
17. pellagra
18. tsutsugamushi fever
19. Friedman test, Friedman's test
20. vulsellum
21. cachexia, cachexy
22. bistoury
23. reovirus
24. semeiologist
25. calenture
    a. granuloma inguinale
    b. byssinosis
    c. ischemia, ischaemia
    d. afibrogenemia
    e. parulis

Modern Authors

1. John Ashbery
2. A. E. Housman
3. Friedrich Dürrenmatt
4. Seán O'Faoláin
5. Muriel Rukeyser
6. James Gould Cozzens
7. Nikos Kazantzakis
8. Knut Hamsun
9. Lawrence Ferlinghetti
10. Archibald MacLeish
11. Dashiell Hammett
12. Pär F. Lagerkvist
13. John Betjeman
14. Eugene Ionesco
15. Jerzy Kosinski
16. Isak Dinesen
17. Theodore Roethke
18. MacKinlay Kantor
19. Salman Rushdie
20. Donald Barthelme
21. Mordecai Richler
22. Allen Drury
23. Bernard Malamud
24. Luigi Pirandello
25. Gerhart Hauptmann
    a. Lawrence Durrell
    b. Marc Connelly
    c. Max Beerbohm
    d. Gabriel García Márquez
    e. Kurt Vonnegut

Money and Currencies

1. numismatics
2. zloty
3. specie
4. do-re-mi
5. ducat
6. markka
7. forint
8. bimetallism
9. cruzeiro
10. koruna
11. ringgit
12. peseta
13. eyrir
14. porte-monnaie
15. dirham, dirhem, derham
16. florin
17. rial
18. nummary
19. Croesus
20. cambistry
21. guerdon
22. Onassis
23. dinar, denar
24. groschen
25. annuit coeptis
    a. rupee
    b. anatocism
    c. bursar
    d. impecunious
    e. solatium

Mountains and Mountaineering

1. bergschrund
2. inselberg
3. Kilimanjaro
4. verglas
5. abseil
6. carabiner, karabiner
7. arête
8. névé
9. aiguille
10. glissade
11. crampon
12. massif

13. rappel
14. cordillera
15. hypsography
16. chockstone
17. prusik knot
18. scree

19. Ararat
20. Pyrenees, Pyrénées
21. Kangchenjunga
22. Aconcagua
23. acrophobia
24. Lhotse

25. Mount Rainier
a. serac
b. Ruwenzori
c. Nanga Parbat
d. moraine
e. kletterschuh

Movie People

1. Daryl Hannah
2. Martin Scorsese
3. Ann-Margret
4. Isabella Rossellini
5. Kris Kristofferson
6. Everett Sloane
7. J. Carrol Naish
8. Dimitri Tiomkin
9. Malcolm McDowell
10. Steven Spielberg

11. Bernard Herrmann
12. Dom DeLuise
13. Dino De Laurentiis
14. Claude Lelouch
15. Nicolas Roeg
16. Donald Pleasence
17. Ronald Colman
18. Franco Zeffirelli
19. Hedy Lamarr
20. Rosanna Arquette

21. Vittorio De Sica
22. Brian Dennehy
23. Hattie McDaniel
24. Jeanne Crain
25. Ricky Schroder
a. Freddie Bartholomew
b. Jon Voight
c. Simone Signoret
d. Gina Lollobrigida
e. Deanna Durbin

Mythology

1. Charybdis
2. Actaeon
3. Hygeia
4. Nausicaa
5. Cimmerian
6. Rhadamanthus
7. Dionysus
8. Deucalion
9. Danaë
10. Tiresias

11. Hephaestus
12. Bellerophon
13. Agamemnon
14. Laocoön
15. Phaëthon
16. Corybantes, Corybants
17. Sarpedon
18. Ares
19. Cybele
20. Minotaur

21. Anchises
22. Menelaus
23. Eurydice
24. cockatrice
25. Iphigeneia
a. Atalanta
b. Momus
c. Galatea
d. Euterpe
e. Dioscuri

Native Americans (Indians)

1. Chippewa
2. wickiup
3. Mescalero
4. Sacajawea, Sacagawea, Sakajawea
5. Tlingit
6. Tuscarora

7. hogan
8. Lenni Lenape
9. Powhatan
10. Nez Percé
11. Tecumseh
12. Penobscot
13. kachina

14. Kwakiutl
15. travois
16. Muskhogean, Muskogean
17. Oneida
18. Passamaquoddy
19. berdache
20. Kiowa

21. Fort Belknap Reservation
22. kiva
23. Shoshonean
24. Paiute
25. Zuni
a. Arawak
b. Kemo Sabe
c. Kickapoo
d. Cochise
e. Iroquoian

Opera

1. regisseur
2. Sparafucile
3. *Così Fan Tutte*
4. fioritura
5. sprechstimme
6. Beppe
7. portamento
8. Schaunard
9. *Hérodiade*
10. comprimario
11. janissary music
12. brindisi
13. tessitura
14. cabaletta
15. *Cavalleria Rusticana*
16. commedia dell'arte
17. ritornello, ritornelle, ritornel
18. Chaliapin, Shalyapin
19. coloratura
20. verismo
21. gibus
22. Micaëla
23. rataplan
24. Galli-Curci
25. Papageno
a. cavatina
b. soubrette
c. *Pelléas et Mélisande*
d. Jacquino
e. solfège

Philosophy and Logic

1. eschatology
2. syncretism
3. Cyrenaic
4. ignoratio elenchi
5. haecceity, hecceity
6. Boethius
7. hylomorphism
8. Carneades
9. dysteleological
10. casuistry
11. ergotism
12. theodicy
13. Nietzschean
14. aseity, aseitas
15. noumenon
16. Ockham's razor, Occam's razor
17. a posteriori
18. Maimonides
19. syncategorematic
20. enthymeme
21. Eleatic
22. Pyrrhonism
23. Fichtean
24. zetetic
25. Kierkegaard
a. Berkeleian, Berkeleyan
b. Plotinus
c. apodeictic, apodictic
d. eristic
e. Comtism

Physics and Electricity

1. enthalpy
2. minometer
3. barretter
4. adiabatic
5. cryogeny
6. poise
7. oersted
8. abmho
9. solenoid
10. shear modulus
11. debye
12. Avogadro's law
13. Klystron
14. capillarity
15. bremsstrahlung
16. ferronickel
17. squegging
18. actinism
19. schlieren
20. Dewar vessel
21. Heaviside layer

22. stellarator
23. roentgenopaque
24. collimator

25. kaon
a. Planck's constant
b. degauss

c. picofarad
d. Leyden jar
e. hysteresis

Political Science

1. autarky
2. Stakhanovite
3. Kuomintang
4. risorgimento
5. Kulturkampf
6. diktat
7. apparatchik
8. suffragettism
9. entente cordiale
10. Tammanyism
11. suzerainty
12. plebiscite, plebescite
13. plenipotentiary
14. ad baculum
15. Knesset
16. Falangist
17. attentat
18. mare clausum
19. sansculottism
20. ultra vires
21. Blanquism
22. satyagraha
23. posse comitatus
24. revanchist
25. oblast
a. hegemony
b. Machiavellism
c. bicameral
d. anschluss
e. gerrymander

Psychology

1. eidetic
2. somatotonic
3. amygdala
4. Krafft-Ebing
5. oligophrenia
6. encephalon
7. anankastic, anancastic
8. hypermnesia
9. norepinephrine
10. dysthymic
11. pyknik, pycnic
12. Wechsler-Bellevue
13. glucagon
14. Zeigarnik effect
15. telekinesis
16. Eysenck
17. acetylcholine
18. xenoglossy
19. hebephrenia
20. dyspareunia
21. Ebbinghaus law
22. algolagnia
23. psychagogy
24. eonism
25. catamnesis
a. erethism
b. Babinski reflex
c. hypnagogic, hypnogogic
d. abience
e. aphasia

Religion

1. soteriology
2. hagiology
3. Karaite
4. theophany
5. proselyte
6. Upanishad, Upanisad
7. chrism
8. Eucharist
9. sabbatarian
10. abbacy
11. simony
12. theopneust
13. suttee, sati
14. ophiolater
15. Wycliffite, Wyclifite
16. Homoiousian
17. Homoousian
18. apostasy
19. Socinian
20. Mishnah, Mishna
21. antinomianism
22. Mahayana
23. kerystic
24. Mennonite
25. nullifidian
a. eschatology
b. Sikhism
c. Cistercian
d. infralapsarianism
e. apotheosis

Sociology

1. miscegenation
2. anthropophagy
3. recidivism
4. levirate
5. telesis
6. bracero
7. phratry
8. avunculocal
9. beena marriage
10. affinal
11. xenophobia
12. anomie, anomy, anomia
13. Kallikak
14. potlatch
15. saturnalia
16. archetype
17. moieties
18. agelicism
19. polygyny
20. gerontology
21. Gemeinschaft
22. brachycephaly
23. Appalachia
24. gynecocracy
25. lumpenproletariat
  a. Weltanschauung
  b. chattel
  c. amitate
  d. petite bourgeoisie
  e. matripotestal

Sports

1. anabolic
2. eephus pitch
3. Yamashita
4. mashie niblick
5. piste
6. fartlek
7. nocking point
8. sphairistike
9. cesta
10. Worcester
11. telemark
12. Marquis of Queensberry rules
13. Naismith
14. Heisman trophy
15. chukker, chukkar, chukka, chucker
16. tarpaulin
17. deke
18. repechage
19. totalizator, totalisator
20. pelota
21. trudgen stroke, trudgeon stroke
22. Wimbledon
23. luge
24. alley-oop
25. oxer
  a. bonspiel
  b. flèche
  c. forecaddie
  d. klister
  e. cauliflower ear

Wines

1. sommelier
2. Lafite-Rothschild
3. Médoc
4. ullage
5. Gewürztraminer
6. Châteauneuf-du-Pape
7. Spätlese
8. botrytized
9. Valpolicella
10. grappa
11. méthode champenoise
12. Bernkasteler
13. ampelography
14. Sémillon
15. *tastevin*
16. petillant
17. Asti spumante
18. Chenin Blanc
19. Trockenbeerenauslese
20. scuppernong
21. Manischewitz
22. Pouilly-Fuissé
23. zymurgy
24. Verdicchio
25. amontillado
  a. chianti
  b. puncheon
  c. Rehoboam
  d. retsina, retzina
  e. Rioja

World Geography

1. Timbuktu, Tombouctou
2. Liechtenstein
3. Kuala Lumpur
4. Adelaide
5. Machu Picchu
6. Qum
7. Abu Dhabi
8. Riyadh
9. Saskatchewan

10. Uppsala
11. Phnom Penh
12. Schuylkill River
13. Djibouti
14. Reykjavík
15. Lake Winnipesaukee
16. Mykonos, Míkonos

17. Württemberg
18. Edinburgh
19. Tallahatchie River
20. Novosibirsk
21. Allegheny Mountains
22. Montevideo
23. Guadalajara

24. Dnieper River
25. Bophuthatswana
a. Marrakech, Marrakesh
b. Portobelo
c. Balearic Islands
d. Sault Sainte Marie
e. Lake Titicaca

Ultimate Death by Spelling

The Esquire Test

1. asinine
2. braggadocio
3. rarefy
4. liquefy
5. pavilion
6. vermilion
7. impostor
8. moccasin
9. accommodate
10. consensus
11. rococo
12. titillate
13. sacrilegious
14. mayonnaise
15. impresario
16. inoculate
17. supersede
18. obbligato
19. desiccate
20. resuscitate

Ultimate Death Words of One Syllable

1. xyst
2. nef
3. dhow
4. pyx
5. cwm
6. mho
7. loess
8. faille
9. ouph, ouphe
10. dalles

-Ie or -Ei Test

1. weird
2. sheikh
3. fiend
4. skein
5. frieze
6. deceive
7. seize
8. forfeit
9. geisha
10. weir
11. heifer
12. Sheila
13. nonpareil
14. codeine
15. Pleiades
16. caffeine
17. plebeian
18. sieve
19. siege
20. ceiling
21. fiefdom
22. wield
23. conceive
24. receipt
25. retrieve
    a. niece
    b. Siegfried line
    c. kielbasa
    d. lieder
    e. heinous

-Ance (-Ant) or -Ence (-Ent) Test

1. aberrance
2. sufferance
3. resplendent
4. impedance
5. cognizant
6. despondent
7. abidance
8. petulance
9. reflectance
10. nurturant
11. antecedent
12. relevant

13. appetence
14. opulence
15. dalliance
16. admittance
17. lieutenant

18. truculent
19. intermittent
20. attractant
21. decadent
22. decedent

23. defendant
24. quittance
25. penchant
a. preponderant
b. retardant

c. disputant
d. mordant
e. adherent

-Os or -Oes Test

1. echoes
2. kimonos
3. fungoes
4. bagnios
5. gringos
6. fandangos
7. lingoes
8. jingoes

9. heroes
10. farragoes
11. caballeros
12. fatsoes
13. dildos
14. majordomos
15. boleros
16. curios

17. bozos
18. albinos
19. gessoes
20. sopranos
21. vetoes
22. pistachios
23. potatoes
24. tomatoes

25. embryos
a. seraglios
b. Merinos
c. fiascoes
d. bassos
e. hidalgos

-Er or -Or Test No. 1

1. estimator
2. facilitator
3. hallucinator
4. mutilator
5. repudiator
6. infector
7. separator
8. discriminator

9. rebutter
10. forfeiter
11. seceder
12. extirpator
13. depredator
14. placater
15. constrictor
16. inculcator

17. insinuator
18. predictor
19. prepetuator
20. enumerator
21. cultivator
22. requiter
23. accumulator
24. pollinator

25. educator
a. consummator
b. proselytizer
c. improvisator
d. arbiter
e. acquitter

-Er or -Or Test No. 2

1. massacrer
2. abbreviator
3. confiscator
4. sojourner
5. formulator
6. masticator
7. embosser
8. subjugator

9. obliterator
10. dissertator
11. absconder
12. punctuator
13. initiator
14. contester
15. tergiversator
16. execrator

17. perpetrator
18. inveigher
19. advocator
20. disburser
21. illuminator
22. extrapolator
23. attractor
24. pontificator

25. alienator
a. denigrator
b. underlier
c. dissimulator
d. irrigator
e. chastiser

-Able or -Ible Test No. 1

1. analyzable
2. assessable
3. biddable
4. censurable
5. codable
6. compassable
7. compatible
8. comprehendible
9. condemnable
10. confusable
11. corrodible
12. cuttable
13. dimmable
14. dippable
15. distractible
16. enforceable
17. erectable
18. excerptible
19. exhaustible
20. expandable
21. expansible
22. fusible
23. gaugeable
24. gelable
25. illimitable
a. illuminable
b. impassable
c. indestructible
d. inducible
e. ineludible

-Able or -Ible Test No. 2

1. infectible
2. invertible
3. irrefragable
4. leasable
5. miscible
6. partible
7. postponable
8. producible
9. provable
10. putrescible
11. resistible
12. salvageable
13. scalable
14. scrutable
15. spareable
16. suable
17. submergible
18. subsumable
19. suppressible
20. tithable
21. tractable
22. traversable
23. destructible
24. unbudgeable
25. unreproducible
a. vanquishable
b. winnable
c. ingestible
d. interruptible
e. locatable

Spell the Plural

1. autos-da-fé
2. ignes fatui
3. courts-martial
4. heirs apparent
5. kielbasas, kielbasy
6. torii
7. billets-doux
8. coccyges, coccyxes
9. anni mirabiles
10. kohlrabies
11. marchese
12. croquis
13. startsy
14. pince-nez
15. metastases
16. mots justes
17. goosefoots
18. kuvaszok
19. oyesses
20. chassis, chassises
a. beaux gestes, beau gestes
b. nouveaux riches
c. entremets
d. plaice
e. nexuses, nexus

Accent Mark or None Test

1. mañana
2. melee, mêlée
3. pietà
4. boîte
5. panache
6. arrivederci
7. porte cochere
8. Götterdämmerung
9. dolce vita
10. mano a mano
11. crepe suzettes
12. aloha oe

13. virtu, vertu
14. zabaglione
15. déjà vu
16. émigré, emigré
17. crèche
18. lèse majesté
19. objet d'art
20. führer
21. ciao
22. gemütlichkeit
23. forte
24. kielbasa
25. tête-à-tête
a. Chicano
b. dacha
c. détente
d. machismo
e. hasta la vista

Webster's Second (One Spelling Only) Test No. 1

1. aficionado
2. chancellery
3. chiromancy
4. colander
5. galumph
6. manikin
7. rumba
8. ukulele
9. gewgaw
10. plebiscite
11. plebeian
12. cerulean
13. Phoenician
14. cosmogony
15. rigmarole
16. valance
17. salmagundi
18. broccoli
19. questionnaire
20. barbecue
a. Babbittry
b. caravanner
c. exhalant
d. khaki
e. ratchet

Webster's Second (One Spelling Only) Test No. 2

1. arrhythmia
2. bassinet
3. chickadee
4. déjà vu
5. katydid
6. Aryan
7. cruet
8. buttinsky
9. chaparral
10. palisade
11. sake
12. czardas
13. a cappella
14. chanticleer
15. canister
16. chancy
17. keloid
18. decrepit
19. ropy
20. duffel
a. bijoux
b. cellaret
c. reducible
d. leucocyte
e. homologue

Ultimate Death Big Fifty Review

1. compos mentis
2. paralogism
3. verrucose
4. niccolic
5. schmierkase
6. nonagenarian
7. abscise
8. crotchety
9. paraquat
10. Naugahyde
11. chlamydia
12. salaam
13. Afrikaans
14. Milquetoast
15. sequelae
16. flytier
17. feoffee
18. *capisce*
19. carrefour
20. sinsemilla
21. amercing
22. bombycine
23. Mah-Jongg
24. tsunami
25. lamasery
26. divvied
27. sororal
28. paparazzi
29. singer
30. rivulet
31. policlinic
32. violoncello
33. statolatry
34. birdieing
35. palling
36. crocheter
37. chthonic
38. mariachi
39. chifforobe
40. glary
41. ekistics
42. gelée
43. consentaneous
44. zombiism
45. olio
46. decedent
47. amanuenses
48. meridional
49. sibylline
50. cubature

Last Rites (Top Twenty)

1. talcky
2. shillelagh, shillalah
3. granary
4. bialys
5. Appaloosa
6. decennary
7. fierier
8. tae kwon do
9. ululate
10. vichyssoise
11. pomegranate
12. pari-mutuel
13. cachinnation
14. bissextile
15. flibbertigibbety
16. whippoorwill
17. cappuccino
18. Kewpie
19. picador
20. shrapnel
a. plumy
b. coaly
c. bimillenary
d. chichi
e. senhor